"There is often an unspoken hierarchy in the recovery community, with IV drug users unofficially labeled 'least likely to succeed.' Mary Beth's story counters that assumption in the most inspiring way. Her tale of trauma, loss, and ultimate victory over addiction is a testament to the strength of empowerment approaches to recovery like Women for Sobriety. If you are struggling with the idea that there is only one way to get sober, you need to read this book!"

—**Adrienne Miller,** Women for Sobriety president and CEO

"Judge O'Connor casts an unflinching gaze over the past to explore the factors that contributed to her demise into drugs, abusive relationships, and self-harm, and the resources that helped her build an empowered life. Harrowing and hopeful, her story assures readers that recovery is possible."

—**Jean McCarthy,** podcast host of *The Bubble Hour,* author of the Unpickled series

"A riveting memoir about a harrowing childhood and the deep abyss of drug addiction—followed by an inspiring story of recovery and a practical guide to building an individual recovery plan—no higher power required."

—**Mary M. French,** administrative law judge, retired

"Recovery, like Rome, is a destination with many roads. There is an abundance of stories where recovery is laid at the feet of some notion of God. But only a small minority of addicted persons actually walk that pathway. Much larger numbers find recovery elsewhere. Mary Beth O'Connor's memoir begins to fill the information gap about recovery for people who, like many younger Americans today, check 'none of the above' when it comes to religious affiliation. Starting in her teens, Mary Beth did about all the drugs you can do. She could have been a poster child for the victims of dysfunctional family life. Yet eventually she pulled out of it. She tried 12-steps and found it wanting. She took charge of her own recovery. She achieved not only abstinence but big-R Recovery, overcoming her inner demons, and demonstrating the competence, intelligence, reliability, and social skills necessary for professional advancement. This is an inspirational story of survival and renewal."

—**Martin Nicolaus,** founder, LifeRing Secular Recovery, author of *Empower Your Sober Self* and *Recovery by Choice*

"*From Junkie to Judge* is an essential addition to addiction and recovery literature. Mary Beth's remarkable and gripping story smashes stereotypes about professionals and drug use. An avowed atheist, she also gives hope to those who've been told recovery requires faith."

—**Lisa F. Smith,** author of *Girl Walks Out of a Bar:*
*A Memoir,* co-host of *Recovery Rocks* podcast

"What a wonderful example of the possibilities that are inside us all! This is a deeply relatable story of childhood pain that is transformed through the trials of addiction and recovery. This compelling account of triumph over adversity speaks to the challenges we all face and the hope of what is possible once we do the work of healing the past. As a person in long term recovery, I found *From Junkie to Judge* to be a valuable resource for those considering a life free of addictions."

—**Arlina Allen,** *One Day at a Time* podcast host

"*From Junkie to Judge* is a story of hard-won grace, and a remarkable tenacity to persevere. Mary Beth narrates an extraordinary journey of transcendence and advocacy. We are so fortunate to have her record, and this guide to recovery—and recovering well—that finds witness in her overcoming adversity, becoming oneself, and blazing the trail for others to follow."

—**John Evans,** author of *Young Widower: A Memoir*
and Stanford University lecturer

"Very rarely do you find a person who has the courage to be so honest about not only their particular experience but the human experience. Judge O'Connor exhibits that courage in spades in her memoir. She takes you in detail through her struggle and her subsequent recovery from addiction and trauma. It is an unbelievable example of the indomitable will to not give up. As a person in long-term recovery and an addiction clinician, it was great to read something that details just how real addiction is, how hard getting sober can be, and wonderful tools to help all of those in the fight. To anyone reading this who is struggling—you are worth it and deserving of all the beautiful things the world has to offer you."

—**AJ Diaz, LMSW, CASAC-T,** co-founder of You Are Accountable

# FROM

# TO

### ONE WOMAN'S
### TRIUMPH OVER TRAUMA
### AND ADDICTION

# MARY BETH O'CONNOR

Health Communications, Inc.
Boca Raton, Florida

**Disclaimer:** Some of the names and characteristics of people have been changed to protect their anonymity. The author does not endorse one specific method of recovery. Before embarking on any recovery program, you may want speak to a healthcare provider or a professional.

*www.hcibooks.com*
Library of Congress Cataloging-in-Publication Data
is available through the Library of Congress

© 2022 Mary Beth O'Connor

ISBN-13: 978-07573-2456-7 (Paperback)
ISBN-10: 07573-2456-8 (Paperback)
ISBN-13: 978-07573-2457-4 (ePub)
ISBN-10: 07573-2457-6 (ePub)

Publisher: Health Communications, Inc.
      301 Crawford Blvd., Suite 200
      Boca Raton, FL 33432-1653

*Cover, interior design and formatting by Larissa Hise Henoch*

# Contents

# Foreword

I FIRST MET MARY BETH O'Connor in the fall of 2018, at a coffee bar during our She Recovers in LA Conference at the Beverly Hilton Hotel. It was a brief encounter, but Mary Beth really made an impact. My frenzied energy likely indicated that we had but a few minutes to chat, so Mary Beth cut right to the chase. She told me that she had become addicted to meth by 17, found recovery at 32, and had accumulated over a quarter century of sobriety. Oh, and she was a federal judge and had written a memoir. I was captivated and would have liked to sit down with her and dig into her story right then and there. Alas, my event responsibilities beckoned, so we bid adieu, and both got back to the task at hand—celebrating women in recovery.

I've had the honor of getting to know Mary Beth since that first meeting. We've spent time together at recovery events, we have a relatively consistent Messenger relationship, and she joined the board of our non-profit foundation in 2020. I also love following Mary Beth on Facebook where she shares tidbits of her life with her beloved partner, Doc.

Through reading this real and raw memoir, I now know Mary Beth on an even deeper level. From *Junkie to Judge* is a triumph —both as a literary project and as a life story. Mary Beth details a childhood and young adulthood rife with trauma and neglect. She reminds us that we become addicted because of what happens to us, not because there is anything wrong with us. Her story is stitched together with poignant details of abuse and pain but also moments of lightness and possibility. She never descends into shame or self-pity, and her generosity in seeking to understand those who hurt her most is nothing short of inspiring.

*From Junkie to Judge* is more than a memoir. As Mary Beth herself declares, sharing her story is her advocacy work. And her work is much needed, especially in this era of massive overdose from a poisoned drug supply. Mary Beth joins others who advocate vociferously for multiple pathways of recovery; it's become clear over the past several decades that people need to be supported to find and follow individualized pathways and patchworks of recovery. That is exactly what Mary Beth did. From the start of her own healing journey, Mary Beth distrusted the idea that only 12-step recovery would work for her—in part because she is an atheist but also because she understands that recovery is not a one-size-fits-all endeavor. Her instincts were right. But always generous and respectful of things that might not work for her, Mary Beth never suggests that non-secular pathways won't work for others. This is an important distinction in the recovery movement. We only get to say what works for ourselves.

Mary Beth took control of her recovery from the start. She researched all sorts of strategies, listened, and watched what seemed to be working for others, tried things out for herself, and kept adjusting. If you ask her what works for her, and continues to work for her, it is connecting with a wide range of secular ideas about recovery and sharing her story with and for others in, or seeking, recovery. As Mary Beth says, taking charge of her personal recovery helped build her confidence and competence, and she uses that process and technique in all areas of her life. Her memoir will inspire others to take charge of their own recovery and lives too.

The stigma associated with addiction prevents the average person from comprehending that women who were once severely addicted can recover and go on to lead fulfilling and amazing lives. But we do. I often say that if you looked at my LinkedIn profile you would never suspect that I spent my young adult years doing and dealing drugs. If you looked at Mary Beth's profile, you couldn't imagine that she had dropped out of law school and spent years shooting speed intravenously. But here's the thing. Neither Mary Beth nor I are trying to hide our past, in fact the opposite is true. We aren't ashamed of where we have come from, and we purposefully recover out loud to show other women—and the world—that recovery is possible.

Mary Beth has accomplished much in her life and much in her recovery. She believes in the concept of being of service to others in recovery, and her memoir accomplishes that and more. Mary Beth offers up the hard, gritty details of her past in addiction because she understands that sharing our recovery narratives can inspire others to choose recovery too. Our stories have power. Mary Beth shares her story with unflinching honesty, grace, humor and, that most important ingredient for anyone in or seeking recovery, hope. With this book, and through her other efforts, this "junkie" turned judge turned advocate, will save lives.

Dawn Nickel, co-founder, She Recovers Foundation
and author of *She Recovers Every Day: Daily
Meditations for Women in Recovery*

# CHAPTER 1
## My First Shot

WHEN I GRADUATED from my New Jersey high school in 1979, I was an honor student and a junkie. I don't mean I smoked a lot of weed or popped too many pills—I shot speed daily. Methamphetamine to the chemist, crank in my hometown, crystal in modern terminology.

I hit a nerve in my right wrist as I injected before the ceremony. When the principal presented my diploma and shook my hand, I bit my lip to suppress the scream that surged from my belly to my throat. Inside the leatherette cover, one note congratulated me for winning the most scholarship money, but another demanded repayment of sixty-two dollars from a candy sale, funds I had used to score a gram of meth.

My classmates avoided eye contact when I staggered off the stage. They giggled and prodded one another, excited to launch the next chapter in their lives. I slumped in the plastic chair, dread suffocating me as I contemplated flunking out of college. *I almost failed last semester, skipping school so often, and UCLA's gonna be so much harder. Maybe I'll get lucky and die of an overdose on a dorm floor.* I snapped the folio shut. *Jesus, is that my best option? How the fuck did I get here?*

Ten months earlier, after snorting crank for three days, I had fallen into the turbulent sleep of an overdue crash. I clawed my way to consciousness, then focused on the clock radio's fluorescent 7:08.

"Cindy," I shouted toward my sister's room. "Is it AM or PM?"

"Goddammit, I'm sleeping. Because it's morning."

I threw off the sheets, struggled to a sitting position, and waited for the dizziness to subside. As I stood, I planted my hand on the bed for balance. Trudging to my mirror, I examined the dark roots setting off my Nice 'n Easy blond hair. Smeared mascara framed bloodshot eyes above sunken cheeks. I held up my hand and watched it shake.

*Shit! I look like that old drunk at the Silver Fox who spends her days chained to a barstool.*

I shuffled to the refrigerator and grappled with the Pepsi tab before I collapsed on the sofa and lit a cigarette. Like every other morning, I snatched my purse from the Formica coffee table and dug for my drug kit.

No crank. Just a few black beauties. Warm tears spurted down my cold face. *It's okay, it's okay. You have the beauties.*

Weaker than meth, but at least these pills delivered an amphetamine high. Should I break them open, discard the time-release ebony granules, and snort the powder for a more intense rush? My nostrils ached from overuse, so I swallowed two. As I waited for the energy burst, I smacked my cheeks. *Pull it together. You need meth. This early, Bubba's your best bet. If you look trashed, he'll send you home.*

I spent the next hour constructing Mary Beth. Shower, blow out, hot rollers, another black beauty, frosted blue eye shadow, maroon shorts, and a breast-enhancing halter top. Scrutinizing my image again, I straightened my shoulders, tossed my hair, and practiced a laugh. Relief! A façade sufficient to hide the depths of my deterioration.

I drove my brown '73 Valiant to Bordentown's four block city center. High school dropout Bubba worked as a mid-level drug dealer. At twenty, he still lived with his parents in a narrow row house. I exchanged pleasantries with his mom as she spread her famous ham salad on Wonder Bread. "Help yourself to a sandwich if you get hungry later."

Bubba beckoned me over and we walked a couple blocks to spend the day with Matt. His wife at work, the unemployed truck driver provided a safe haven in a tacit exchange for drugs. Proud of his chiseled body, Matt would use speed and then spend hours weight lifting.

As we approached the two-story brick apartment building, Bubba tugged at his loose pants. Naturally plump, too much crank and too little food had reduced his waistline.

"Mary Beth, if I'm not careful, I'll be crazy skinny like you."

"Hey, I put on a couple of pounds."

"Hmm, I've never seen a collarbone stick out like yours."

*Jesus. He's on this again. Yo, Bubba! Just last week you gave me enough meth to choke a horse.*

Shrugging, I strolled backward, facing him, hoping to appear casual as we neared Matt's apartment. "So, I heard they arrested Dennis for pointing a gun at a cop."

"Yup. During a parole check. He'd been up for days and thought the fuzz was gonna shoot him. Won't be seeing him for a while."

"Good. He tried to force me to suck his dick a couple of weeks ago."

Spinning around, I beamed at Matt as he let us in, my mouth watering as we sashayed to the glass kitchen table. Bubba set aside ten vials filled with speed for clients to pick up throughout the day.

He poured a mound of the glistening white crystals from a sandwich-sized baggie and waggled his finger at us.

"We gotta make this last all day, minus the tastes I'll offer my customers."

From a folded denim sack, Bubba removed a razor blade and silver straw. He chopped the meth *rat-a-tat-tat*, like a sous chef dicing vegetables during the dinner rush. He carved out three long lines. As the crank provider, he snorted first. The speed disappeared in an instant. Bubba thrust himself up and knocked the chair to the floor. "Man, oh man, oh man. My skull's about to explode."

He exhaled four times in staccato, then waved me over. As the woman and his occasional sex partner, I had second dibs on the drugs. After pecking him on the cheek, I sidled into position. I rolled the metal cylinder between my fingers, then bent down, pressing a finger against my right nostril to increase the suction of the left. I moved the straw along the line as I attempted to ingest the crank. "God damn it. Nothing."

Months of heavy drug use had clogged my nose. Despite several efforts, I couldn't inhale the speed. Matt scraped my line into a pouch he made of tissue. I swallowed, then gagged when the damp paper clung to the inside of my throat. Panic threatened to engulf me as I choked. Bubba jumped to his feet and nabbed a Bud. After several swigs, I gargled to propel the crank toward my stomach.

Matt already had snared the silver straw. I fixated on him as he vacuumed up his portion. "Fuck. That's good shit."

Bubba nodded with pride, grabbed a deck of cards from the hutch, and began to shuffle. Matt skittered around the apartment, rearranged magazines, and scrubbed a Teflon pot with steel wool. Clutching my half-empty pack of Salems, I shifted to the olive-green recliner and waited for the slower impact from injesting the drug. Leaning back, I propelled the footrest forward. Thirty seconds later, I slung my legs over the chair's side. My Dr. Scholl's sandals flapped as I jiggled my feet.

Renoir's *Luncheon of the Boating Party* hung above the buffet. My mother had purchased a larger version of the same print at Quaker Bridge Mall because it was pretty and matched our furniture. A flash of fury overwhelmed me as I recalled my stepfather backhanding me across the face because I hadn't dusted it to his satisfaction. As my second cigarette burned down to the nub, my cheeks began to glow, and a familiar heat traveled from my chest to my fingertips. I tilted my neck and expelled a slow "aah."

Bubba whirled around. "There's my girl."

I stretched my arms to the ceiling, then shimmied my shoulders. Bouncing over to the pressboard stereo cabinet, I flipped through all two dozen albums, then selected Pink Floyd's *Dark Side of the Moon.* The boys joined me in the living room to wait for round two. For the next thirty minutes, we debated my drug consumption options. Matt lobbed the nasal spray to me, I tried to draw in the liquid but to no avail.

"Why don't you stir it in your soda?"

"Tried that. Nasty taste."

"Well, sweetie," Bubba said, "I think we need to pop your cherry. You're gonna have to shoot up."

An ecstatic tingle pulsed through my body as I anticipated a new high. To prevent Bubba from witnessing my ear-to-ear grin, which might worry him enough to change his mind, I gathered the paraphernalia. Matt snagged a pristine hypodermic, a set of works, from his wife's dresser. Eyeballing my share, Bubba grasped the razor blade and swept crank from the pile into a tablespoon.

Having watched others, I knew how to prepare the shot. Removing the orange cap from the set took more force than expected. I gasped when I heard the resounding snap of success. I drew up a small amount of water and slowly squirted it onto the meth. With the flat end of the plunger, I crushed the particles until they dissolved into liquid. To avoid losing even one drop, I scraped the residue on the spoon's inner rim and watched it flow toward the mixture. I wadded up a tiny piece of cotton, centered that ball in the speed puddle, then positioned the needle against it, to suck the elixir into the syringe. To remove any air bubbles, I flicked the plastic barrel and guided the crank to the top. Matt handed me his belt and I tied off my upper arm.

Bubba smacked the pit on my inner elbow to raise the blood vessels. I twice clenched and unclenched my hand before making a fist. I slammed my arm on the glass tabletop, almost knocking the ashtray to the floor. Bubba placed the works at an angle, tapping until the point punctured my skin. He wiggled the hypodermic a bit and then withdrew it.

"You have baby veins, so it's easy to miss. You gotta push hard enough so they don't roll. Not too hard or you'll go through them."

On the second try, as he eased the tip forward, a minute curl of blood penetrated the syringe. Bubba retracted the plunger and bright red fluid gushed in, mingling with the clear speed. I loosened the belt. He pulled back slightly until a fresh droplet emerged, indicating the needle remained in place. Bubba mainlined the blood-speed amalgam with one graceful stroke.

My muscles twitched as I visualized the drug racing toward my brain. An ether taste rose from my throat. I gazed upward and coughed. My eyes wobbled in their sockets. Spasms in my gut made me hunch over. Adrenaline and euphoria flooded every cell. A blaze ignited inside me and irradiated the room. Gripping Bubba's thigh, I opened my mouth to describe the shimmering paint, gleaming mirror, and throbbing music but could not formulate the words, or even a thank-you.

I giggled and held up my palms the way a child does when spotting a stack of gifts. I clutched my seat as the glorious power flowed through me, and I wondered if this was what happiness felt like. I took a deep elated breath. And sang my new mantra.

"When can I do it again?" ●

# CHAPTER 2:
## Conception

MY LIFE HAD STARTED SLIDING DOWNHILL within weeks of my conception, before my eighteen-year-old mother had realized she was pregnant. On the flight to Los Angeles to start college, Mom told me that my father, John, had adopted me. I may have missed a few details because I was distracted by an escalating panic as the thought, *How the hell will I find meth in LA?* gnawed through every neuron in my brain. I had a gram vial in my underwear because I was afraid to travel with any quantity, so withdrawal threatened to hit shortly after touchdown.

I do recall that Mom reminded me of her high school popularity. She'd met Don in 1960, her senior year, while working at Dunham's department store. He epitomized the man she'd wanted to marry: good-looking, a business major at Rider College in snobby Lawrenceville, and bound for the executive suite. Mom's assessment had been that Don wasn't the brightest bulb, so, despite his claim that he preferred clever women, she'd known better than to outshine him. She'd exhibited the level of intelligence she'd thought he would appreciate, like dropping the occasional five-dollar word but feigning ignorance of politics.

Mom had pulled out all the stops, dying her hair blond, wearing pencil skirts over a girdle that squeezed her already tiny waist so tight she could barely breathe, and hiding her cat eyes in her purse because, as Marilyn Monroe advised, guys don't make passes at girls who wear glasses. She had fantasized about their fabulous future while clutching the commemorative pillow from the Kappa Phi formal where she'd dazzled Don's fraternity brothers. She said they'd taken a secret weekend trip down the shore, which she'd hoped would seal the deal, although she'd known she rolled the dice by having sex. He had broken up with her the next week, consistent with my grandmother's warnings that upscale boys only chased working-class girls for one thing and then lost interest after foolish dreamers gave up their virginity.

As I listened to my mother, I wondered why she was dumping this on me now. Was she thinking about her life when she was my age? Was she making an effort to develop an adult relationship with me, more like friends? Or perhaps she imagined that by sharing what she went through, I would feel obligated to help her later? After all, my scholarship to a top-tier college seemed like it was putting me on an opposite path than the one she'd taken.

"When I missed my period, I'd hoped it was stress. Understand, 1960, an unmarried pregnant Irish Catholic girl. Disaster. No chance of getting a top-notch husband. And I assumed Grandmom would throw me out. Where would I go? And how would I raise you on minimum wage?"

Mom said she'd flipped back and forth from terror to picturing Don on his knees presenting a diamond ring. She'd begun dating John, a sweet boy with a low-level office job, who adored her. "I didn't even have to try. To him, I was fabulous." She'd thought about how her parents didn't understand her, like the time she'd run up debt buying clothes with her employee discount. When Dunham's had called because she was behind on the payments, Grandmom had carried on about her irresponsibility. "I told her off good. You're happy in dowdy housedresses. I need to outshine the girls at Don's college."

"I know, Mom; you've told me this before. None of your debts have been your fault." I wanted to say "not the credit cards or car payments, and not even when you drained my savings account." I held my tongue because I didn't trust she wouldn't twist my arm or slap my face. After all, she seemed oblivious to the other passengers, who must have been able to hear her. Or she might have been enjoying the imagined sympathy.

Mom brushed a few strands of hair off her face, threw me a quick scowl, and plowed ahead. Grandpop O'Connor had arranged a meeting with Mom, my father, and all four parents. Grandpop had pushed hard for Don's parents to make him marry her. To cover up her sin, according to Mom, but I wondered if also to protect her. "He needs to do the right thing. He had his fun and now he has to pay the piper."

Mom said her eyes had pleaded with Don, but he never opened his mouth. His family had insisted their son's promising future wasn't going to "be ruined by a girl like that." Grandpop had sputtered spit. "What about her life?"

Though the details were new, I'd known John wasn't my biological dad for years, yet feigned ignorance to avoid a "why didn't you bring it up" discussion. In high school, for a blood type experiment, I'd asked Mom for John's and hers, which didn't match mine. She hadn't followed up, and I'd altered the data, so the teacher wouldn't think I'd made a mistake or want to talk about the family secret.

Plus, I hadn't seen John since I'd spent the weekend at his house when I was thirteen. At the bowling alley, I'd met a gorgeous nine-teen-year-old. John had answered the door when Kurt arrived to take me out and hadn't hesitated to wish me a "have fun" as I flew down the stairs. Kurt had shared a high-powered joint and we'd fucked in the woods. Afterward, he'd adopted the role of teacher, explaining the importance of condoms, with no apparent awareness that the better safety tip would've been not to have sex with grown men. I'd returned to John's, bedraggled and unable to walk straight, and I hadn't seen him since. So finding out he wasn't my biological father hadn't shaken my world.

Anyway, luckily for Mom, the Catholic Church had an elaborate system for unwed mothers, providing a Philadelphia facility where she could relocate for the duration and even routing her mail through Boston. The priests would've arranged for adoption, but my mother had rejected that offer despite my grandparents' refusing to house us both. "You can't expect to traipse back here with a child on your hip and pretend you've done nothing wrong." Instead, Mom had moved back, and I'd been left at a nearby convent where the nuns cared for me. She'd dropped by when she could, she swore. And Mom had taken me out one day to push me in a borrowed baby carriage near Don's apartment. She'd even succeeded in running into him. "He just asked how I was, patted you on the head, and took off with his buddies."

My heart sank a little, knowing my father hadn't changed his mind when he saw me. I thought how even then, before I was born, none of them, not my parents and not my grandparents, had considered my best interests. My father had avoided tying the knot and hadn't asked for visitation. My grandparents had focused on salvaging the family's reputation. Mom had insisted on keeping me, I think only because I was her best option for getting out from under her parents. Either Don would change his mind or she'd convince John to take us in. In the meantime, she had enrolled at Trenton State, picked up her social schedule, and squeezed in convent visits.

She did marry John, and I'd moved in with them at around six months old. With my sister, Cindy, half-sister biologically but not in my heart, we'd visited those nuns occasionally after church. I'd presumed all Catholic girls did so. They would ask about school and Mom would encourage me to perform, like singing my exuberant rendition of "Supercalifragilisticexpialidocious."

I am confident the nuns satisfied my basic survival needs. However, I doubt I received much nurturing from them or my mother. Even Mom's descriptions made it clear she flitted through for cursory check-ins. I have wondered if Mom would've bonded with me more had I lived with her right away. And part of me wants to think she tried, since she did defy convention to keep me. But she also chose to spend minimal time at the convent in those early months, establishing a pattern that saddens me still. When I began dating my husband, he commented on my ongoing demands that we snuggle, which reminded him of the baby monkeys who hadn't been touched enough and never quite recovered. ◉

# CHAPTER 3
## First Kidnapping

MOM AND JOHN HAD LOTS OF FRIENDS and we often socialized as a family. My mother, her sisters, and their girlfriends created the Whamahaw Club. The meetings started with a song about "weary housewives and mothers and half-assed workers." The Whamahaws met monthly to commiserate, catch up on the latest gossip, and share amusing anecdotes, all while serving mixed drinks and hors d'oeuvres featured in women's magazines.

In the summer of '67, they invited husbands and kids to a picnic to introduce some new members. Cindy and I leapt out of the Dodge Dart and veered toward the voices emanating from the backyard of the maroon Cape Cod. I sprinted to Mr. Miller and beamed, revealing my two missing front teeth. The lanky grill master bent down and cupped my chin. "Well, lookie who's here. The Holub girls. Let's see, a cheeseburger for Mary Beth and a plain hamburger with nothing on it for Cindy-Lou. Right?"

We nodded and scurried off to horse around with the other kids for a half hour, then picked up our well-done charcoal-broiled burgers and a handful of New Jersey's famous Charles Chips. We sang in unison, "Thank you, Mr. Miller."

From the wives' circle, Mom gestured for me to park myself at her feet. Her blue sundress shimmered next to my complementary salmon shorts and paisley gold top. Mrs. Miller tickled my neck as she settled into her lounge chair. "She looks so much like you, Pat. It's no wonder she won the beauty pageant."

I had heard this often but failed to see much similarity between my round face and my mother's striking countenance. My dirty blond mop did not compare to her platinum coiffure. She moved with grace whereas I grew so fast I was clumsy and, to use her phrase, tripped over every crooked blade of grass.

"Sometimes beauty works against you. Did I tell you how we almost lost her? No? Well, when Mary Beth was three, she was outside with her boyfriend, Chucky, who lived in the apartment next door. The buildings made a square, with a lawn where the kids played games. Chucky taught her to build Lincoln Log houses. Mary Beth would make up stories for his GI Joes and her dolls, like they all happily drove to the shore but ended up arguing about whether to ride the Ferris wheel. They were so in love, they decided to marry, have six kids, and live on a fire engine."

My mother took a long draw from her Pepsi, and the Whamahaws standing near the trees stepped closer. I swallowed hard and used a fingernail to make red ketchup swirls on the paper plate. I wanted to crawl away but knew that would disrupt my mother's moment. I tugged at her skirt, but she brushed me aside.

"One day, some neighbors came over for gin rummy. We glanced out the windows now and again, to keep an eye on the kids. I can still see them, like in a movie, the sun shining bright as they chased each other, giggling like little idiots."

Mrs. Miller raised her hand as if to comment, but Mom plowed ahead.

"Suddenly, Chucky raced into the apartment, ashen white, trembling from head to toe." My mother gripped my shoulder and squeezed. "What did Chucky say to Mommy and Daddy?"

The women's eyes fixed on me. I glanced at Cindy riding Dad like a pony, then, in slow singsong, provided the phrase she sought. "Chucky told you, 'Somebody stole Mary Beth.'"

"That's right. Somebody stole Mary Beth." She paused as the other women exclaimed "Oh my God" and "Dear Lord."

"As best we can figure, a teenage boy hurtled toward them from the parking lot, grabbed Mary Beth, and fled out the opposite side of the property."

Mrs. Miller clutched her chest. "How horrible!"

Mom wiggled in her seat. "Look! Even now, goose bumps, imagining him watching her for weeks, waiting for his chance."

The women nodded and Mrs. Miller rubbed my shoulder.

"The men threw down their cards and dashed outside with Chucky. Sobbing, he managed to say 'big man' and point in the correct direction. John and his posse bolted out of the complex in pursuit."

"Oh, Pat, you must've been petrified!"

"I almost fainted from the shock!" As I expected, my mother slumped backward and pressed her palm to her forehead. "Anyway, the men rushed to the corner and spotted him. John told me Mary Beth peered over the boy's shoulder, her big blue eyes pleading for help. He was skinny and couldn't outrun them while carrying her, probably heavier than he'd guessed, with her baby fat."

My mother pinched my cheeks, so I bit off a giant mouthful of burger and chewed so hard I bit my tongue.

"After a few blocks, he dropped her, hightailed it over a fence, and ran off. They saw his brown crew cut but not his face. So they never did find him."

Mrs. Miller leaned down from the edge of her seat. "You are a very lucky girl."

Mrs. Miller was right. I was lucky the boy hadn't hurt me, although I suppose I'd felt as surprised and upset as Chucky. I remember the apartment and the square, but, due to my age, I don't recall this boy snatching me up. I can envision it in detail though. My mother burned the images of this kidnapping into my brain by retelling the story throughout my childhood. I still can feel myself bouncing in the boy's arms and, although I wasn't there, I can see Chucky announce my abduction.

I picture my mother outside the apartment crying, "No, no, my baby!" I'm sure she worried about my safety but would bet she grasped the sympathy value of this crisis when friends comforted her while they waited on the porch. Her frequent performances suggest this, and that she never appreciated the impact on me of hearing this tale from a young age. Or perhaps she thought this would teach me to use life's challenges to advantage through good storytelling that garnered the spotlight.

We lived in that apartment for another year. One night I awoke from a deep sleep and saw a woman with bushy red hair peering into my room through the window. She reminded me of Chucky's mother but with luminous skin and huge teeth. She examined me, then scanned the room but didn't seem to notice Cindy in the next bed. I recall a hot flash while a chill ran up my spine, which I'm not sure is possible, but that's how it seemed to me.

I tried to lie motionless while I watched her through one half-opened eye. Her fingers splayed against the glass. I had to pee but dared not move. After what seemed an eternity, she sighed and slid away.

I ran to my parents' bedroom down the hall, panting in panic, and shook Mom hard. "There's a funny-looking lady."

"What? What are you talking about?"

"Red hair. Staring at me from outside."

"It was a nightmare. Get back to bed!"

My knees almost buckled as I flashed on the woman clambering through our window. I opened my mouth twice but couldn't formulate an effective plea. I glanced at John, but he lay prone, snoring.

"Back to bed. If there's a crazy lady, you don't want to leave your sister alone, do you?"

My stomach sank as my mother gestured toward the door. I swiveled toward my room, shuffled back, then paused in the hallway to slow my rapid breath. I tiptoed to Cindy and stroked her hand, then climbed into bed, forgoing the bathroom to protect my sister. After allowing myself a few tears, I shook my head and whispered, "Don't be a ninny." I tried to stay awake, but my eyelids closed several times, then flew open when I thought I heard a board creak or a tap on the windowpane.

I'd wager I did conjure up this odd hag although I can't be sure because no one checked. Rather than alleviate my distress, when bored, my mother might smirk and ask, "Have you seen the funny-looking red-haired lady lately?" At first, my heart would plummet to the floor at this question. Later, I told this story to friends, sometimes as a horrific event and other times as a childish fantasy.

These two incidents contributed to my profound sense of being unsafe in the world. For decades, apprehension subverted sleep. I dreamed unseen monsters chased me through dense forests or down steep mountains. I attempted to scream but could emit no sound. I searched dank caverns for my sister, terrified I would never find her.

I developed various techniques to calm myself. I whispered with Cindy about Christmas gifts or sang songs from *Mary Poppins*. I gave each finger an identity, like a talking puppy and a fairy godmother. My left thumb became teacher Mrs. Cassidy and the pinkie Fireman Joe. We acted out fairy tales, discussed trips to Hershey's chocolate factory, and reviewed my school lessons. We played together almost every night until I dozed off.

By fourth grade, I had an active story line to pick up each night. I visualized myself as Cinderella and created scenarios in which the prince saved me from peril. By my teenage years, I devised harrowing ordeals, such as being taken hostage and beaten. In my imaginings, friends or teachers noticed my suffering afterward, admired my ability to survive, and assisted my recovery. I used this method to settle my mind and fall asleep until my forties, when I realized that immersing myself in trauma might have been contributing to my lifelong anxiety.

Even now, when writing about this kidnapping, dismay resurfaces over my mother's lack of concern for my well-being and how she telegraphed this so she could garner a bit of attention for herself. These experiences reminded me that I was not safe in this world and my mother did not care. ●

# CHAPTER 4
## Carving Knife

DESPITE HER LIMITATIONS, my mother had many positive attributes. Although not well educated, she was exceptionally smart. My grandpop told me that when my mother was three, she could put together a jigsaw puzzle with all the states from memory. In the eighties, she won *Jeopardy* when she nailed the vague final question about Cliffs Notes, a study guide she'd heard mentioned on *The Cosby Show*. She also could be very creative when attempting to control the behavior of Cindy and me. She taught us the "Who Can Be Quietest the Longest" game, which I never won despite my best efforts.

And Mom cautioned us about the large green containers at the supermarket. "Until you girls turn five, I can put you in that bin and send you to the used kids store. Some parents do it for no reason, but I'll only return you if you keep disobeying me." When Cindy and I ignored orders or talked back, she would holler, "Don't make me ship you off to the used kids store."

Sometimes when she seemed particularly close to the edge, I would warn my sister, "Knock it off! She'll throw us in the car and drive us to the used kids store." Other times, I would threaten Cindy,

"If you touch my doll one more time, I'll tell Mom to send you to the used kids store."

One day before shopping at Two Guys grocery, I ran to the green bin, stood tiptoe, pushed up the heavy rubber lid, and peered inside. I swung around and placed my hands on my hips. "There's no kids! Just clothes."

Mom smiled. "Those are donations for the used kids."

I still chuckle when I see similar bins with a sign seeking contributions for foster kids.

Once in a while, she'd mention that I was a brain like her, but more often I confounded her. Like the time our cat moseyed into my room, so I leapt off my bed to cuddle him. Prince didn't agree with this plan and fled down the stairs, so I ran after him, at one point grabbing his legs before he slipped away. I chased him into the kitchen, where he squeezed behind the stove. I tried to capture him by putting my arm into the crevice between the oven and the wall, but Prince moved farther away. I stuck my head into the gap to increase my reach. He appeared to sneer at me and escaped out the other side. I attempted to back out but couldn't pull my head through.

Panic overwhelmed me as I struggled to free myself. I yelled for my mother. The stove muffled my calls, and I doubt my voice reached her. Tears streamed across my face as I began whimpering, "Mommy, Mommy." It seemed to be hours, but probably was thirty minutes, before my mother ambled out of her room and nearly tripped over me.

"How the hell did you manage to do this?"

In retrospect, I cannot blame her for laughing.

And Mom did support me sometimes, like once at the dentist when I was five, when the nurse shoved cotton in my mouth. "Please, stop. Can't breathe." She instead grabbed another roll. As her fingers passed my teeth, I bit down hard. The nurse screamed in pain and apparent disbelief. My mother cackled. "She warned you!" It was a new story for her collection, but one I enjoyed.

Yet, despite some moments of connection with her, my world felt tenuous. Mom's marriage to John is a prime example. He was easygoing, had a ready laugh, and was an interested father in the early years. He would spin us around, expressed pride in my great report cards, and convinced our mother to let us get a dog. A plump man of middling attractiveness, it seemed to me that Mom mesmerized him, like when I would catch him staring at her as she impressed party guests. John's buddies would comment, "You lucky dog" and "I don't know how you managed to snag her."

I think my mother appreciated that John married her and treated me as a daughter. But she resented losing out on the big house and upwardly mobile life she'd dreamed of with Don. In her mind, John and all the things he provided were second-best replacements. She made it clear that, while she craved Chanel N°5, she'd settled for Estée Lauder. A typical dressing down of John involved complaints about our tiny apartment or a litany of disappointments rolled into one. "We need to go to New York once a month, go to that club where the Rat Pack shows up sometimes, and get great seats at the big Broadway hits. Make my friends jealous. But all you want to do is bowl and watch TV. You are so booooring."

I didn't understand the details but knew my mother was miserable. My ears pricked up anytime she raised her voice, because her unhappiness tended to explode into rage. This could be a synthesis of such events, but I have a memory of John commenting that she'd overcooked the pork. Mom burst out of her chair. "So I'm not the ideal little homemaker you imagined? Look at me! Did you think you married a meek housewife who would be fulfilled because she cooked the perfect dinner? If you want a divorce so you can find your mouse, that's fine with me."

Cindy and I glanced at each other, then at our plates, to avoid making eye contact with her. Our mother ran upstairs and slammed the bathroom door. We could hear her muttering to herself as she banged the wall with her fists, based on the sound. Despite the frequency of these outbursts, John looked like a little boy, stunned to find he lived in an unfair world. He stared at his plate for a few minutes, then grabbed his beer and retired to the backyard.

Even though we were alone now, Cindy whispered, "Is she that upset over pork chops?"

"Doubt it. She likes carrying on."

Soon after, when I was six, we moved into a small two-bedroom apartment in nearby Bordentown. One night, my mother's wails woke me. As I pushed back my blankets, I heard John sputter, "I . . . I . . . I just don't understand. What do you want from me?"

My feet landed on the rough carpet and I tiptoed to the door. I cracked it ajar and a small shard of light crept into the room.

"I can't take it anymore! I swear, I'm going to do it."

I peered down the hall toward the main part of our flat. I could only lay eyes on Mom, who stood at the end of the corridor, facing the living room, where I assumed John sat. The harsh illumination forced me to squint. She stood barefoot in her white blouse and ice blue pedal pushers. Disheveled hair, smeared lipstick. She held a carving knife over her wrist.

Although I'm not sure I heard the words, I knew she was threatening to cut herself. I imagined blood spewing from her arm as it had from my foot when I'd stepped on a nail in the yard. I slumped onto the floor as tears dripped from my eyes. My head banged against the bed frame, but I managed to stifle my yelp. I gripped the ruffled hem of my yellow baby doll nightgown with both sweaty hands and listened for a while as the argument moved into their bedroom. I thought about talking to my finger friends, but sadness overwhelmed me and I didn't have the energy. I turned onto my side as my mother's words transformed into the exhausted sobs that lulled me to sleep.

The next morning, I shrugged when Cindy asked why I had slept on the floor, seeing no reason to add to her worries. And I knew better than to bother Mom with my concerns. To her, my emotions were an inexplicable irritant. If my face crumpled because she said something that upset me, she would order me to "Stop being so sensitive" or wave me away, saying, "You're being ridiculous." A blubbering child sent her over the edge. "Stop that racket! Go to your room or I'll give you something to cry about!" So I swallowed the lump in my throat and shuffled down the hall. As we walked past our mother's boudoir, as she called it, Mom issued a common pronouncement: "Make yourselves cereal for breakfast. But I have another headache. So first, bring me two Excedrin and a glass of water."

I used to say that my earliest memory was my mother about to slit her wrist. But in writing this memoir, I realized my brain had tricked me because, I think, this moment clarified the nagging dread that inhabited my core. Life was unstable, horrors lurked around every corner, and my mother was absorbed in her own pain. I didn't understand why she suffered like this or was willing to take us down with her, but I couldn't ignore the evidence. Even still, looking back, I can see that my mother usually didn't intend to hurt us. She just focused elsewhere—on her unmet desires, frustrations, and drive to be special.

But she made sure we were fed, housed, and clothed. To the best of her understanding, this was her job. And she did it. ●

# CHAPTER 5
## Goldfish

JOHN'S GRANDPARENTS, NANNY AND POPPY, babysat us weekdays once our mother landed a secretarial job when I was four and Cindy two. In their sixties, Nanny and Poppy owned a small home in the working-class DeCou neighborhood. Poppy would wait for us each morning next to the large oak, smoking his pipe, which Nan wouldn't allow inside. Cindy would bounce up and down while he unlatched the metal gate, then rush to him because Poppy handed out hugs like they were free. We'd fly through the house, past the tiny sitting area with the heavy black telephone with the rotating dial, which Nan displayed, like a sculpture, on a three-legged table. To her, it was a sign of modernity and a pretense to being middle class, as if she didn't realize that everyone now had a phone, although she warned us never to answer it during a storm because "lightning can run through the line and kill you."

Nanny could be hauling canning jars of fruit from the cellar or preparing Poppy's breakfast at the table in the petite kitchen. Sometimes we caught her pinning her long silver mane into a bun, as her mother taught her when she was a girl. Or she might be "putting on her face," powdering her wrinkled visage and applying a touch of rosy cream rouge.

Nanny fulfilled the role of efficient homemaker, assigning a specific task to each day of the week, such as laundry Monday and gardening Sunday, and loved her "no more hand scrubbing" wringer washing machine. She wasn't much of a cook, so Nanny taught Cindy and me to use the manual eggbeater to turn ice cream into "pudding," maybe to keep us busy when she cleaned up after a meal. She fried hamburgers and fed us mayonnaise toast and buttered kaiser rolls. If we begged, she'd let us eat cereal at lunch, which I slurped up with the Tony the Tiger spoon that I'd ordered after I'd collected Frosted Flakes box tops for months. In the yard, Nanny planted an extensive flower garden, and Poppy converted the outhouse into a shed for her tools. Nearby, he installed a swing set and a sandbox for us.

As Mom dropped us off one day, we tumbled out next to the concrete post with a loop on the side to tie up horses, before there were cars, Poppy'd said. He squatted and pecked each of our cheeks. "Girls, we have a big surprise. Nan and I bought you a bright yellow motorcycle. It's in the barn. Go take a look."

I asked, "Poppy, are we big enough?"

His eyes crinkled and he patted my butt. "Don't fret, you'll see."

Cindy flew past me and up the walkway. I sped across the lawn to beat her to our present, but we had to work together to open the door. I clutched the handle and pulled until it cracked ajar, then Cindy pushed against the bottom to help. We paused as our eyes adjusted to the dim light that filtered through the red slats. The sweet smell of fresh hay wafted toward me. I spotted the brown pony we'd ridden at nearby Carney Roses Riding Academy leaning down and enjoying her breakfast.

"Poppy, that's not a motorcycle! That's Silkie!"

"Yep, she's old and they were gonna send her to the glue factory. I thought, *My girls love Silkie.* So I rescued her."

"What's a glue factory?"

"Never mind, Mary Beth. She's here now."

Poppy would lead us by the reins as we rode Silkie through the neighborhood. I would sit tall, sway from side to side with each step, and listen to the *clop-clop* of her hooves on the tarred street. Poppy might jog a bit because Silkie preferred to trot, but at his age such exertion was short-lived. He told stories about the families that lived in the houses we passed, pointed out needed repairs, or reminisced about childhood visits to his uncle's dairy farm. Now and then, a friend would run out with a carrot. Poppy would take a breather so they could pet Silkie while she chomped on the snack, but only Cindy and I could ride her.

About two years later, John's car flew past the front window of our duplex as he pulled into the driveway. I flipped over our *Mary Poppins* album and plopped back onto the floor. Cindy danced with Baa Baa White Sheep, her favorite stuffed animal. The screen door slammed as our mother entered from the backyard. I sat up and watched the trail of smoke from John's Chesterfield King cigarette float across the porch.

Mom dropped the laundry basket filled with rumpled sheets she'd taken off the clothesline, marched to the record player, and flipped the off switch. I cringed as the needle scratched the vinyl. She sat on the sofa and stroked the tufted beige upholstery.

"Girls, I'm sorry to have to tell you this, but Poppy died."

Cindy asked, "Whaddaya mean?"

"He's dead. Gone. Like the time your goldfish was floating belly up so we flushed him."

I scrunched my forehead as my mind considered and rejected various interpretations. "No, Mommy, Poppy's too big for the toilet."

Cindy nodded agreement, threw Baa Baa high, and caught him midair.

"Jesus Christ! I didn't say . . . Listen, Poppy died. Like the goldfish. He's dead." She jumped up, grabbed the basket, and tromped upstairs.

Cindy leaned over. "Poppy isn't a fish."

"I know. I think he's sick, in bed, like when I had chicken pox."

That Saturday Mom said we should wear our best dresses. Cindy put on my favorite navy blue, made entirely of vertical pleats, so the skirt fanned out when you twirled. My red satin was pretty but just hung straight. I pushed Cindy so hard as she spun around showing off that she slid into the hallway.

Mom took one look and wagged her finger at me. "Mary Beth, I don't want to hear you complain about that dress. You grow too fast, so it doesn't fit. We can barely afford to keep you in clothes."

Cindy laughed. "Yeah, too bad, Mary Beth. Plus, all I get to wear are your hand-me-downs anyway."

John drove us to a majestic white house with a circular drive. I jumped out of the sedan and gallivanted toward a long black car to better view its lace curtains and polished brass ornaments.

"Mommy, why do they have such a fancy station wagon?"

She did not reply but instead gestured for me to return to the fold and precede her up the stairs, next to the Buklad's Funeral Parlor sign. I hesitated as my eyes adapted to the dimly lit interior, then recognized family and neighbors sporting their Sunday best, just as they had for a recent wedding.

In the foyer, John stopped to whisper to a sobbing Aunt Doris. Mom paused at the entrance to a wood-paneled room that included six rows of chairs with a path in the middle. Various small groups sat nearby or stood along the walls, talking in hushed voices. Mom started to move us down that corridor.

John gripped her arm. "Are they old enough to see him?"

Cindy and I hesitated, waiting for her reaction. She shrugged hard to force him to release his hold. "They aren't babies!"

She proceeded in quick steps, her heels click-clacking on the wooden floor. I knew to follow. Cindy grasped the hem of my dress and trailed behind. As my mother reached the end, she leaned over and pointed to the knee rest. When we kneeled, as we did in church, she shook her head. "Stand on it."

I steadied Cindy as she lifted her leg to mount. Once in place, we saw Poppy lying in a wooden box with green lining. He wore a suit rather than his usual work pants and flannel shirt, and held large white flowers. His smile was stiff and his skin waxy, like the candles at Holy Angels. I reached in to smooth a wayward hair but retracted my hand as the icy cold raced from my fingertips to my soul.

"Poppy is in heaven now. This is the last time you'll see him. Tomorrow they'll bury him at the cemetery near Nan's." She swung around and left us.

Cindy frowned and stretched her neck to look into my eyes. "What's a cemetery?"

"It's that park, with the statues."

We lingered as others visited Poppy. They peered inside the casket, crossed themselves, and sometimes straightened his already straight tie. Often, they said, "He loved you girls so much." This made me happy and sad, but I couldn't put my finger on why. I thought about

Poppy as the crossing guard for my school. He looked so different in his black uniform as he waved cars through the intersection or twittered his whistle to hurry the kids along. When he turned toward me, I would skip down the sidewalk. As I neared, Poppy's face would light up and he'd smile so wide I'd worry his dentures might pop out. He'd take my hand, escort me across the road, and hug me before he sent me on my way.

An old lady from down the street tapped me from behind, drawing me back into the room. We waved to Poppy and beelined for Nan, but grown-ups surrounded her. We had to entertain ourselves because none of our cousins materialized, so we went back several times to see Poppy. I was reading the cards on the bouquets to my sister, proud I could decipher "sympathy," when our mother corralled us by the shoulders and rushed us to an exterior room.

"You're upsetting your father. Quit chatting about the goddamn flowers."

Cindy asked, "Mommy, when will Poppy wake up?"

I scanned the room and locked onto Nanny dabbing her eyes with one of the handkerchiefs we'd given her for Christmas, so I didn't anticipate a hopeful response but pivoted toward my mother just in case. She stooped to our level.

"He's not. Your father and I aren't going to be married anymore. We'll live apart. You two will move in with Nanny. She'll be lonely without Poppy. She needs you there to cheer her up."

My heart sank and tears flowed.

"We planned to tell you later, at home, but . . . so many goddam questions. Look, you know Dad and I don't get along. This will be better for everyone. There's no reason to boo-hoo about it."

I focused on my mother's face. She nodded firmly, relaying the hopelessness of any effort to change her mind. Cindy collapsed to the floor with the blue dress flaring into a circle around her. I lifted her chin and rubbed my nose against hers.

"Don't worry, Nan's nice and we'll be together."

Poppy's death created a void for Nanny, Cindy, and me. After we moved in, once I understood he wasn't coming back, I refused to leave the house because the loss of Poppy and the sudden separation from my parents eviscerated me. I'd even lost Silkie because Nan sold her back to Carney Rose's, she said to save money. Although I don't remember my time at the convent, I now wonder if the first abandonment exacerbated my despair. I must've still had hopes then that my mother would be the mommy I craved because, if I'd already given up this fantasy, I wouldn't have been so heartbroken when I realized she didn't want me.

I spent my days in the recliner watching television. I bit my fingernails until they bled and clenched my jaw so hard that I wondered if a bone might snap. The monotony of the flickering TV could lull me into a numb, disembodied state. If Cindy or Nanny headed my way, I would force myself to imagine Poppy in the pitch-dark underground so I would be crying when they neared. I yearned for someone to notice my sadness and despair. Nan might toss a "Go outside, Mary Beth" as she passed, which I ignored. A bored Cindy occasionally pestered me to play but fled when I shouted, "Leave me alone." After a few weeks, my tears ran out, I gave up, and I adjusted to my new life.

Nanny seemed quite willing to have us live with her, and we ended up staying for three years. But she blamed our mother for the divorce and warned us against becoming flighty and "caring more about yourself than your responsibilities." Nan said we didn't live with Mom because she hated being tied down to kids and instead went out carousing every night, which Mom's breathless stories of night-clubs and lobster restaurants reinforced. I'd bet no one considered the option of John getting custody, yet as an adult I thought it interesting that Nan focused her criticism on Mom. John stopped by once a month for a quick check-in or to take us out for dusty road sundaes, but we did see our mother regularly. Not weekly as she later claimed, but she visited and sometimes we slept over at her apartment.

Being at Nan's, when she babysat us and when we lived there, provided the calmest and quietest part of our lives. I do think my mother convinced John to send us to live with Nan so she could be a single woman on her own for the first time. Though I doubt she thought about our happiness, I'm sure she trusted Nan to care for us. It's true that emotional support wasn't her strength, but Nanny was straightforward and practical. She didn't engage in drama or create chaos. So, ultimately, whatever the motivation, these were the best of my childhood years. •

# CHAPTER 6
## School

EVEN MORE THAN riding Silkie, I loved school. Kisthardt was small, with one class of about fifteen students per grade. The L-shaped brick schoolhouse had a playground in the center, monkey bars and swings on the tarmac, and a hopscotch diagram painted nearby. A scruffy softball field comprised the back lot, though I don't think Kisthardt had money for equipment because I only recall neighborhood pickup games. We did put on plays, with students responsible for their own outfits, all homemade except my mom would drop off a boxed Bugs Bunny or whatever cartoon character sort of fit my role. These costumes were repurposed for the Halloween parade. Beginning with the oldest, the sixth graders, we students marched around the block. The stay-at-home moms stood in front of their houses to clap, and passersby honked and waved.

One kid would come or go over the summer, but otherwise I was with the same classmates from year to year. My best friend, Tony, hailed from a large Italian clan and knew how to navigate the grammar school social structure, a skill I struggled to master. When hit with "stop being bossy" pushback for trying to organize an activity,

Tony would step in and say something like "C'mon, sounds fun." And he shared my intellectual curiosity. In kindergarten, we'd sit on the floor and race to complete jigsaw puzzles or discuss how to construct a high-rise with building blocks.

In first grade, Mrs. Stuckey arranged the desks in rows and seated us by height. Because I was tall, she relegated me to the back. When I couldn't read the blackboard, they made me get glasses, first in my class, so the kids pummeled me with four-eyes and blind as a bat insults. When I was nine, I caterwauled in frustration because the popular wire frames couldn't bear the weight of my thick lenses, forcing me into an ugly "brainiac" style. My extreme prescription worked to my advantage later though, at thirteen, when my optometrist prescribed contacts to slow my vision decline. My mother seemed relieved. "Goodbye Coke bottles! And you've grown out of your baby fat. Now you'll be able to land any boy you want."

Mrs. Stuckey also taught me to read. In those days, at least in my working-class world, no one learned at home. I caught on with ease, as if I already knew and just needed to be reminded. Immersing myself in animal stories or adventure tales took me out of my chaotic life and into a world of happy endings. But, despite my best efforts, artistic assignments flummoxed me.

"All right everyone, quiet. While I'm grading your spelling test, sketch a picture of your family at your house."

I debated about who to include as my family. If just Nan and Cindy, I'd have to explain why I left out my parents. If they were included, I'd be lying because I didn't live with them, which a few kids knew and might bring up. Anyway, that was a lot of people to draw and people were hard. I wiped my palms on my dress to remove the sweat.

Tony turned to me. He mouthed, "You can do it!"

I nodded twice and opened the top of my desk, removing my six-pack of Crayolas while Mrs. Stuckey handed out construction paper. I bit my lip and stared at the blank sheet, then colored the bottom green and the top blue. On the right, I placed a square house with a triangle roof. I drew two stick figures, one twice as tall as the other, which was nearly accurate even though only two years separated Cindy and me. Then I scrawled yellow lines for my hair and squiggled brown to suggest her curls. Blue eye dots for me and brown for Cindy, two red mouths that looked askew, so I didn't dare try noses. As I stared at the page, my cheeks burned as I imagined standing at the front of the room with this disaster.

A quick glance around verified my inadequate effort. I saw flowers, puppy dogs, and swing sets. I rested my forehead on the desk and tried not to bawl, which would expose me as not just a failure but also weak. Then I remembered the newspaper comics I read every day. I sketched two bubbles above my stick girls and added a conversation.

"Play catch?"

"Okay."

This astounded Mrs. Stuckey. "Come with me, Mary Beth. Class, we'll be back in a jiffy. Sit and finish your work." She escorted me around the school to show the other teachers my picture. "I've been at this twenty years, and no first grader ever thought to do this." Each scrutinized my drawing and congratulated me for a job well-done. I beamed, thrilled with the attention, but was baffled by all this praise for a bit of dialogue in an embarrassingly simple picture.

That summer, I read everything I could lay my hands on. Since she couldn't afford to buy them, Nan borrowed books from neighbors who had kids a few years older than me. I devoured my first novels, *Black Beauty* and *The Secret Garden*. I perused the entire local

newspaper, which sounds more impressive than it was since Nan sub-
scribed to the low-brow *Trentonian*, not the relatively erudite *Trenton
Times*. Two weeks into the new school year, my teacher, Mrs. Cook,
took me to the librarian and told her I could check out any book I
wanted, even from the sixth-grade section. I was thrilled to have the
entire library at my disposal and barely minded my new nickname,
"Miss Smarty Pants." Plus, a teacher again had plucked me out of the
crowd as deserving special treatment and for a talent I enjoyed.

In third grade, they distinguished us based on academic success.
A student teacher worked with the chosen five for several hours each
week on advanced reading and math. I always sat beside Tony but
also befriended Doreen, a recent transplant. She and I shared that our
parents had divorced, a disgrace we'd been instructed to keep secret
although my mother focused on the "people will use anything they
can to put you down" aspect. Admitting this felt liberating. I regretted
my honesty, though, because Doreen's father came by to see her every
weekend and she seemed stunned to learn that even my mother did
not visit me weekly. I exaggerated how often we saw my parents, made
up excuses about Mom working hard so she could save money and
get us back, and changed the subject. If I would've had the words to
categorize my emotions, betrayal would've topped the list, although
anger and hurt would've been close behind. The next time I saw my
mother, I couldn't look her in the eyes, with the new knowledge that,
on top of leaving us at Nan's, she even failed to live up to the visitation
rules for divorced parents.

After Poppy died, I often succumbed to my anxiety, like when I
left, at school, my hated green-and-black-checkered lunch box, plain
compared to the other kids' colorful cartoon character versions. After
class, as usual, I smiled at Mrs. Stuckey and traipsed out with Tony.

"Will your Nan let me come over and play?"

"I don't think so. My mother might come by later."

"Really, on a school day?"

I shrugged, and Tony split away and headed home. Halfway up the block, I froze in my tracks as a pulsing wave of terror flooded my body. *Oh no! I left my lunch box. What'll Nan do with my sandwich tomorrow? Mrs. Stuckey will think I'm stupid.* With my brain focused on this horrific chain of events, it didn't occur to me to just return to Kisthardt to get it. Or perhaps, in my child's mind, school closed as soon as the students left. I did race to the corner to look for Tony for help, but he was long gone. I buckled at the waist and grabbed the street sign pole to steady myself, and the dam of tears broke. I turned and dashed home howling. By the time I ripped open the gate, barely noticing Cindy waiting next to the tree, Nan had run from the kitchen to the front porch.

"Mary Beth! What's going on?"

I paused, brushed the sweat off my brow, then, between gasps, squeaked out the critical information. "I forgot my lunch box. At school."

"For God's sake. It'll be there tomorrow. Now get in the house and change."

Cindy slid under my arm and patted my belly. "Nan says don't worry."

My breathing slowed and the roar in my ears receded. I unclenched my fingers and stumbled into the house.

While I feared the dire consequences of any simple mistake, my panic had escalated because looking like an idiot to Mrs. Stuckey risked the loss of my intellectual superiority status. I completed all the homework and raised my hand to answer every question, despite knowing this irritated the other kids sometimes, because I reveled in being seen and the confidence I gained.

Another similar anxiety-inducing event occurred in fourth grade. When I received my Iowa Skills Test scores of straight ninety-nines, I struggled to calm my shaking hands and to keep my butt in my seat rather than race to the wastebasket to rip up the report. At home, sobbing, I handed these results to my mother.

"What is the matter with you? Why are you crying?"

"I didn't get any hundreds."

"Jesus Christ! Mary Beth, these scores are percentiles. That means ninety-nine is the highest. So knock it off and go to your room."

As relief washed over me, I barely noticed the brush off. Only one thing mattered. My score was perfect, so I had held off calamity for the moment.

This pervasive anxiety was related to high-impact events like an evil boy kidnapping me, Mom's threat to cut her wrist, and being dumped at Nanny's. But I think it was the lack of bonding with my parents that took the largest toll. I don't remember Mom playing with me, asking me about my day, or offering to help if I mentioned any challenge. Even Nan and John rarely did, though Poppy had, but he was gone. Plus, I was the oldest, loved Cindy, and felt the burden of protecting her. This isn't to say I didn't argue with her or swat her in anger. But I tried to be a good big sister. I absorbed the lesson that I could count only on myself, which meant relying on my wits and not on others. When I went into group therapy years later and people spoke about what they "needed," mostly assistance or support, I was astounded. I just needed to pay close attention to all eventualities and course-correct to avoid catastrophe. The problem, as I saw it, was my lack of perfection in doing so. •

# CHAPTER 7
## Allan

AFTER SEPARATING FROM JOHN, Mom hunted for a new husband. Twenty-five at the time, she initially seemed to enjoy the single life. But she lived on a secretary's salary and complained about the clothes she couldn't buy and drove us through lovely neighborhoods to point out her favorite houses.

The first boyfriend Cindy and I met was accountant Lester, a sweet low-key man, like John. His daughter, Samantha, always wore Sunday-best dresses and a barrette in her curly hair. The five of us enjoyed excursions to local sights, movies, and kid-friendly restaurants and shared some holidays. Cindy and I savored our time with them and generally behaved. Like me, Samantha and Lester loved books. He brought a new Nancy Drew each visit. I would read the first chapter aloud for everyone. Mom beamed when he said, "She's smart as a whip, like you, Pat."

Despite everyone's best efforts to snag him, Lester ended the relationship. Although Mom charmed us during our excursions, I would bet he bailed because her true colors emerged. Because she really did have everything going for her, except her emotional volatility and vicious mouth. She told Nan she didn't like him much anyway, another stick-in-the-mud like John, but grumbled to her sisters that he'd lied about his intentions. "Guess he was like all the rest, just wanted one thing."

Soon after, Mom prepped us to meet her "new beau," Allan. "He lives with his dad and brother and isn't used to children. I'm lucky he's interested, since I have you two. So no back talk, no bickering. Smile, look pretty, and be pleasant. Now, what do you think, the black jumpsuit or the lavender mini?"

With the long buzz of the doorbell, we glanced at our mother for guidance. "Follow me and stand near the sofa." When she opened the door, Allan pulled her close and kissed her long and hard with his fat wet lips. "Baby, the kids."

He examined us, then grinned. "Sorry, girls, just can't keep my hands off this sexy thing."

Cindy hid behind my legs when introduced. Mom frowned and turned to me. "Allan, this is my oldest, Mary Beth."

I tilted my head up, gazed into his eyes, and extended my hand for a shake. "Nice to meet you."

Allan roared with laughter. "Well, the little professor. C'mere and give me a hug."

Cindy gripped my skirt and tugged. I pivoted and plunked her onto the couch, then strode toward him. He lifted me from my armpits and flung me into the air, catching me just as I dropped level with his waist. I sat backward onto the coffee table to regain my equilibrium. Allan took a step forward, I thought to toss me to the ceiling again, so I straightened my arm in the universal "stop" signal.

"So, do the fraidy-cats like steak and shrimp cocktail? Course ya do. Pat, get their coats, I'm dying for an Alexander's filet."

The maître d', as Mom taught on the ride over, ushered us to a table near the fireplace after Allan slipped him some cash. When I climbed onto a chair, Allan commanded, "Get down, you wait for the man," so I stood until he seated our mother, then Cindy, then me. He ordered Shirley Temples for "his girls," which turned out to be ginger ale topped by a cherry, in a fancy glass, with a giraffe stirrer he let us keep.

Even at eight years old, I could tell he wasn't my mother's intellectual equal, making grammar mistakes she would've hammered me for and pish-poshing Mom's mention of my academic achievements: "She's pretty, that's what counts." But he did have a similar magnetism. Allan slicked back his jet-black hair, dark lashes fringed his eyes, and he flashed large white teeth with every smile. Not quite medium height but broad shouldered and muscular. The waitress flirted with him, which caused my mother's brow to furrow, except sometimes she smirked, like she'd won the prize.

They'd arrive unannounced at Nan's most Sundays. We saw *Peter Pan*, picked out bikinis at the Jersey shore, and ate our first prime rib. At Grandmom O'Connor's birthday party, Allan appropriated her spot at the table and yanked Mom into his lap. He bragged he earned extra cash by loan-sharking to coworkers at the steel mill. "Once in a while I've gotta make an example out of a deadbeat, but it doesn't take much to get these pussies to pay up." When this pronouncement met dead silence, Mom chimed in, "He's very entrepreneurial."

The next week she dropped by alone and divulged their marriage plans. "He has a good job, and we can live together again, in his house." I wagged my head, meaning I understood, which she took as assent. "Good, I'm glad you're happy." As the screen door clicked shut behind Mom, we turned to Nan, to see if she would pipe in, but she just shrugged and kept mopping the floor. Cindy pushed me into the corner.

"I don't wanna. I liked Lester."

"I know. We go fun places. But he barely talks to us. And I don't believe his hugs."

"Won't Nan be sad if we leave, Mary Beth?"

"I guess so. But kids are supposed to live with their mother. Maybe Mom'll be happier because he likes restaurants and wears pretty shirts."

In anticipation of merging the families, Allan insisted we meet his father at the home they'd built in Bordentown, a mile from Nan's. The stone-covered ranch house stood at the front of a large lot in the middle of a short dead-end street. Allan pulled into the driveway. "See that garage we're building? On top, an apartment for my dad. Then you girls can move in. Well, after we update the house, the way your mom wants."

We entered through the kitchen, dominated by a Formica table with six vinyl chairs. Soon-to-be Grandpop M, a short, round, balding man in his late fifties, stirred something in a large pot on an old stove. "Well, who is this? Mary Beth and Cindy? Do you like rigatoni?"

I nodded and inched closer. The sauce smelled sweet and had an odd texture. "That's not spaghetti sauce. It's just squished tomatoes."

Grandpop M guffawed. "I guess you've never eaten Italian home cooking."

Cindy and I ran through the house, peering into the three bedrooms. We investigated the cellar and gazed at the tools in Allan's workshop. Cindy tried to lift the rifle that leaned against the wall near the back stairs. "Leave it alone. It's bigger than you are." We exited into the yard but scurried back when I broke a cornstalk in Allan's garden, just in time to catch him picking out pool cues. He tried to teach us, but Cindy had to stand tiptoe and I almost ripped the green felt with my first stroke. Allan snatched the stick from my grip. "You're both useless. Maybe in a few years."

At dinner, he regaled his father with stories we'd heard Mom tell him: how I won the beauty contest, "how the women in Pat's family are all knockouts," and how Cindy only ate vanilla ice cream. Afterward, the four of us set out to see the town, Cindy and I in the back of the massive Lincoln Continental.

Mom smiled at Allan. "I think that went well. Your dad seemed to like them."

"You must be kidding. Word one, out of your brat's mouth, complaints about the food he spent all day cooking for them. What an ungrateful little bitch." Allan threw me a quick hard glance. I gulped, looked down, and traced the edge of the red seats with a finger.

My mother reached out and took his hand. "He thought it was funny. She just never saw that type of sauce before."

"Get her under control. She never shuts up. Question after question. Says whatever pops into her skull. She's too smart for her own good."

Cindy poked me in the shoulder. "Yeah, smarty pants. Stop talking so much."

After she yelped from the pinch I gave her leg, Allan stopped so fast I bashed my head on his seat. He grabbed the headrest with his right arm and raised himself a few inches. "Shut. Up. Both of you. Not. Another. Word."

Eyes wide, Cindy crumpled into the seat. I slid toward the door, out of sight, but had to pause to peel the underside of my sweat-drenched thighs from the leather.

"Don't talk to my kids like that. You're frightening them."

"Good. They should be scared. If they don't watch it, I'll knock some sense into 'em." Allan sped to the next intersection and jammed on the brakes, then bent toward Mom. "Don't you ever, ever take their side over mine. Do you understand?"

My mother gasped and opened her mouth, as if to respond, but Allan's left fist plowed into her face. I heard his knuckles impact her cheek, like the thwack of a rubber ball against a wall. Mom's half-emitted scream turned to a whimper. My stomach dropped to the floor, and I covered my face. Cindy's sniffles floated to my ears. I shook myself alert, put my finger near my lips, and mouthed a shush because I worried about her drawing Allan's attention. I realized my shallow breaths were making me light-headed, so I focused and slowed my heart rate. I could see my mother's corded neck and the effort to swallow. A car behind us honked and Allan shifted into gear. Mom walloped the dashboard.

"Pull over! Pull this car over."

Allan peeled into the parking lot of a men's clothing store, and we scrambled out. Mom'd barely slammed the door shut before he hit the gas and barreled into traffic. "See, Cindy, it'll be okay now." I yearned to ask my mother how we'd get home and maybe even seek out a reassuring caress. But Mom leaned against a light post and closed her eyes. Cindy and I paced nearby, holding hands. After Mom's order to be careful, no dirt on your good shoes, we competed in a kick the rock the farthest contest.

Allan returned about ten minutes later. Mom straightened up as he approached, wiping her tears. "Sorry baby. Don't know why . . . just upset because I wanted the visit to be perfect."

We watched as he whispered into her ear. Brow furrowed, she said something like "never again," then let him pull her close and rock her from side to side. We froze when our mother waved us back into the Lincoln. She stomped over and pulled my arm so hard I worried my shoulder would pop out of the socket. Cindy followed, her tiny body racked by sobs. My mother later told me this was right before the wedding, so she'd brushed off the incident as Allan's understandable stress.

Mom left us at Nan's for another nine months after the marriage. Even after the Bordentown house renovation, I couldn't bring myself to ask why. As much as I dreaded moving in with Allan, even though he was on his best behavior on the few occasions we saw him during this period, I still felt unloved because she'd broken her promise that we'd be together. I began telling myself to "knock it off" whenever I felt sad or, especially, if tears welled. I directed Cindy to convince her friends we stayed with Nan because we wanted to once I decided our mother preferred to unload us on her. I still think I was right, but at some point, no rational explanation existed for leaving us at Nan's. So we moved into Allan's house.

To be fair, I imagine Mom pushed out our move-in date, hoping to solidify their relationship without the added conflicts kids create. Perhaps she thought the extra time would allow Allan to settle in and increase the chance of success in the marriage. Considering she had evidence of his proclivity to flip to violent rage, I agree this plan was worth a shot. That is, since she insisted on marrying him. ✽

# CHAPTER 8
## Bordentown

MY NINTH SUMMER, we moved into Allan's house on Heiser Avenue. Mrs. Halko, from across the street, told Mom he'd been calmer since the wedding. As a boy, he'd seemed to manage the wound inflicted by his mother when she abandoned him. But when he'd returned from the Vietnam war, Allan had been volatile, getting drunk and yelling at Mr. Halko or anyone else within his vicinity. The cops even brought him home several times with a fat lip or black eye, although he'd later announce his victory with some variant of "You should've seen the other guy."

Allan was in a good mood the first month we lived with him, I assume because my brother Albert had been born two weeks before. When friends visited to meet the newborn, Allan paraded around introducing his son. "Strong sperm, so I knew it'd be a boy to continue the family line." Sometimes he distinguished between us. "This is my real son and these are Pat's daughters." But mostly he appeared to enjoy his new role as family man, like taking pictures with all five of us for the photo album. He'd even show off the upgrades Mom had selected for the house. "Too fancy for my taste, but you've gotta let the little woman have some say on decorating."

Cindy and I settled into a summer routine. Laurie was my closest Heiser Avenue friend and Sharon was Cindy's. An avid *Tiger Beat* reader, Laurie had an outstanding 45 record collection and always knew what was in or out. Her chin-length hair flattered her round face and bright eyes, and she tanned just by standing near the window, which I envied because I burned to a crisp within an hour of sun exposure. She dressed in all the modern styles—colorful minis, hip-hugger jeans, and white go-go boots.

Since her parents paid for baton and dance lessons whereas my mother always promised "next year," Laurie taught us to twirl and to master her jazz routines. We loved *The Monkees* television show so, since there were four of us, we acted out episodes. I always played Mike, the smarter, more serious Monkee and mediated "whose turn is it to be Davy?" disputes among the others.

The neighborhood kids had engineered a path through the woods behind our expansive backyard. They'd cleared brush and covered a permanent mud patch with a rickety wooden ladder. We all used this route to talk privately during our treks to pinball and pizza at Hilltop Shopping Center. We built a fort, where we practiced flirting and choked on stolen cigarettes. Only a few families had erected fences, so the hide-and-seek boundary extended to Crosswicks Creek, the "crick" in local lingo, that ran behind the homes. We caught catfish, and the boys shot water rats with their BB guns. At low tide we explored a muddy island, even though occasional screams announced that a snake had wiggled over someone's foot. Small leeches nestled between our toes, so we girls would sit on a log while the boys removed the bloodsuckers. I didn't know the source of this rule but was grateful for it.

From the adjacent swamp, we gathered punks—cattails with bushy stalks— laid them out to dry in Halko's backyard, then lit them up like a torch to repel mosquitoes. The town also sent around an exterminator, who would pause at the top of the street, then activate a machine on the flatbed that emitted a toxic cloud. Despite the parents' warnings about breathing poison, whoever first spotted the truck would yell "mosquito man." We'd dash to our bikes and follow close to the gas plume while the mosquito man drove down the street, because it made us dizzy.

I enjoyed this period, getting comfortable with kids we'd grow up with rather than wondering when or if we'd be leaving Nan's to live with our mother. I'd watch Mom cook Allan's preferred meals of pasta or steak as I bounced Albert in my lap and described the book I'd finished that day. Allan welcomed our friends, offering them treats and asking after their parents. Even so, his attack on my mother lurked in my mind. I never mentioned it, though, and tried to comply with Mom's original "be nice and don't talk back" instructions and noticed she did the same. But one August day, as she washed dishes in the sink, with me rinsing and Cindy drying, she must've forgotten.

"I work at the office and cook a nice meal. Why did you refuse to buy a dishwasher when we upgraded the kitchen?"

Allan was sitting at the table paying bills, but then I heard the chair legs scrape the floor. Before I could turn my head, he bounded toward us, grabbed Mom's shoulders, and spun her around. Cindy ducked and I jumped in front of my little sister. Allan half twisted from the waist, then swung his arm. His open palm smacked Mom's face so hard, it sounded like a bone splintered. My mother's head wobbled back and forth as she rubbed her cheek. Cindy and I gasped. My jaw trembled as dread overwhelmed my body and my soul.

Mom shouted, "Not in front of the girls!"

Allan sneered while stretching his arms high, so his undershirt lifted and exposed his rounding belly. As he sauntered to his seat, my stomach heaved, I'm not sure whether in disgust at his slick white paunch or fury that he'd assaulted my mother. He stared at her as he picked up the next bill, pulled it out of the envelope, and flourished it overhead. Mom flipped around and clutched the edge of the sink. Cindy's hand shook, so I extracted the plate she was holding and placed it in the drainer.

That Saturday a dishwasher arrived. I was so repulsed by my mother's exuberant "Thank you, baby" to Allan that I gagged. By the time he left the room, I'd flipped through disbelief and disappointment and landed on scorn. I opened my mouth to say "I guess that's the price of a punch" but swallowed the words when I saw her crumble after Allan turned away.

Dishwashing turned out to be a hot-button issue more generally. One day as I dusted Mom's Renoir print, I paused to consider the colors, wondering how they could be both muted and saturated. I was drawn out of my reverie when Allan stomped toward me with his heavy work boots, holding a white and gold Corelle dinner plate. My heart pounded so hard, blood roared in my ears. I strained to hear him.

"You wanna get me sick? Eating off a filthy dish?"

"No, no. It went through the dishwasher. I thought it was fine."

He took two steps and halted. "Did you check it?"

"I'm sorry. I didn't notice. I'll wash it by hand now."

He slid the plate onto the end table, with some torque, so it wobbled and made that ringing sound. As I wondered if I could squeeze behind the sofa, he hurtled toward me. For a stocky man with short legs, his speed astounded me. I raced to my right. He lunged as I maneuvered past him. Allan snagged my shoulder but couldn't get a grip because the marble coffee table separated us. I flew through the kitchen and flung open the door so hard it slammed into the radiator.

His footsteps neared as I reached the porch. Yet I hesitated. *Run to the woods? Get help from the neighbors?* I decided to flee to the street. As I tottered on the first step, Allan seized my waist from behind. He dragged me backward. I think my feet left the ground. I screamed, "Help me! Please. Help."

Allan propelled me forward into the kitchen, and I landed on my hands and knees. He placed his boot against my back and forced me to the ground. I flailed and wiggled, trying to escape. Allan bent down and put his hands around my throat, pressing as I gasped and choked, almost out of breath, but not quite. Just as I wondered if he intended to kill me, he let go and hovered over me, silent. Then grabbed me under my armpits, hoisted me to my feet, and dumped me in a chair. He stooped to my eye level. "No one will rescue you. You could howl all day long. None of those people will dare stand up to me."

I wiped my tears and nodded.

"Now wash that goddam dish before I break it over your head." He thrust back on his haunches and strolled to his room.

I allowed the fear to roll through me for a few seconds before shoving it down. I rose and paused so my unsteady legs could find their balance. Perusing the sparkling dinner plate, I located one tiny dot of food hidden in the pattern. With trembling hands, I scrubbed it clean.

These first years with Allan, I mostly felt enraged and frustrated. I would beat my bed or stomp around the yard after an incident or when just remembering a beating. Sudden surges of adrenaline became a familiar sensation, a reaction to danger. I jumped at loud noises, unexplained movements flashing in my periphery, or anyone approaching from behind. My sleep struggles increased. Often I awoke throughout the night, my ears already attuned to any sign of activity in the house. Sometimes I couldn't bring myself to shower or could barely nod when friends spoke to me. I'd clasp my hands tight or count syllables with my fingers when others spoke, hoping for an even number because odds felt like the world was unbalanced, which meant I might be sucked into a dark, chaotic chasm so deep I'd never again see the light of day. I became forgetful, such as not taking the steaks out of the freezer for dinner, despite Mom's calls to remind me. I'd promise to do it right away, yet about once a week she'd return from work and find an empty counter where the defrosted meat should be.

"Mary Beth."

I would leap off my bed and rush to the kitchen. Halfway down the hall, my pace would slow as I remembered. By the time I rounded the corner, I would be struggling to choke back tears. "Sorry, sorry."

"I don't understand. How can someone so smart be so stupid? The basement door is literally next to the phone. Did you forget in the two seconds it took to hang up?"

I could sort of recollect her call, but then there was a blank, so I had no explanation and shared her exasperation. It would've been easier, and safer, to heed her orders. Because she'd become abusive, too. Before she mostly screamed or called me names, with occasional whacks across the butt or the face, but now she vented her furor. She'd race toward me and pound me anywhere she could land a punch. Indignation surged through me during these frenzied treacherous outbursts. I avoided her to minimize the risk but at least didn't worry she might kill me.

Mom saw some of Allan's intimidation tactics and the milder

violence, but the worst occurred when she wasn't there. I never told her the rest, in part because she didn't intervene when she could. And I worried that disclosure would result in another beating for tattling. Even when Mom asked, I lied about the bruises, shrugging off the question with a "you know what a klutz I am." So maybe she didn't comprehend why I was more distracted, assuming she cared enough to ponder this rather than just focusing on the inconvenience to her to muster up dinner.

Perhaps because of Mom's example, but more likely a shared need to feel powerful for a few seconds, once in a while I unleashed my anger on Cindy. I'd push her or holler above her as she lay on the floor. Small conflicts with Laurie or Sharon could infuriate me, too. We once argued over whether to play the Archies' "Sugar Sugar" or the flip side "Melody Hill," with all three of them aligned against me. I felt betrayed, I think because they didn't appreciate how important this was to me. Of course, it shouldn't have been that significant. When they wouldn't let me argue or berate them into agreeing, I stormed out of the house, wracked by sobs.

Underneath, too, was popular Laurie's rejection of me at school, where she brushed me off to sit at the cool kids' lunch table. Although inundated with compliments from my Bordentown teachers, which buoyed my mood at times, these students' braniac label seemed hostile. When combined with towering over my classmates and my budding breasts, I didn't feel special but rather peculiar. I strove to exude lightness and joy, to fit in, and managed to be the first to land a boyfriend, who even gave me a silver filigree ring he stole out of his grandmother's jewelry box. So my perception might've been askew because my life weighed me down and depression crept in from living under constant threat.

Because no matter how much I tried to obey Allan's many precepts, I failed to satisfy him. Like when completing his long list of daily chores, such as delivering milk to the cats. Their dishes were outside, just beyond the porch perimeter. One day I hauled out a full gallon of milk from the refrigerator. Allan watched from the glider as I strolled by, hopped over the two steps to the yard, and uncapped the container. I paused and closed my eyes, to allow the soft breeze to caress me, and listened to Allan's pigeons coo, the ones he raced, that lived in the coop out back. Then I crouched to the bowls but struggled with the heavy jug, so some milk splashed.

Allan leapt to his feet, barreled across the porch, and flung the screen door open. As he hustled down the stairs, I started to rise. When I was halfway up, Allan shoved me into the yard. I stumbled and one hand scraped the dirt, so I sort of bopped along the grass. Before I could straighten up, Allan planted his two meaty palms on my backside and propelled me forward. The momentum caused me to catapult across the lawn. My feet slid out from under me. I hit the ground hard, my skull and entire right side taking the brunt of the fall.

Allan rushed toward me, so I curled into a ball. He stood with a leg on each side of me. I refused to look up. He screamed insults. But I couldn't decipher most of the words because my head buzzed and brain clanged. And my terror prevented clear focus. Allan moved his leg across my quaking body and stood alongside me. This time I heard "stupid cunt" and "fucking idiot." He pulled his leg back and kicked me in the stomach. His final "be more careful" resonated in my ears as he stormed away.

I hugged myself tighter, held my belly, and gasped for breath. Resentment at being treated like this due to a minor mistake washed over me. I grabbed mounds of grass with my fists and threw them across the yard, then cried and cried. As I returned to the house, I looked up and saw Albert's eyes barely above the frame as he watched from his bedroom window.

It never occurred to me to call the police. Having lived with John and Nanny, I knew Allan's extreme hair-trigger reactions were not universal. But many parents spanked kids then, so what I suffered didn't seem that far out of the norm. And I'm not sure the cops would've done anything in those days. At least not without broken bones and multiple visits to the emergency room. Unless I was sure they'd take him away permanently, I wouldn't have risked it anyway. The price would've been too high once he came back home. ☀

# CHAPTER 9
## Shift Work

ALLAN HAD A GOOD JOB at the steel mill. But our lives revolved around his ongoing schedule changes. One week he worked days, the next 4:00 p.m. to midnight, then midnight to 8:00 a.m. I never understood why the union agreed to this. Allan groused that his body didn't know when it should be awake and when asleep. And I think this exacerbated his explosiveness.

For midnights, he was asleep when we arrived home from school, a problem because we entered through the back, near his bedroom window. So I devised a protocol. For our initial challenge, the porch screen door, I would pass my books to Cindy, then grab the handle with one hand and the top clasp with the other, which I tugged simultaneously to prevent the loud reverberating snap. Cindy would scooch past me onto the porch. I followed and eased the door shut.

She lowered our books to the concrete floor, opened the glass storm door, and held it while I crept forward. My hand would shake as I focused on sliding the key into the hole. I'd turn the knob all the way to the left, pause, and visualize a firm push—enough to succeed on the first try, but not so hard as to bang the radiator. Cindy would nod encouragement, and I usually pulled it off. Either way, we listened while we caught our breath. Had we awakened the beast, or were we safe for the moment?

Although Allan rested, he'd come down hard if we didn't do our chores. We could clean our room with low risk because it was on the opposite side of the house. We could even dust the living room, adjacent to his bedroom, although we skipped vacuuming that week. Still, we would whisper, "Shh!," or spin around and glare at the other for the slightest noise. Putting the dishes away proved a particular complication because they'd clack, so I taught Cindy to place each bowl and plate in the cabinet, one at a time.

The 4:00 p.m. to midnight stint offered a reprieve. Allan slept when we readied ourselves for school and headed to work before we returned home. That week, we would mosey down the street from the bus stop and chat with Sharon and Laurie. We warmed the oven for Elio's pizza while we changed out of our school clothes. After we ate, we completed our homework and part of Allan's task list. We might gab on the phone or head out to play with the neighborhood kids. Mom was relaxed, too, and we'd sometimes giggle while eating our dinner.

But when Allan worked the day shift, he'd roll in thirty minutes after we did. Cindy and I would dash home and peel off our school outfits as we rushed through the kitchen. We hustled from chore to chore, the most obvious first, such as straightening the clutter. Every two minutes, we'd pause to listen for his truck as it turned the corner. A shout of "He's coming" signaled the race through the living room and to the front door.

His truck's booming engine would grow louder as he neared. Peeking out of the heavy blue drapes, we watched him drive past.

The transmission groaned and gravel crunched beneath the tires as he hauled ass into the driveway. We spied on him as he trudged to the mailbox. He then headed back up the drive and toward the kitchen as he flipped through bills and grocery store flyers.

I would grasp the door handle with both hands. When Allan reached the halfway point, I yanked while Cindy scooted out, me on her heels, easing the door shut. We tiptoed down the brick steps, slid behind the towering evergreen tree, and escaped into the neighborhood, grinning at each other in relief. We never returned home until after our mother had. Allan often complained we hadn't been around to serve him or take orders, but, with Mom right there, he'd just intimidate us or land a wallop or two.

Although these strategies protected us somewhat, my heart still contracts when I see a truck in the same rust color as Allan's. Well into adulthood, I dreamed about glancing up to find him towering over me. Awash in terror, I'd spin my head from side to side in search of a place to hide, despite knowing nowhere was safe. In my sleep, I reexperience Allan lumbering behind me shouting, "You'd better run." Even awake, my stomach ties in knots if triggered to recall his footsteps heading toward me, a furious giant bear about to attack.

But at the time, I tried to talk myself out of my sadness. I didn't cry much after the first year, and when I did, it mostly was in frustration. Once in fifth grade a classmate asked about a puffy eye I had from a hard smack. I let a few tears drip, but my friend didn't pursue the subject and I never explained. I told myself to stop overreacting because, after all, the assaults didn't happen all the time, sometimes not for months. And I thought the beatings weren't that bad, not compared to the book *Sybil*, in which her mother tied her to the piano and thrashed her within an inch of her life. Even Laurie, who lived so close, was stunned when I told her a few details years later. She knew Allan was dangerous but didn't realize the extent of the mistreatment.

Cindy and I didn't talk about him as much as you might imagine. We warned each other about what inspired a beating, like slurping spaghetti or referring to our mother as "she" rather than "Mom." And, as sisters, we consoled each other. Cindy's outrage lasted longer than mine, which stunned me because I'd shoved my emotions so deep. Instead, I put on my thinking cap and developed techniques to reduce the threat. •

# CHAPTER 10
## Protecting the Siblings

ALLAN DID HAVE A CHARMING SIDE. For parties he'd show off his best 1970s tight polyester pants and flowered satin shirts and slick back his jet-black hair with gel. He'd pat Mom's ass, and she'd make a show of swatting him away. He'd work the room, talk deer hunting with the men, and compliment the women. Vacations brought out sweet Allan, too. We trekked through the Virginia historical sights, headed to Disney World and Miami. He loved fancy restaurants and barbeque dives. When the family presented well to other tourists, he'd give us a "you girls made me proud." So Cindy and I did our best to look pretty and keep our mouths shut, except for the occasional "yes, Daddy" or "Daddy, you're so funny."

At home, on the other hand, even Christmas was a minefield. One year, Allan read the sports page in his lounge chair, a recliner infused with his power. Mom had selected beautiful French provincial furniture, yet Allan insisted he needed a Lazy Boy. Dismayed and saying "that will ruin the room," she chose a gold velvet and dark wood version and stuck it in the corner. He'd often brandish his pipe before hunkering down. "Ooh, my king's throne, just for me. I'd better not catch any of your butts in my spot."

When Laurie and Sharon came to see our gifts, I distinguished between the gifts "Mom gave me" and those "my dad in North Jersey sent." After they left, my mother berated me because this upset Allan, who'd also paid for the presents. Mom said he deserved recognition— a valid point, since he contributed a significant portion of our upkeep and most of our nicer things. I was thoughtless to ignore that, especially when he could hear every word from his chair. But I struggled to give him any credit, with the beatings always at the forefront of my mind. Mom insisted I apologize. I must've sounded sincere because he chilled out for a couple weeks, consistent with the usual pattern. A blowup, whether verbal or physical, whether directed at one of us or our mother, would be followed by quiet for a while, until the next explosion.

Cindy and I could predict certain triggers, such as talking back or skipping our chores, but sometimes he didn't seem to notice or just glared for a few seconds. Other times, a minor transgression was an affront to his authority. Maybe he'd had a bad day at work, maybe gained a few pounds, maybe someone cut him off on the drive home, or maybe he woke up that way. Every day, in every interaction, we scrutinized his face and body language for clues. We listened to his tone of voice for hints the conversation was about to go off the rails. But all this concentration and effort only reduced the danger level. No matter what we did, we could not eliminate the threat.

For example, Allan demanded we not reach across the table during dinner. We all did this anyway because the food sat in the middle. Plus, if we asked him to pass a serving dish, half the time we'd get "you've got two hands" as a tossed-off comment or accompanied by his pounding fist. So we had no choice but to engage in one risky activity or another.

A couple of years in, Cindy stretched her arm toward the Betty Crocker scalloped potatoes. Allan grabbed her wrist and squeezed hard. "What have I told you? A thousand fucking times."

Cindy tried to withdraw her hand, but he refused to let go, so she bobbed her head and managed a tight-lipped smile. Allan scowled, released her, then scooted on his rear end, so he faced her. Mom sighed and focused on her plate. My temperature rose and my palms sweat. I decided I was done sitting on the sidelines, especially when my sister confronted danger. She wasn't just younger, but smaller. And Cindy froze in her tracks when he attacked and felt devastated for days afterward.

"Dad. Dad. If you're such a big man, why do you need to pick on little girls?" For a moment, I felt like the Hulk from Albert's comics—like I had grown six inches taller with muscles to match. But then I clutched my thighs under the table, bracing for his reaction. Still, I kept my head high and back straight.

Allan swiveled in my direction. His expression yo-yoed between anger and surprise. "What did you say? You'd better watch your mouth." Albert fussed with his sippy cup. Allan turned toward him. "It's just you and me against these crazy bitches."

Pride surged through me. I'd knocked him down with a few words and he hadn't known what to do. I got away with it. Afterward, Cindy congratulated me. "That was frigging amazing. How'd you come up with that? And you stared right at him, like you weren't afraid. But I know you were."

That night, though, I woke from a deep sleep with a sour taste in my mouth to Mom's screams from their bedroom. I heard Cindy stir as well, so I peered at her through the dark. "Albert will be scared. We've gotta get him."

As on prior occasions, we shoved back our covers and tiptoed to the bedroom door. I cracked it open. At the end of the hall, Albert had done the same. I gestured for him to run to us. The tensed muscles of his baby face formed a grimace and he didn't move.

"Cindy, it's your turn."

"No, you're faster and he's too heavy. Allan almost caught me last time."

"That's why I want him to run to us. He just has to go one way." Cindy shrugged.

"All right, all right. I'll do it." I swallowed, with effort, and exhaled.

My heart raced as I ran to Albert. When he raised his arms, I bent over and picked him up. Albert clung to me. I eased his door shut so they wouldn't know he was missing, then dashed back, trying to keep my footfalls light. As I cleared the entry, my sister softly closed the door. Cindy and I argued in hushed tones about whether Albert would sleep with her or me.

I drew my brother into the debate. "Albert, you want to sleep with me. I'm your favorite, right?"

"Albert, I pushed you on the swings yesterday. And wasn't Mary Beth mean when she begged Mom not to cook your favorite broccoli?"

He giggled. "I'll do eenie meanie miney mo."

Cindy propped herself on her shoulder. "Shh. Mary Beth, did you hear something?" I detected the sound of branches scraping the window, the hoot of an owl, and the ticktock of the grandfather clock. But nothing else. I drew Albert's warm body close and dozed into a light sleep, yet cocked an ear toward our parents.

About an hour later, Allan tromped through the living room, in our direction. In near unison, we three siblings lifted our heads part-way, to hear better. Allan paused at Albert's room and the hinges creaked when he, I assumed, opened the door. "Goddammit, where's my son?"

I clung to my brother as Allan headed toward us. Albert whimpered, not afraid for himself, I think, but for his sisters. After all, he was the maniac's beloved child. Allan barely turned the knob before he barged in. We all lay still as he loomed over my bed. He snorted, raising the hair on my arms as he reached down and threw back the blankets. I realized my nightgown was bunched near my thighs and worried he could see my underwear.

"Mary Beth, I told you. Stop bothering Albert at night."

Allan picked him up by the waist. Albert's tears gleamed in the bright light coming from the hall. "Come with Daddy. We'll scarf down milk and the chocolate Tastykakes the girls like." Allan carried Albert to the kitchen. The rattle of glasses and plates almost concealed the echoes of our mother's sobs.

I envisioned my brother in his highchair, watching his father storm around. I thought he must be wondering if tonight's explosion had petered out or if this was but a brief respite. Even as a child, I recognized that Albert suffered from Allan's brutality against the rest of us. I could see it when he fled the room at a raised voice or ran behind my legs for cover. But I doubt his father, who purportedly would do him no harm, ever considered Albert's trauma from witnessing the violence.

I began to have strange ideas about protecting my siblings. For example, my mother had given me a comb, brush, and hand mirror set, which I kept on my dresser. At night I'd brush my hair one hundred times, an early beauty technique copied from Marcia on *The*

*Brady Bunch.* Next I'd comb it smooth, then use the mirror to check the back. I believed I needed to place these three items in a specific order on the dresser. Brush, comb, mirror. The brush had to rest on its bristles, the comb teeth face left, and the mirror glass down.

But I tended to get lost in reverie, then jerk to awareness as a wave of trepidation washed over me, because if I failed to follow the proper procedure, something horrible would happen to Albert. I imagined him being struck by a car and lying in the street, bloody, body twisted. I saw him dive into the pool and hit his head on the bottom, then rise in a dead man's float. Hands shaking, I would pick up the hair set, start over, and do it right. But I knew this might not be enough to save my brother. He was going to die because I didn't pay attention for the few seconds needed to follow the rules.

Through the years, I was reminded of the hairbrush ritual. My freshman year of college, my psychology textbook described an experiment about superstition. Pigeons had to push a button to eat. Sometimes the birdseed would slide down the chute and sometimes not, based on a randomizing algorithm. The pigeons developed elaborate dances, based on what they'd been doing when the seed dropped. This sounded to me like the hairbrush ritual. I wondered if I'd connected my bedtime grooming with Allan beating my mother at night. However, probably unlike the pigeons, my logical brain understood my efforts didn't impact events. But the predominant part of me feared the consequences if I failed to carry out the process correctly. The risk might be low, but the penalty was unacceptable, so I felt compelled to do it. I also later learned that similar brain circuits are involved with addiction and obsessive-compulsive disorder and wondered about the various times I succumbed to OCD-like tendencies.

This also related to my decades-long apprehension that one small error would plunge me into catastrophe. Perfection was mandatory. Even when I knew my foreboding was unfounded, even after many years of resolving challenging problems, the anxiety persisted. Always on alert, always vigilant, but always assuming my efforts were insufficient to avoid calamity. I still struggle with putting that expectation behind me.

Despite all this, when I was eleven, I began baiting Allan. The first time, during one of his racist or sexist tirades, I can't remember which, I scanned the dinner table. Cindy, Albert, Mom, and I, trapped, cowed, forced to endure his rant. My eyes bounced from Allan to the tree outside to my sister's clenched jaw. I rocked back and forth. I tried to speak but ended up muttering vowel sounds. I told myself *just do it*. I slammed my feet into the floor and spit out the retort I'd spent the past week refining. "It's sad all you have to be proud of is being a white male."

I'm pretty sure all four of them, in unison, sucked in as much air as their lungs could hold. Enough color drained from Allan's face to wash the Italian out of him, then surged back scarlet red. I fought the urge to stand and beat my chest. Instead, I adjusted my glasses and pushed my hair behind my ears. Under the table, I pressed my hands to my churning stomach and wondered what he'd do to me. Albert slid under the table, Cindy turned to Mom, and Mom traced the tablecloth pattern. Allan leaned over and jabbed his finger into my forehead with each sputtered "bitch" and "whore." He leapt to his feet, gripped my chair and twisted it, so I tumbled to the floor. Allan grabbed me under my arms and dragged me to my bedroom. He banged the door behind him, on the second try because the first caught my foot, which I noted in passing. I attempted to flip onto my hands and knees, but he thrust me back. He bent over, then screamed "who," wallop to the face, "do," another wallop, "you" . . . and in the middle of the third wallop Allan lost his balance and pitched backward into the wall. He righted himself, then slumped forward, hands on his knees, I think because he was huffing so hard he needed a break. I gagged on my regurgitated supper but forced it down. I tried to crawl under the bed, but the frame was too low to the ground, which I knew but somehow forgot. Sobs reached my ears, so I touched my cheek to verify the tears were mine. Allan clamored over me and left.

This didn't deter me, at least not always. When Allan began a tirade about something I'd done or hadn't done, I might shout my defenses or hammer his inconsistencies. "I've only been home five minutes. I haven't had time." Or "Yesterday you told me to put the dishes away first." And I used my intellect against him. If Allan made a grammar mistake or factual error or used faulty logic, I sneered and pointed out his stupidity to prove I was smarter and thus superior to him in at least one way.

I chose to release my tamped-down rage like this because I thought it displayed the depth of my disdain. Even when I later smiled at a nice gesture from Allan, I'd throw in a slight sneer to remind him. I expected this rejection, too, would escalate the friction between us but couldn't stop. My outbursts energized me and provided an emotional release. The adrenaline rush, with its increase in heart rate and respiration, felt like excitement as much as terror. Once I started the ball rolling, my body was amped up, and my mind hyper-focused, to anticipate his next step and to respond. Plus, I felt strong when I stood up for myself. I had to say "I am a real person. I am not your slave. I am not your punching bag." My brain was my weapon, my path to victory. Well, not counting the beatings. Still, it was worth it to humiliate him and live to tell the tale. ◦

# CHAPTER 11
# Moving Out

LATER THAT YEAR, a battle between Allan and my mother escalated to an unprecedented level. As usual, dinner did not go well although I can't recall the specifics. They might have fought about money, my mother's "slutty" dress, or a disrespectful glance I gave him during an earlier tirade.

As soon as I cleared the table, I scurried to my bedroom, secured the door, rolled onto my bed, and flipped open a book. Cindy eyeballed me as she dialed the white princess phone installed after we had begged for months. She gestured me forward, so I bent down but still had to strain to catch her words.

"I'll see if we can go to Sharon's." She wiggled the handset at me as the busy signal buzzed. "I'll try again in a couple minutes."

A final clang, clang reached us as my mother finished scrubbing the pots and pans. The faucet petered out, then there was a long squeak and the squelch of slowing water. Slow thuds as her feet hit the thick carpet on her way to the master bedroom. I turned my ears in that direction. Silence.

Albert poked his head in, carrying a Hot Wheel in each pudgy hand. I smiled. "All right, you can play near the dresser. Don't bother us." He plopped his chubby toddler butt on the floor and made zooming noises as he raced his cars. Cindy and I chatted about my boyfriend, Benny, and the almost real topaz ring he'd given me.

"NO! NO! STOP!"

Our three heads jerked toward the wall that separated us from the living room. Our mother screamed, a high-pitched shriek, cut off mid-wail. Cindy scrambled to the far corner of her bed and pulled her knees to her chest. I chewed my inner lip. Allan's fist landed hard and Mom crashed into the bookcase. I couldn't see this, but little interpretation was needed for these familiar sounds.

"You stupid bitch. I warned you to shut your fucking mouth."

Another sickening thump as a punch landed and then the sound of breaking glass. Footsteps headed to the kitchen.

"Don't you run from me."

The side door slammed.

"PLEASE help me."

Albert moaned so I flipped my attention to him—eyebrows drawn, deep grimace, thin rivulets streaming down his cheeks. Cindy raised her hands and shook her head, in despair, I assumed. I felt big sister pressure to manage the situation. I rose and opened the door, crept along the hallway, stood at the kitchen's edge, and gazed toward the porch.

Allan had cornered my mother against the wall, wedged against her as he crushed her. I pressed my fists to the sides of my head as he bellowed, "Why the fuck don't you listen" and "I'm the man of this house." His hands gripped Mom's throat and he choked her. I shifted to my left and glimpsed her face, stiff, frozen. She tried to speak but could only gurgle. My mother's eyes rolled back in her head.

A sour taste filled my mouth, and my heart threatened to burst from my chest. *Jesus Christ. He's finally going to murder one of us.* My siblings slinked down the hall. Albert tugged at my shirt and wiped the snot from his nose. Cindy's wide eyes implored me to do something. I wanted to rescue Mom yet could not force my feet forward.

"Mary Beth. Mary Beth." I realized Sharon's mother was calling from outside, through the open front door. I stepped in that direction, glanced at her, and turned back to watch the beating. Mrs. Fischer issued an order. "Mary Beth. Get Cindy and Albert and come here."

Allan yanked Mom by the neck and smashed her head into the concrete. I pivoted on one foot and spun my siblings 180 degrees, so none of us had to see the blood. I waved Cindy forward, grabbed Albert's hand, and led him out. Many of our neighbors had gathered in the street, positioned such that they witnessed Allan throttling my mother. As I paused on the lawn, a few glanced my way, then averted their gaze. In my mind, I begged them to save my mother, but my constricted throat prevented the words from reaching my lips. No one intervened.

Allan's prior warning was spot-on. They must be terrified of him. For one thing, everyone knew he loan-sharked to earn extra income and acted as his own enforcer. I'd heard my mother, at a Heiser Avenue picnic, describe a detour on the way to dinner, when Allan had driven to the worst part of Trenton to find a guy who owed him money. The man was working on his car, standing tiptoe as he leaned over the engine. Allan had sneaked up behind him, bent over, clutched his shins, and jerked his legs backward. The delinquent debtor's face had smashed on the radiator as he hurtled to the ground and slammed onto his stomach. Allan had kicked him in the side twice, knelt down, extracted the man's wallet, and confiscated his money. He'd swaggered to the truck, waving the bills. "Prime rib tonight."

Mrs. Fischer hustled us across the yard and toward her house. She rushed us past our side porch so fast, I couldn't get a clear view. As Sharon ran out to embrace Cindy, I heard police sirens approach. Mrs. Fischer strode inside and cradled Albert on the sofa. Cindy and I followed Sharon to her room. They sat on the bed facing each other. I collapsed onto the floor, lay flat, and put my hands over my face. Cindy began sobbing, so I sat up, crosslegged. I rammed a knee to the carpet until I winced, then the other, and back again, which I found oddly soothing. Cindy touched her forehead to Sharon's and kept repeating, "Oh, my God. Oh, my God."

"What happened?"

Cindy curled into her best friend's lap. A jealous twinge shook me before I responded. "He was strangling her on the porch."

I squeezed my eyes shut but failed to interrupt the flow of tears. *You can't cry. You'll freak out Cindy and Albert, even worse. Stop being a baby.*

Cindy stepped up to finish the story. "We really thought he was gonna kill her."

"Your dad is nuts. Still. Geez. That knocks me out."

My sister thrust herself up. "You don't live there. It's a frigging insane asylum."

Sharon's brother Billy stuck his head in, eyes darting from Sharon to Cindy to me, in either excitement or concern, maybe both. "The pigs handcuffed Allan."

We ran to the picture window and saw the cops shove him into the back seat of the cruiser. I breathed deep and relaxed my clenched fists.

Cindy swiveled around. "What'll happen now?"

In vain, I wracked my brain for information about husbands getting arrested. "I don't know. I mean, they can't lock him up forever." Cindy frowned, so I offered a more comforting assessment. "They've got to keep him for a while at least. I think."

This was one of the rare instances when the neighbors called law enforcement even though, during each assault, my mother would howl in anguish, shriek her panic, and plea for help. And the officers arrested Allan just this once. During the other visits, they took him aside and instructed him to go somewhere to "cool off" because in the 1970s they viewed domestic violence as a private family issue.

About two hours after the police departed, my mother came to the Fischers' house. We cracked open the door to Sharon's bedroom and Albert waddled in. The adults spoke in whispers, though an "oh Pat," and "of course, of course" floated by. Then Mrs. Fischer raised her voice. "Kids, come on out."

I picked up my brother, and we shuffled past the happy family pictures lining the hallway. Albert clutched me tight. I had to loosen his grip to suck in some air. My mother had washed her face yet overlooked the mascara streaks beneath her half-closed right eye. Dark red splotches covered her neck, and she sounded hoarse when she spoke.

"I'm taking Albert to Grandmom and Grandpop's. You girls will stay here."

Cindy nudged me. So I piped up, "For how long, Mom?"

"I don't know."

"What will we wear?"

"I gave Mrs. Fischer a key. You can pack up a few things."

As I handed Albert to my mother, I nodded. Mom started to speak again but turned aside. I stared at the dried blood matting down some blond curls. I fretted over whether we'd ever see them again. Maybe she'd abandon us to the Fischers. My chest heaved as I studied my baby brother. *He needs her the most. Maybe we'll go back to Nan's. We liked it there.* As they drove away, neighbors paused before they remembered to give the usual wave. Mrs. Fischer asked, "Who wants Elios pizza?"

When I was in my twenties, my mother swore she'd told my grandparents the whole truth about Allan's violence. My Aunt Catherine verified that they saw the bruises on her neck, which they categorized as one more histrionic cry for attention. Mom said her parents forced her to return because the idea of her being twice divorced horrified them. "You've already destroyed one marriage. Don't ruin another." She ranted about how they'd never supported her. They hadn't funded her quest to catch a high-value husband, hadn't allowed her to bring me home, and hadn't protected her from a dangerous husband.

The police released Allan after a twenty-four-hour hold. Although attuned to any movement, Cindy and I averted our eyes and kept quiet as we walked past our house to the bus stop. The window sheers fluttered, but he remained inside.

We all moved back within the week. As usual, our mother disregarded the beating or how we might be impacted. Also as customary, Allan at first stuck to his best behavior, so she plastered on a smile and tossed endearments his way. Cindy and I sometimes fumed to each other and other times felt buoyed by optimism that we'd enjoy a respite. We wondered, but never dared ask, whether Allan actually had been arrested or the outcome of any charges. And no one ever mentioned this in our presence, so I still don't know.

The following weekend, my mother miscarried, which is how I learned she'd been pregnant. Back from the hospital, Allan tried to hug her as she wept. She shrugged him off. "This is your fault. You killed my baby." I overheard her tell Mrs. Fischer, "This was the only child I ever planned." Since the new information was inconsistent with her haphazard interest in Cindy and me, I mused over why she wanted a fourth child. I guessed she said this to gain sympathy from Mrs. Fischer rather than having any earnest interest in adding to the family.

Two months later, as we exited the school bus, we saw a moving van in front of our house. We'd heard stories about moms sneaking out when the dad wasn't home. My legs wobbled and my muscles released tension I'd held since the first beating in the Lincoln. Cindy jumped up and down. "We're leaving, we're leaving." We pranced down the street, pausing only to hold hands and squeal a few bars of "Joy to the World."

At the new place, we all savored our relief and the peace and quiet. We'd relocated to a small rental two miles from Allan, to stay in the school district, Mom said, but I never understood this decision. The small ranch home could be seen from the highway, so each passing car posed a risk. I expected that, eventually, someone would spot us and inform my stepfather. I would have preferred to change schools than live with such a high likelihood of discovery.

I told Cindy and Albert we had to play in the backyard, not the front. When we waited for the school bus, I scanned the highway for Allan's truck. On the return trip, I worried he'd borrowed a car to follow us. I didn't disclose where we lived to my friends, and I reviewed what I knew about each kid on the bus. Were their parents connected to Allan in any way?

And I wondered if my mother intended to leave him or instead hoped this dramatic event would change his behavior. Looking back, I doubt she wanted to be a single mother of three. Dropping us at Nan's again would've resulted in her parents vociferating about her selfishness and irresponsibility. I'd bet she concluded the best option was to find a way to keep the good parts of her marriage, like the decent income and vacations and good-looking husband, but at least reduce Allan's vicious tendencies.

The next month, we came home to find his truck in the driveway. Even though a nagging voice had half convinced me our departure had been a farce, I stopped dead in my tracks and ripped off a fingernail with my teeth. Torn to a nub, it throbbed when Cindy grabbed my hand for the trek to the front door. Allan rushed us as we crossed the threshold and pulled us close for a bear hug and an "I missed my girls." Mom smiled as she prepared lasagna with meat sauce, his favorite Italian dish that she could cook. During dinner, I couldn't speak. At least, thanks to years of practice, I managed to stifle my tears until he left the next morning. I wouldn't give him the satisfaction of knowing he had power over me. I refused to undermine my ability to assert myself now that I'd again have to battle his efforts to crush me.

We returned to his house a few days later. On the ride back, I sat in the truck bed, crossed my arms into an X on my chest, and screamed into my armpit when the engine roared loud enough to cover the sound. Cindy looked to me for reassurance, but I just couldn't carry it off. My mother had promised he'd seen the light, agreed he'd done wrong. Even at this young age, I knew she was deluding herself. He verified this when, on the phone, he bragged to his brother that "Pat couldn't stay away," in a tone that suggested a sexual draw, and then "I'm gonna have to work harder to keep them in line."

I began to blame my mother for forcing us to live with Allan and ignoring the maltreatment. Plus, when the cycle of abuse continued,

her erratic outbursts and physical attacks on us escalated. She'd back-
hand me across the face or pummel me indiscriminately with a book
or wooden spoon for sassing her or because I "looked at her funny."
Today I recognize that she had lost control due to the strain of living
with Allan, but at the time I just viewed her as another enemy.

When I reflect on this period, I recall anxiety and sadness, mixed
with feeling debilitated and hopeless. I was trapped in a world of
brutality and stress, with radical consequences if I violated confusing
and ever-shifting rules. I had to fend for myself and survive as best I
could. I lived in a long dark tunnel and saw no way out. •

# CHAPTER 12
## Molestations

WHEN I WAS NINE, my mother bought me two "training" bras, baby blue lace with matching panties. She shook the stack of undergarments at me as I sidled past Allan as he read the sports page. He laughed. "A brassiere for those bumps? It's not like I can see her nipples."

I snatched the underwear from my mother's outstretched hand and clutched the bundle to my chest. But I regretted that decision because the lace reminded me of Mom's skimpy lingerie, so I crumpled it into a ball.

"Leave her be. She's already an early bloomer. Takes after her mother."

Allan paused his perusal of the Phillies report and scanned my body. "You're right. Long legs and big boobs. Boys will be following her scent any day now."

I dropped my eyes, to hide my embarrassment and my elation. A grin burst across my face at the suggestion I might resemble my beautiful mother. I didn't think so but would be thrilled to even approximate her appeal. The back of my scalp prickled and I bounced on my toes, similar to a runner readying for a race.

"Mary Beth, I signed you up for White Gloves and Party Manners. They teach girls to act ladylike. You're so clumsy, you really need the help."

Allan snickered. "God knows she could use some sophistication." He slid his tongue over his lips. "Ever since they changed the school dress code, all you girls wear are slacks. And the way you both whiz around here, I'd might as well have two more boys."

Although in 1970 White Gloves was an anachronism, I enjoyed it. They taught us to set a proper table and use the correct fork. A lady never slices her dinner roll, she breaks off and butters one small piece at a time. No rubber bands for ponytails, to avoid split ends, and baby cream your elbows for smooth skin. For graduation, Mom bought me an A-line peach dress with a lace collar, white patent leather shoes, and thin white knee-high socks, almost stockings. Also, of course, white gloves. Allan dressed in his suit to escort me and glows in a picture as I curtsy before him.

Mostly, though, I wore polyester slacks and blouses, switching to cotton pants or jeans for play. I grew so fast my grandmother sewed embroidered trim on the bottoms to avoid needing a new wardrobe every few months. I did have some pretty dresses, such as the teal with a vibrant scarf, which made me look about twenty in the class picture. Minis were in, but young girls didn't go above mid-thigh. I was wearing my new favorite pink dress, which was purchased about a month earlier, for the first day of fifth grade, when my teacher took one look and sent me to the principal's office. He phoned my mother and ordered her to pick me up and take me home to change. When she arrived, the principal made me stand before them. About to be inspected, I tugged my skirt down in front, but this raised it in back.

"If she lifts her arms, the boys can see her underpants. I don't know how you let her leave the house."

My mother huffed. "It's not 1950 and she's a big girl. I don't need to get up to send her off to school." She did examine me, though. "I'll have her try on all her outfits after work."

After this "too short, not too short" exercise, my mother told me to sit on the sofa. She went to her room and nabbed a book entitled something like *Where Do Babies Come From*. I'd heard vague rumblings about "the talk." Laurie had whispered about getting your period, and a girl in our class claimed she had the "curse." I knew we'd view a film at school this year on our changing bodies. One movie for the boys, one for the girls.

My mother flipped through the book, which covered breast development, new hair, and menstruation. It also explained that parents made babies when the penis entered the vagina, which surprised me because I wasn't aware I had a hole there. Mom asked if I understood. "How do you make twins?" She later said she'd felt relieved, fearing I'd ask for sex details. A few months later, red spots appeared on my underwear. I found my mother alone, her nose buried in Jaqueline Susann's *Valley of the Dolls*.

"Oh good, you're up." I lowered my voice. "I got my period."

She headed toward her bedroom and I followed halfway, then paused to wait. Allan muttered irritation at being disturbed. "Jesus. I have to get a pad for Mary Beth. First period."

My mouth dropped open and a hot flush suffused my body. How could she tell Allan something so private? I dreaded new unsavory looks and wondered if he'd stare, trying to make out the sanitary napkin.

My mother waved me to the bathroom. She gave me a few pads but never told me how to dispose of them. So I'd sneak used napkins into my closet and shove them inside an empty box, until no one was home, then I could stuff a batch deep into the garbage bin outside. Later, in the wastebasket, I saw Sharon's pads neatly rolled in toilet paper and realized her mom had taught her the proper way. Even then, I categorized this as another example of low-level mothering, part of Mom's pattern of doling out enough information to survive but not enough to thrive.

By spring, now barely eleven, I was the tallest in my class, and my breasts had continued to grow. On a shopping expedition with my mother, I picked a paisley turquoise bathing suit. The top had a skirt that hid my stomach, which was flat, but I could "pinch an inch" if I really tried so I thought I was fat. Sewn in were two bra cups, a bit small, which created cleavage. En route to the Halko's pool across the street, Allan stopped me in my tracks. "Come stand next to me." His heavy-lidded eyes perused me from head to toe. "Your tits fill that out?" Mortified and disgusted, my stomach roiled. I attempted to rush past, to the door, but he latched onto my wrist. "I guess you're a woman now." Sweat glistened on his brow as I wrestled my arm free and bolted.

Although I couldn't articulate why, not even to myself, anytime I had to be in the house with Allan, I tried to cover up with a loose top, with limited success due to my burgeoning bust. Plus, I was conflicted, as I wanted to wear cute clothes, like the other girls. My discomfort wasn't just from Allan. I'd noticed other older men staring at me. Bus drivers, teachers, cashiers, family friends. Kids at school made comments, too, sexpot or hot chick, and boys snapped my bra when they could get close enough before I twisted out of their reach.

Then, near the end of sixth grade, my mother contracted a neurological disorder and was hospitalized. On the 4:00 p.m. to midnight shift for the first week, Allan wasn't home in the evening. Grandpop M cooked supper or brought us cold cuts and Italian rolls for sandwiches. Other than that, as the oldest, I assumed responsibility for the household. I played with three-year-old Albert, bathed him, and read Dr. Seuss until he nodded off. To compensate for my time, I ordered Cindy to do half my chores.

Three nights in, I woke from a deep sleep, Brut aftershave in my nose and arm hair standing on end. Allan towered over me, shaking me awake.

"Be quiet and come with me."

I squinted at him, struggled out of the tangled bedding, plopped my feet on the shag rug, and shuffled into the hall. Allan gestured toward his room. *Must be headed to the steel mill. Wants me to sleep there with Albert.* Sometimes he did this when he worked midnights if my mother's bowling league ran late. The smell of beer wafted by, which confused me because he didn't drink before work. Still, I complied.

Allan waited near the window as I climbed into the side of the bed closest to the door. I pulled the sheet up and fell back into the slumber from which I'd never fully awakened. I barely noticed him creep in next to me. But when he thrust his body hard into mine, my eyes flew open as my brain jolted into consciousness. Allan rubbed my neck and pushed his erection against my backside.

"Give me a kiss."

I continued breathing deeply, pretending I slept. I felt repulsed by the image of his large wet lips on mine. I wiggled away from him, to the edge of the bed.

"Give me a little kiss good night."

I muttered, "Quiet. Sleeping."

"You need to take your mother's place."

As I puzzled over this, Allan pressed down on my shoulder, forcing me to turn toward him. I feigned grogginess, leaned in, and bussed him on the cheek. Then reclaimed my original pose, except I pulled my legs into a fetal position. My adroit brain failed me. I tried to analyze the problem, but my mind was stuck on one useless thought. *He's going to do something bad.*

Allan began pushing up my nightgown. Petrified, I couldn't grasp the concept of a father doing this. Nonetheless, his focused brazenness convinced me that, no matter what I said, I wouldn't be able to dissuade him. He panted in my ear as his fingers advanced higher on my thigh. Tingling electricity where he caressed me, aroused, but more focused on his next move. As if I was waiting for someone to stab me or throw me from a bridge. My vocabulary did not include "rape," but I understood he intended to have sex with me—whether I wanted to or not.

Time slowed as I waited for the horror to unfold. When Allan reached my panties, he brought his arm around farther, to get his fingers underneath. Just as I remembered I had my period, he felt the sanitary napkin. Shame washed over me as Allan's hand recoiled. "Get outta here" rang in my ears as I leapt out of his bed and fled through the house to the relative safety of the room I shared with my sister.

I crawled under my bedspread and smashed my pillow onto my head. My body trembled and I sobbed, in brief spurts, struggling to suppress my tears. Once under control, I peeked out of the covers toward Cindy, who still slept. I considered waking her but couldn't bear to tell her how he'd groped me.

I wriggled out from my sanctuary, slumped against the headboard, and ransacked prior conversations for information about my mother's return. I counted the days until my period would end to calculate the odds he'd make a second attempt before she returned. I speculated about his opportunities to ambush me again, maybe when Mom went bowling or took Albert shopping.

Allan did not emerge in the morning while we got ready for school. His truck was hauling ass up the street as we exited the bus after school. I stopped dead in my tracks and fought the urge to run. He slammed on the brakes and rolled down the window. "Your mother's resting. Don't make any goddamn noise!"

I wrapped my arm around Cindy's shoulders and squeezed. "Okay, Dad, whatever you say." For a few months, I walked on eggshells, but he didn't approach me, not even for the usual intimidation or punch.

On my next birthday, thirteen, Allan presented a birthstone ring, an emerald-cut aquamarine, set in real gold. Mom said, "This is a big day, starting your jewelry collection," and pressured me to give him a hug. I loved the ring for its beauty and wanted to trot it out for my friends as additional evidence I was grown-up. But it was from Allan, and wearing it seemed like a silent agreement that all was forgotten. Each time I slid it on my finger, I cringed for a moment. Mostly I slipped it on before school when he wouldn't see. If he insisted I wear it to a party, I spent much of the event with hands clasped behind my back.

Allan began to barge into my room when he thought I was alone and changing my clothes. At random intervals, he pressed close, backing me into a corner, sometimes with an erection but always making sexual comments. "I love summer; your big tits, little tops get me so hard," or "Get on your knees and I'll teach you to suck dick." I'd say nothing and avert my eyes, except when he clamped down on my cheeks and tilted my head up. My knees would go weak, so I'd collapse against the wall, brace myself, and wait for him to tear my clothes off or push me to the floor.

But he never did. However I couldn't know that at the time, so I lived in fearful anticipation. I understood my stepfather was more interested in his sexual excitement than his duty to a sort of daughter. I saw his behavior as an expression of dominance, like the physical abuse, to crush me. He could control himself but chose not to. And why would he? To him, I reasoned, I was just an object to possess or fulfill his desires.

When I was around twenty, my mother asked if Allan had molested me. I smell bacon when I remember this, so we must've been in the kitchen. Her back was to me so I could discern no clues as to why she asked. I considered and rejected the possibility she was concerned. Instead, I decided she wanted a denial, to ease her conscience, so I acceded to her tacit request. I didn't trust her enough to share anyway. But to me, the question indicated she suspected, which enraged me for a brief second before I snuffed out that useless emotion. Mom also said Albert had told her about some of the beatings he'd witnessed. "I would've stopped Allan if I'd known."

I shook my head in the negative. "What did you ever do that would have made me believe that?"

This certainty about my mother impacted another event, some-time in junior high. I can't pinpoint when precisely, except that I recall a typical New Jersey summer day, hot and humid and sticky. Cindy and I had moved to the garage apartment when Grandpop M bought his own house, so Mom could turn our room into a den. Enjoying the privacy, I wore my bathrobe and underpants. I sat on the shag carpet watching *General Hospital*, smoking a Salem, and flipping through our albums, looking for Pink Floyd's *Animals*.

The door banged against the faux wood paneling as Allan's best friend, Jerry, barreled in. He resembled Allan, only slimmer and even better looking. Because our interactions were limited to "hi" and "doing great" at various gatherings, I first thought he'd forgotten Allan's father had moved out. Jerry swayed from side to side, then fell into the wall. He surveyed the room, I now think to verify we were alone. He leered down at me, mouth agape. My face flushed as I realized he could see my breasts. I scrambled to my feet and tightened the soft belt, and stepped back two paces, until my calves hit the sofa. Jerry lurched at me, reeking of alcohol. "Show me that sexy body."

*Oh shit, just like Allan.*

I planted my feet solid, extended my arms, and held him at bay. "No, absolutely not."

"Just wanna look." He karate-chopped my inner elbow, which collapsed my barrier, and grabbed me by the waist. I managed to turn so my back was to him. His fingers scrambled to pull my robe open, and I struggled to keep it closed. Feelings flitted by so fast they barely registered. Surprise, apprehension, irritation. Then the phone rang and we both froze.

"I bet that's my mother, to tell me what to defrost for dinner."

We paused our contest. Jerry relaxed his hands, so they now rested on my hips. His hot breath warmed my right ear. But he didn't retreat as I'd hoped he might when I said "mother."

I seized the receiver. "Hello. Yes, hi, Mom." I turned my head and nodded at him. "Okay, I'll get the T-bones out of the freezer."

As I asked my mother when she would be home, Jerry slid his arm under the robe and squeezed a breast. He held on while I tried to wiggle away from his grip. Jerry reached for my panties with his poured rubbing alcohol on them to elicit the biting pain.

After about thirty minutes, I heard a key in the lock, the front door opening, and my sister's voice. "Jesus, Mary Beth. Why are the records all over?"

I recalled this event through the years, but it wasn't until I told my husband that I appreciated the full significance. Yes, this was another sexual assault, which contributed to my core belief in an unsafe world. But more notable, I was speaking to my mother on the telephone while being molested. Yet, it never occurred to me to seek her help.

Did Jerry anticipate this? He hadn't appeared worried. Maybe he'd known Allan had crossed the line multiple times and yet I'd told no one. Maybe he had deeper insight into my relationship with my mother than I'd realized. Or maybe he'd just been too drunk to care. ●

# CHAPTER 13
## Alcohol

THE SUMMER AFTER Allan molested me, when I was twelve, my best friend, Sally, called.

"Want me to head over? Stole a bottle of Boone's Farm Strawberry Hill wine from my sister's secret stash."

"How fast can you get here?"

I rarely invited people to the house because they might witness an Allan tirade. But my parents were out for the day. The odds were slim that either would return early, and it was worth the risk. I planned to use getting drunk to increase my social status. Like me, other kids had sipped alcohol, but none had consumed half a bottle of wine. This could be my chance to lead the pack in something other than grades.

Plus, drinking looked fun. Pre-Allan, I hadn't been exposed to drunken excesses. Family members toasted with a glass of wine on holidays, had a beer or two at picnics or when watching a game, or sipped cocktails at parties. Alcohol lightened their mood, increased the loud talking, and led to funniest story competitions. Couples held hands and kissed. Men flung kids onto their shoulders and sprinted around the yard until they had to stop to catch their breath. Women ignored antics they otherwise put the kibosh on.

But Allan drank daily. One beer and he was jovial and pleased with the world. Two, he'd grouse about work or the idiot neighbors. Three, he would turn on a dime whenever events did not proceed perfectly, by whatever standard he chose to apply that day. A pleasant meal could deteriorate into a raging rampage. At parties, Allan sometimes bellowed his anger over minor disagreements.

Once, he fought his friend Vaughn in the kitchen until Mom issued a "take it outside." Cindy and I ran to the window and watched them pummel each other in the backyard. Vaughn was bigger and more athletic, but Allan was vicious and powerful. We watched as he slammed his fist into Vaughn's face, causing him to fall to one knee. As Allan approached for a second round, Vaughn ripped Allan's shirt from his body, leaving only the cuffs. The fight was so loud and lasted so long that someone called the police. We watched the cops handcuff both men and haul them away. I'd noticed the cops didn't tell them to just cool off, like when Allan beat Mom.

This didn't impact my opinion about drinking, though, since Allan's outbursts seemed to be about him, not the booze. Plus, I could close my eyes and reexperience the warm glow from the few sips I'd been allowed. So when Sally phoned, my heart skipped as I imagined an afternoon of giggles and fun conversation.

I waited by the picture window and danced around the living room with one eye focused on the street, ready to pounce when she arrived. After about fifteen minutes, an eternity, Sally flew past on her Stingray with the high handlebars and banana seat. I raced to the side door, wrenched it open, and leapt onto the porch. Sally slid off her bike and kicked the stand into position. She cradled the contraband, hidden under a rosy scarf in the wicker basket, the white cap peeking out.

"I chose pink because it matched the wine's color."

"Good thinking."

I snagged two of the Flintstones glasses, the ones that used to hold Welch's grape jelly, handed Sally the red Fred, and kept the green Barney. We scrambled down the basement stairs and strode to the "bar," really wooden boards nailed together, because Allan never got around to finishing it. To set the mood, I turned on the neon Budweiser sign that hung on the paneled wall behind. Sally unwound the scarf until it encircled the bottom rim of the glittering Boone's bottle.

"Open it, Sally. Open it."

She unscrewed the top, took a whiff, and scrunched her nose. I waved her away and half filled the cups.

"You first, Mary Beth."

I swallowed a swig. Before I could express disgust at the sickly sweetness, the heat of the alcohol hit my bloodstream and overrode such complaints. I opened my mouth wide, sucked in a quick breath, and issued an "ooh, ooh." My temperature seemed to rise five degrees, so I fanned myself, dramatically of course, then set Barney on the counter so I could drum my feet into the concrete floor. I raised my glass to Sally and gulped down the remainder. She lifted her eyebrows and took a sip as I refilled my cup to the brim.

We relocated to the gold sectional. I fell into the cushions, then plopped my feet on the coffee table. As Sally drank her first portion and I my second, we reviewed our fall class schedule. We both had been selected for the academically advanced track.

"I'm glad we'll be together, MB. My sister says McFarland is hell. A lot of cliques. I don't want to get lumped in with the brainiacs. Can't we be smart *and* cool?"

"We are smart and cool!"

She laughed so hard she choked on her wine. "This shit is sweet, and I don't mean the sugar."

Now I bent over, whooping. "Stop, stop, you're going to make me throw up."

During the rest of the afternoon, we finished off the bottle, played pool, and sprawled in the yard, too dizzy to stand. Sally started a story about her grandmother's cat, but I interrupted with exploits of swiping root beer mugs down at the shore and almost getting caught smoking behind the bowling alley. I regaled Sally with my romantic exploits and reminded her that when I broke up with Robby Bash in fifth grade, I threw his ring into the mud underneath the swing set. We both became hysterical as I explained, "I don't remember what he did. But I'm sure it was unforgiveable."

At 4:00, I rushed her out before Allan returned and brushed off her hug in a sudden panic that he might notice I hadn't completed my chores. I made my bed, put the dishes away, and ran to the woods to hide out until I had to return for dinner. While I lay on my back in the shade of the tall trees with cool leaves beneath me, I analyzed when and how I could get drunk again.

I began sneaking Allan's beer, initially a can to chug behind the house. To cover my tracks, I swapped cold Buds from the frig with warm ones from the cellar. Within the year, I focused on six-packs. I would slam two beers, then share the remainder with Sharon and Cindy. With Sharon's parents at work, we guzzled the brew, chain-smoked, and played spades with the ABC soap operas in the back-ground. We'd be buzzed just enough to explode with enthusiasm at winning, or losing, a hand. Due to my secret higher intoxication level, I might rant about an argument with a boyfriend or a mean comment from my mother. My companions' apparent befuddlement at the intensity of my diatribe barely registered.

I loved being drunk, especially the first half of the event, when I felt confident, interesting, and engaged with the world. Life seemed manageable, delicious, and precious. I even craved the deeper connection to my despair at the three-quarter mark, which felt like an honest expression of pain. This lifestyle also provided distractions beyond the drinking, like evaluating how next to get alcohol. Drink during the day, then feign illness to avoid dinner with the family? On the weekend, how early could I begin to party and how late could I stay out? How would I sneak back in after curfew? Did I want to invite my sister or a girlfriend? Then binge, lose a day to a hangover haze, and make plans for the next drunk.

When I was thirteen, I sought out older boys, even men, who provided alcohol. The drinking age was eighteen in New Jersey, which meant easier access. Michelob became my preferred beer, but I also drank schnapps and cheap wine like Mad Dog 20/20. I graduated to vodka by fourteen, which I consumed almost every weekend, often mixed into lemonade made from the cans everyone kept in the freezer.

I drank to get as high as possible and often ended up curled in a ball, mumbling incoherently. Once, I lay on a doghouse, unable to raise my head, watching the boys do donuts with a car in the field next door. Drunk one midday, I twisted my ankle in a rut in Sharon's dirt driveway. The next morning, I woke in agony, my lower leg swollen and purple. Allan refused to take me to the emergency room until his pigeon race finished. I complained, "That's hours from now." To which he responded, "You walked on it all yesterday, so it's obviously not that important." Even though I knew he had a point, I fumed and spent the day cursing him out to my friends on the phone.

At fifteen, I frequented bars. With the right makeup and my Far-
rah Fawcett hair, most of the local tavern bartenders served me. Sally
and I would don sexy shirts, tight jeans, and high-heeled boots to
walk a mile down a dark street to New Heights Inn in the middle of
winter. By sixteen I qualified as a regular at the Silver Fox, the favorite
watering hole of the local drug dealers and addicts. My drink now was
rum and Coke, preferably Bacardi 151 for the bigger bang.

So, like many addicts, alcohol was my gateway drug, which
worked in the beginning. The science tells me the trauma and various forms of abandonment by all parental figures predisposed me
to substance use disorder. My brain interpreted imbibing addictive
drugs as a survival need and ordered me to consume more to keep
my agony at bay. Sharing that bottle of Boone's with Sally spiked my
dopamine levels. I felt euphoric, a lovely state my brain encouraged
me to reproduce. But over time, due to constant chemical overload,
the rush was smaller and the crash deeper. I struggled to get inebriated at just the right level to enjoy the ride. Every time, at some point
I turned into a weeping, raging drunk. Still, this was a more profound
emotional release than I allowed myself sober, which compelled me
to do it again and again.

When high from alcohol, I avoided my parents as much as possible, made easier by living in the garage apartment. Still, I sometimes
ran into them on the porch or had to join the family dinner. If I
drooped in my seat, Cindy would make a show of sitting up straight
in her chair as a signal to me to do the same or answer for me if she
thought I couldn't follow a question. Yet, although it seems likely they
suspected, my parents never mentioned my drinking.

It is difficult to reconcile being beaten for spilling milk with
silence about escalating alcohol use. It reminds me that they did not

care about providing appropriate parenting or guiding me to become a productive and happy human. Instead, they lashed out to release their own emotions and justified it based on the most recent irritant. I also wonder if they knew that addressing my evolving addiction would take more energy than they were willing to invest. ●

# CHAPTER 14
## Pot

POT ATTRACTED ME BY REPUTATION. My brain latched onto every hint that smoking weed spawned joy and serenity. In newspaper articles, college kids kicked back, toked on joints, blared rock music, scarfed potato chips, and rolled on the floor in paroxysms of laughter over *Road Runner* cartoons. TV news complained about rebellious teens who got high and tuned out. At the 7-11, I spotted mellow hippies, in their peace sign–embroidered jeans, purchasing Zig-Zag rolling papers in the white-and-gold cardboard dispenser, with the bearded man and inscription in French.

My first direct exposure escalated my interest. When I was thirteen, Allan's buddy visited a few months after the Boone's experience. Eyes bright red, he sashayed through the house, trailed by a pungent earthy scent. This introvert twirled Cindy, joked about my dyed golden hair, and settled into the sofa. He rested against the cushion and closed his eyelids in the middle of Allan's anti–women's lib diatribe. I imagined his mind drifting away from that nastiness to a pristine mountain lake where a cool breeze and chirping birds soothed his battered soul, like a scene from one of Mom's romance novels. After he left, my stepfather turned to my mother. "Was he on marijuana?"

Finally, a week later, my childhood friend Tony bragged he could buy a half ounce of Columbian weed from his brother for $20, a prohibitive price for me, with a weekly $5 allowance. I clutched Tony's shoulders from behind and propelled him out of the garage apartment and across the driveway. As we strode over the Fischer's threshold, I tossed an order toward Sharon's bedroom. "You guys, come 'ere."

I plunked myself into a kitchen chair, nabbed a lighter off the table, and sucked down a drag from my cigarette. Tony paused at the door.

"Jesus, don't be so goddamned polite. Get your ass in here."

Cindy and Sharon nodded to him as they rounded the corner.

"So, Tony can score pot. If we all chip in five bucks."

Cindy jumped in place, but Sharon's face melted into a frown.

"I don't get my allowance until Saturday. I only have three dollars."

"Cindy can lend you the rest. Right?"

"Yes, no problem. Let's do it!"

I twisted in my seat to look Tony in the eye. "When can you get it?"

"Um, I don't know. Maybe today. Guess I can try."

"Great, we'll give you the money. You run home. You'll be back in an hour? Grab some rolling papers or one of those baby pipes, like we saw at the mall."

"I guess so. Okay."

While we waited for Tony, I laid out the plan. We'd roll the joints in the kitchen but smoke down the hill near the creek. We giggled and poured Charles Chips into brown paper bags and stacked Tastykakes for transport. I pictured me, center stage, as I regaled my friends with this new step toward adulthood; at least that's how I viewed it.

"I bet we'll be the first in our class to toke the Mary Jane. Cindy, you're not even a teen yet. So you will be, definitely. But even me. Other people brag they did it, but it's always at a party in another town, so I think they're liars."

We spent the next hour taking turns racing to the front window in hope of spotting Tony. At Cindy's "He's here," I trotted up the street and hustled him along. He dropped a baggie onto the table. Sharon dumped the contents on a plate and spread the weed thin.

Tony relayed from his brother that the golden-brown color and low ratio of stems and seeds indicated quality. He fingered a large pinch, then laid it on the nearly transparent Zig-Zag. He tried to roll it, but the paper ripped, so he started again with half as much grass. He licked the adhesive and held up the doobie, a term Tony'd learned from his brother, for approval.

"Is one enough?"

"Mary Beth, how about we start there."

"Fine, but bring it along, so we can roll another afterward."

After I busted through the door, I tripped over a rock as we scrambled down the incline. We settled onto the half-rooted log we used as a bench. Tony took the first toke, held in the smoke for a second, coughed it out, then handed the joint to me.

I drew in deep, grateful that my cigarette history had prepared me well, held my breath for as long as I could, then exhaled slowly. Dizzy, maybe from the weed, maybe from lack of oxygen, I gripped my ankles to ground me. My jaw slackened and my brow unfurled. In fact, all my muscles relaxed, beginning at my neck, the warm wave descending through every vertebra, down to my toes. Until this moment, I hadn't realized my natural state was tightly clenched.

I focused inward and noticed new feelings: carefree, exuberant, languid. Even my breathing seemed easier, rising from my diaphragm, not stuck in my chest.

The day passed, simple but lovely. In between doobies, we skipped rocks across the water, played the Miss Mary Mack hand-clapping game, though not well, and lay next to one another jabbering nonsense.

Living in the apartment over the garage allowed Cindy and me to hide our drug use from our parents because, although we couldn't rely on this, they didn't seem to care what we did behind closed doors. We smoked cigarettes there, which they pretended not to notice. Still, we'd jam a towel under the door to prevent the pot smell from drifting out. When we were grounded, which was often, Cindy would sneak Sharon in so we could share a joint. If we heard Allan or Mom open the porch door, we'd make a big production of hiding her, but they rarely entered our sanctuary; so much so that Allan's assaults typically occurred when he caught me in the house as I did chores or gathered food. All the more reason to barricade myself in the apartment.

Soon most activities revolved around smoking weed, which was even easier to get than alcohol, now that we'd been hooked up and expanded our circle of reefer-toking friends. As one example, each Sunday that year the three of us walked a mile to St. Rafael's. We weren't religious, nor were our parents. In fact, at this point I'd never met anyone who spoke about God outside of church. Attendance was more a social norm. And our parents insisted, although I never was certain if this was for the religious instruction or to get us out of the house. For Sharon, Cindy, and me, the walk was a chance to talk about Saturday night escapades or the upcoming week. Plus, Suzanne's Bakery sat in front of the attached parking lot. As we approached, Sharon would say, "Do we need to go to Mass? Could go for a few tokes and a ladyfinger."

I would nod. "Well, we do have our parents' cash for the church collection basket."

On one particular day, we headed to our usual spot behind the adjacent Catholic school. Cindy and Sharon sat against the concrete wall. I crossed my ankles and lowered myself across from them. Cindy pulled a deck of cards from her pocket, and Sharon proffered a joint, which we puffed while we played gin rummy and devoured creamy pastry bliss.

We froze in unison, startled by a whistling priest headed along the path from the administration building. Cindy gathered up the cards while Sharon stubbed out the doobie and slid it under her butt. We started chatting about an upcoming birthday party.

"What are you girls up to?"

I turned as if surprised and hoped he couldn't see the cold sweat running down my neck, partly from guilt for being selfish and spending the donation money and partly from nervousness at the consequences I'd face if a priest called home. An image of my mother hollering "stealing from the church" while Allan grabbed his belt hovered in the back of my brain.

"Oh, good morning, Father. We're waiting—for the next service."

The priest nodded and continued his trek toward the church.

Cindy stared at me, mouth half open, which I interpreted as admiration. "You lied. To a priest. You're gonna burn in hell now. For sure."

I laughed but wondered whether I ought to make a quick stop at confession.

I'd start most days buzzed from pot. I realize this may seem odd now, but when I entered Bordentown Regional High School in the mid-'70s, the main patio was a designated cigarette smoking area for students and was where the druggie group also toked dope. Most teachers used a different entrance, which I attributed to a "see no evil" attitude.

One morning, while the wind howled and blew around empty sandwich bags, Sally, my boyfriend Will, and I prepared to toke on a joint. As rockers and potheads, Sally and I wore knit sweaters and tight Levi's, not the shiny polyester outfits of the disco crowd. In winter, everyone enrobed themselves in heavy coats to protect against the bitter chill, so we'd covered up with our black class of '79 jackets. Maybe I'm not remembering correctly since it was freezing, but I see Will in a worn denim jacket, which matched his scruffy beard and almost too short jeans.

As most students rushed into the warm building from the bus, we joined the cool kids clumped together for warmth. We huddled in a circle, heads bent, to prevent the wind from snuffing the lighter. Will took the first hit, drew deep, then exhaled a mixture of smoke and fogged breath. Still in a tight cluster, we passed the doobie since we'd never violate the "don't bogart that joint" rule. My geometry teacher, Mr. Wolski, snuck up behind Sally and insinuated his head into a small gap.

"What're you doing, kids?"

Although aware of the rumor that dozens of math quizzes had flown out of long-haired, Harley-driving Mr. Wolski's apartment window while he nodded off after toking some killer weed, Will dropped the stubby roach into the snow. I stomped on it with the two-inch heel of a knee-high boot, careful not to grind it to dust, in the hope we could finish it later. As we broke formation, Sally passed me her Marlboro. I put it to my lips, glanced at Mr. Wolski, took a drag, and almost coughed because I preferred mentholated cigarettes.

"Just sharing a cig."

Mr. Wolski brushed a fluttering strand of hair off his cheek and rubbed his mustache. "Mary Beth, go inside. Wouldn't want you to get into trouble."

Around this time, I began saving my lunch money to buy weed, eating a ten-cent ice cream sandwich to tide me over. I'd also swipe extra change or a couple dollars, however much I thought she wouldn't notice, whenever Mom told me to get cash from her purse. By the end of my freshman year, I smoked daily. At school, after school, skipping school, and on the weekends. Sally and I imbibed before first period gym, then lounged in the weight room. We'd burst at the seams as we watched the volleyball players, some very serious, others barely trying, and many making weird faces at the point of maximum exertion.

After our lunch tokes, we'd reek of pot in Mr. Foster's biology class. Our academic honors cohorts would inhale our new perfume and shake their heads but also looked impressed. The room would explode when a classmate, allergic to the fumes, sneezed. Mr. Foster just shushed us, either oblivious to the impetus or because he viewed this activity as outside his purview.

When not high, or not high enough, I often acted out. I targeted Mr. Foster more than other teachers. He was sweet and let it slide when I expressed my generalized rage, although I'd jump on any minor mistake he made. "No, Mr. Foster, you're wrong." I'd explain the error, sometimes roll my eyes, and might even add, "You sure you're qualified to teach this class?" But if in a deep marijuana haze, I struggled to focus enough to follow the material, much less have the ability or desire to engage with my teacher. Luckily, I could learn the lessons from the textbook, and somehow Sally and I managed to carry out the lab experiments, sometimes with a little help from our friends.

Weekends were different only in degree. One Saturday Cindy and I rode our bikes three miles home from Will's, wasted on pot and vodka. I was so intoxicated I couldn't lift my head. Cindy rode in front, and I followed her back wheel because that's all I could see, which worked for a while. Then she made a sudden turn. I failed to react and plowed straight into a large industrial garbage container. Two guys from the nearby bike store straightened the rim as I used their towel to stop the blood from the gash in my forehead. I blamed Cindy for this accident, vehemently and repeatedly.

"You were supposed to watch out for me, not let me ram into a frigging massive metal bin."

"I tried, Mary Beth. It's not my fault you're an alkie and pothead."

Laying blame on Cindy was hypocritical, as I couldn't look out for my friends any better. A couple weeks later, one hot and humid summer day, Will and I were stoned on weed and decided to walk to Anthony's Pizza, two blocks from his house. His doormat snagged the lip of my sandal, so I grabbed the porch rail to avoid falling on my face.

"Jesus, Mary Beth, be careful."

"Coming into the heat from the air conditioning disoriented me."

"Yeah, sure, that was it."

I ignored this "you're too high again" dig and tried to latch onto Will's hand to remind him of my girlfriend status, but our sweaty palms glided past each other. After I wandered into the street, twice, Will took the outside position. I could feel dots build up below my eyes with every blink from my melting mascara but felt too lethargic to wipe them off.

As we entered Anthony's, a blast of polar-cold air hit my face. I careened toward a table and swayed into a chair while Will ordered slices at the counter. I clutched the seat with my left hand and struggled to light my cigarette with my right because my dangling head oscillated. A loud thud reached my ears, then what sounded like bones cracking as they hit the floor. After a few failed efforts, I managed to swivel in that direction and caught a glimpse of Will's inert body sprawled on the linoleum. As I visualized him fainting and floating down in slow motion, howls of laughter exploded from my belly. I intended to go to his side and assist, but the eruption stole my breath. When he complained that day, and for the year thereafter, that my maniacal outburst rang in his ears as he regained consciousness, I only could spew, "Sorry, so high, couldn't help it."

I also exposed myself to danger for alcohol and pot sometimes when I'd hitchhike to the house of anyone who offered to share their drugs. Once, at fourteen, I headed into town to get high, denim hot pants to accentuate my legs and a rosy halter that clung tight from the heat and humidity. A middle-aged man with streaks of gray in his hair picked me up. I stretched my long legs across the dash and watched his eyes skim my body. I asked him to drop me where Route 206 crossed the main street into Bordentown, thinking this would be less inconvenient for him. As we neared, he said he'd be happy to drive me to my destination if I showed him my tits. At first, I felt more exasperated than afraid. But his sideways glance reminded me of Allan, so I jumped out of the car at the next light.

Two months later, my chemistry teacher caught me as I thumbed a ride in that same location. He lectured me the entire drive about the dangers of getting into cars with strangers. Although I pshawed his concern, it warmed my heart how the teacher's attention somewhat balanced out the way my parents looked through me. And I could tell he really was concerned. As I thanked him for the lift, he grabbed my wrist. "Mary Beth, I'm serious. You're playing with fire."

This didn't stop me, though. Once at fifteen, Sally and I took a ride from a guy who shared a joint with us. He asked if we wanted to smoke his stash at his house. Of course we did. We never hesitated, even when he drove us thirty minutes into the countryside and up a long dark road, where it turned out he did live and where he did have weed. After a couple joints and a nice chat, he drove us home.

As I look back to that time, my decisions to ignore risks to obtain drugs arose from several sources. Sometimes I barely registered the danger that permeated my daily life anyway, so a bit more seemed inconsequential. Other times the fear energized me as adrenaline throbbed through my body and mind. I invited chaos to feel alive and engaged with the world. And, like many abused kids, I longed for peace and used drugs to overcome my profound sadness and constant vigilance. With pot, I felt that I was part of the world and wasn't just watching from my pain cage. Plus, dealing with Allan had worn me down. Pot and alcohol helped numb me so I cared less about whatever he did that day and stopped wasting energy fighting back. And being a druggie offset my struggle to get out of bed each morning because my how-I'll-get-high-today plan energized me. So in the short run, drugs provided benefits. That's why I kept taking them. •

# CHAPTER 15
## *Sex*

AS A TEENAGER, I believed my attributes were limited to brains, a pretty face, and a good body. My mother shared these qualities but demonstrated she valued her ability to attract men over her intelligence. She batted her eyes at cops to get out of tickets, stretched toward the upper shelf at stores to garner any nearby stocker's attention, and wore fitted silk blouses and tight skirts to work. Men would squeeze her elbow and compliment her lovely children while never taking their eyes off her face or her tits.

"Your husband's a lucky man. I hope he takes good care of you."

Mom would giggle and whisper, "Of course, thank you, so kind." When she gained weight after she married Allan, probably from stress or depression, she would whisper about how she nonetheless attracted men. "They say, 'You're just more voluptuous. You still surpass these other ladies.'"

So I learned that a shiny façade garnered attention and accolades. But I also understood Mom's beauty camouflaged rage and bitter unhappiness, evident even after such encounters. Sometimes she'd radiate confidence for an hour. Usually, though, the afterglow dimmed within minutes. Cindy failed to walk fast enough, someone bumped into her, or I suggested a different route to the car, which only could mean I thought her an idiot. Once home, Mom would stare at a portrait of Marilyn Monroe, her idol, a charismatic but damaged beauty.

I didn't trust my own looks and compared myself unfavorably to my mother. Several factors contributed to this. Mom valued nice clothes and wanted me to reflect well on her. But to keep me stylish, in light of my growth spurts, she would've had to spend more time shopping with me than she was willing to invest. To compensate, she'd buy me too big pants, which a few months later were too short. By seventh grade, I resorted to sneaking some of her outfits, which fit better, plus displayed my cleavage and long legs. Mom stopped controlling my hair decisions, so I grew it to my shoulders and dyed my now ash blond mane back to its original golden sheen. At my request, she bought me hot rollers, like hers, so I could create volume and waves.

I deemed myself ugly in my thick-lensed specs, which distorted my eyes. At thirteen, my confidence grew when the insurance company paid for contact lenses because my vision was so bad, an unusual cosmetic improvement in my 1974 working-class town. Now that my eyes were visible, I noticed they'd turned a different shade of blue, with green and gray tints. I taught myself to bring out the various hues with the cheap makeup I bought at Two Guys, enhancing the blue with brown shadow and the gray with taupe.

I finally could see that I was pretty, sort of. With my height and figure, I looked two years older than I was but still a mid-teen. Boys, but also men, reacted as I passed by, which excited me. I felt special when I noticed the glances, even if a little shaken by the long stares at my breasts or legs, which reminded me of Allan's unwanted attention.

Mom seemed happy with my features for the first time since I was little. To her it meant I could outshine the other girls. "It's not just about being attractive. It's attitude. Stand tall, swing your hips, push out your chest. If you can't win your competition against the other girls, at your age, it doesn't bode well for your future." Since I sometimes faced a hostile reaction to my intellect, I latched onto this advice because I hoped being pretty would boost my social standing. I wanted all the boys to prefer me. Of course, an impossible task. I became unnerved for weeks when an unattractive boy, who I didn't even like that much, rejected me and chose a classmate who, I thought, was less desirable.

To improve my odds, in eighth grade I wore a tube top and hot pants to school. Mom didn't know since she never dragged herself out of bed until after I left the house. Looking in the mirror, I admired my womanly body and wondered how big my tits would be once I grew up. I puffed my boobs out, per Mom's instructions, but my shoulders hunched as I imagined running into Allan in the kitchen, so I grabbed my purse and headed to the bus stop before he woke.

Laurie traipsed out of her house as I approached. She seemed surprised by my outfit. "Mary Beth, are you sure they won't send you home for wearing that?"

"Why? Other girls wear shorts."

"Other girls don't look like you."

In each class, the teacher scrutinized me but said nothing. My classmates, however, harassed me for being a sexpot. As the day wore on, I no longer felt attractive—just exposed.

That summer we rented our usual shabby, but near the ocean, vacation duplex. Allan stayed home to work on his brother's house, which relieved my stress enough that I didn't pursue alcohol or pot. After a day spent lounging beneath a beach umbrella and bodysurfing, Cindy and I walked to the hamburger stand. We wore bathing suit tops and shorts as did most of the other female customers. Although the suit had fit earlier that summer, my breasts threatened to burst out. I hadn't styled my hair, but the sea salt had encouraged the curl. I had refused to leave the house until I applied carnation pink blush, blue mascara, and pale rose lip gloss.

As we sauntered toward the Frosted Mug, I stumbled when a pebble caught between my toes and my flip-flop. Cindy laughed so hard, she bent over and held her belly.

"Jesus, Mary Beth. You think you're so grown-up. You can't even walk straight."

I tossed the rock in her general vicinity, hiked up my bikini bra, and spun around. A gold MG convertible zoomed by. "Hey, that's Mom's fave sports car. The one she has to own before she dies."

We ordered, then sat on a white picnic bench, half shaded by an awning. Still, sweat dripped from my neck and armpits. I patted myself down with a few paper napkins. From the corner of my eye, I noticed two guys hop out of the MG and stroll toward the counter.

"Whoa, Cindy, two foxes. The blond is gorgeous. And the other guy is built. Maybe they're surfers."

"Do you think any of the boys in our school will grow up to look like that?" We snickered and swigged the sweet root beer.

A shadow crept across my arm. I tilted my head and grinned at my reflection in the blond's silver aviators. He dipped his chin and the sunglasses slid lower, exposing seafoam-blue eyes.

"Hey, can Eddie and I join you?"

Cindy kicked me under the table as I slid over to make room.

After he wiggled into position next to me, the flaxen demigod lifted my dolphin necklace to get a closer look.

"I'm Chet. Do you girls live around here?"

Cindy leapt up and corralled our mugs. "Mary Beth, give me a dollar for refills."

My bosom lurched in Chet's direction as I struggled to get a bill out of my pocket. A tingle swept across my face as I swerved back into position and slapped the cash into Cindy's open palm.

"Ah. Mary Beth. And is that your friend?"

"No, sister. Cindy. We're here for the week. We've been vacationing at Beach Haven for years." *Don't act so stupid. You sound like an old lady. Lighten up. Smile.*

"Eddie and I live nearby. Grabbing a burger after band practice. Psychedelic Euphoria. Kind of like Hendrix mixed with Zeppelin."

"Wow! Where do you play?"

"Nowhere yet, but we're going to start gigging at clubs soon. My dad's pestering me to get a job. You know, now that I graduated. But I said no fucking way. I gotta focus on my music."

Eddie jumped to his feet to pick up their order and smacked Cindy on the butt as she passed with our mugs. Her eyes popped wide and a wave of brown liquid spilled onto the dirt.

Between bites, Chet regaled us with stories about sneaking into rock concerts and displayed his encyclopedic knowledge of musical history. He instructed us to list our 45 records and then would name the B side. Eddie challenged him to recite the song list for Steppenwolf's *Born to Be Wild* and Deep Purple's *Machine Head*.

Cindy beamed. "Jesus, Mary Beth, he's a genius like you."

Eddie glanced over. "What do you mean, genius?"

"Mary Beth's super smart. Last year, in seventh grade, she got all As, even in algebra and French."

Eddie's shoulders stiffened and he squinted at Chet. He tapped my wrist. "How old are you?"

"Thirteen."

"Chet . . ."

"Eddie, Eddie." Chet swatted the air. "Look at her. She's all woman."

A spark of pride and a blush of embarrassment competed for dominance.

Eddie continued, "Really, Chet . . ."

Chet lifted my chin. "You are a beauty. Listen, I've got to drop Eddie off and do some shit at home. How about I pick you up at 7:00 and we go to the amusement park?"

Cindy kicked me under the table again.

"Okay, yes. See you then." I swung my legs around the bench. Chet rested his hand on my thigh.

"That's your real address, right? Don't leave me hanging."

I nodded as Cindy pulled me up and toward the street.

"Mary Beth, I can't believe Chet wants to take you on a date. You think Mom's gonna let you go?"

"I'll tell her he just turned seventeen and the car was a birthday present. That will make him sound rich. Plus, it's her dream car. She'd better be fine with it. I have to go out with that babe." Cindy chortled so hard she snorted like a pig, which caused us both to squeal all the way back to our beach pad.

My mother did let me go. She suggested I add the purple floppy hat to keep my hair in place on the rides. "Don't jam it. You still want volume when you remove it."

When Chet honked, we both ran onto the porch. She waved as I bounded down the steps in hip-hugger shorts and a pink paisley crop top that covered my bare breasts but also emphasized their heft. My flat stomach and belly button gleamed white. I pushed the seat back so my legs wouldn't bend, then gave Chet a quick peck on the cheek.

He took me on a few rides, bought me a fresh-made waffle with whipped cream and strawberries, and lost ten bucks trying to win a stuffed animal. A new experience for me, this brought to mind the dates described in the preteen books I'd read. I felt honored when Chet put his arm around me and pulled me close. Older teenage girls studied his face and two bumped into him. He didn't notice any of this. He focused on me.

"Walk on the beach?"

"Sure, great." We held hands during the three-block trek to the shore except when I let go to rub the sweat onto my rear pockets.

"With the bay on one side and the ocean on the other, you freeze your ass off here in the winter. Once I get a record deal, I'll live in Philly and buy a beach house just to use in summer."

"Man, that will be so boss. You can have like a massive"—I threw my arms straight up and flung them to my sides— "penthouse apartment. And you already have a fab car. It would be perfect."

"You are a crazy girl. What do you know about penthouses?"

My finger headed toward my teeth in anticipation of biting off a nail, but I caught myself and adjusted my shoulder strap instead. "I read. Plus, it's in *Green Acres*." I switched to a singsong, "I just adore a penthouse view."

Chet snatched my hat, tucked it in his belt, and ran his fingers through my hair. Relieved that I had used the spray that left my hair bouncy and natural, according to the label anyway, I circled his waist with my arms. He leaned down and kissed me, gently at first and then with pressure. Before Chet released me, he flicked his tongue just inside my mouth.

"Let's sit on the dune and look at the stars."

Although the waves shimmered in moonlight a few yards from the shoreline and faint light from oceanfront homes almost reached the beach, dingy black surrounded us.

"Stretch out darlin'. I want to melt into you."

Chet rested on one shoulder, leaned over me, and kissed me with more tongue. I concentrated on his technique and tried to respond in kind. He straddled me and suckled my neck. Breathless, the word "swoon" flitted across my brain. He lowered my straps and slid my top down onto my stomach, so my boobs popped out. Chet pawed my breasts, then placed his lips on a nipple and licked. Electric tingling flowed from my belly to my vagina. I squinted into the inky black and wondered if anyone could see us.

He yanked my hand to his rock-hard dick. "Rub it, baby."

I followed Chet's orders and he groaned as his cock twitched. His powerful reaction increased the wetness of my crotch. A cold ripple undulated from my throat to my toes. I pulled his face closer, hoping he would retreat and be satisfied with making out.

Chet sat on his haunches, unbuttoned my shorts, and tugged them off, panties inside. He spread my legs apart and kneeled between them while he unbuckled his pants. He shoved his dick toward me, so I stroked it up and down, like in my mother's Harlequin romances.

"Shit, shit. Knew you'd be good. Jesus." Through my satisfied smile as I attempted to tell him I had never touched a boy before, Chet leaned back, put his hands under my backside, and lifted. He rammed hard inside me. Again and again. I gasped and shook my head but later wondered if he figured this was passion.

I thought I felt blood and panicked, worried he might mention this, which would be unbearable. I managed to swallow the agony of the first thrust and experienced relief when each lunge created less pain.

Chet's hot nose slid across my cheek. Then he bit my earlobe. His heavy breathing drowned out the surf. "Ah, ah, fuck, fuck."

He fell on me and his full weight crushed my body. Struggling to breathe, I wondered if this was normal and if he realized I was suffocating. Too weak to push him off and probably without sufficient air to talk, I still worried he'd think I wasn't cool if I asked him to move.

After about five minutes, Chet rolled over and adjusted his pants. "That was great, honey, you are something else."

I didn't want to stand and have him see my naked body in its full glory, so I wiggled into my underwear and shorts while lying on the sand. As I adjusted my top, I banged my skull on a piece of driftwood. Woozy already, I felt grateful when Chet pulled me to my feet.

"Well, we'd better head back. I need to meet my friends at the bar and there's no way they'll let you in. But I can come by Friday before you leave. We can go out on my dad's boat."

Chet kept his word. He had me jerk him off, but the bay was too crowded to have sex. He mentioned that he'd told his doctor he'd banged a thirteen-year-old. They had laughed about how young I was, but the doctor said at least I wasn't likely to give him a venereal disease.

My friends and I considered the age difference a sign of my maturity and sexual appeal rather than viewing Chet a criminal, although I expect he committed statutory rape even under the laws of 1974. At the time, conflicted and confused, I had been aroused when he touched me. But, like Allan's molestation, I didn't want to have sex.

I did brag about my conquest but mostly felt sad, sort of like my heart was breaking. I consciously chose not to process those emotions and instead pushed my feelings into a deep cavern, next to the molestations.

A couple months later, as I closed the porch door, footsteps charged toward me. From the length of the stride, I knew Mom approached. I turned into the kitchen, planted my feet, and braced for impact. She slammed a book across the left side of my face. A metal clasp grazed my cheek and I realized she held my diary. A paralyzing tingle raced down my spine as my mind reviewed the contents.

"What is wrong with you? You stupid sleazy idiot."

"What? What?"

"You had sex. On the beach."

As her arm swung at me again, I leaned backward and avoided the blow. Momentum pivoted her to my right. I turned and bolted through the porch, up the garage apartment stairs, and into my bedroom. She followed, screaming "whore" and "slut." Woozy from the panic coursing through my body, I staggered to the narrow gap between the twin beds. This trapped me but also limited her movements.

My chest heaved as I waited. She barreled around the corner, panting from a combination of fury and exertion. I dipped my head and covered my face with my arms. She slugged me on the shoulders with the diary a few more times.

"Knock it off. It was just a story."

After I said this four times, she calmed down. I straightened up, looked her in the eye, and repeated my lie. "It didn't happen. I made it up."

Her beet-red visage began to return to its natural alabaster and her breathing slowed. "You should be careful about what you write."

She huffed out of the room and never mentioned this again. No discussion of the risks of early sexual behavior. No expression of concern about reputational damage difficult to overcome in a small town. Nothing.

When I better understood her history, I realized my mother probably feared I, too, would derail my life with an inopportune pregnancy. This may explain why she felt compelled to read my diary, although this behavior fit well with her general failure to comprehend the concept of boundaries. Or she simply may have worried that my promiscuity would reflect badly on her. Or maybe she'd had a bad day and utilized this opportunity to release her frustrations by beating me.

At the time, I did realize other mothers might have initiated a more adult sex talk. But primarily I noted how I could redirect her by telling her what she wanted to hear. Although I fibbed as a child, mostly to avoid punishment, my ability to deceive improved as a teenager, like my off-the-cuff lie to the priest, skills developed by observation and practice. I recognized that duplicity provided a useful survival strategy. I became an expert, but often this sophistication proved unnecessary because no one really cared about my explanations or even the truth. Plus, I understood that my parents' vehement attacks only tangentially related to my actions. ●

# CHAPTER 16
## *Pills*

I ADOPTED A NEW MONIKER—brainiac druggie. I explained this choice as combining my life's best parts. The alcohol and pot, even the sex, fit my new identity. And I knew this label announced my commitment to mood-altering substances.

I dreamed of the more powerful drugs I'd heard older kids preferred. *Go Ask Alice*, a made-for-TV movie released when I was in junior high, educated me about the variety of pills available. And I homed in on how lackluster Alice became interesting when she joined the popular drug-taking crowd. She dressed cool, landed a hot boyfriend, and dropped uppers for energy and downers to relax. She died of an overdose at the end, but that didn't register with me.

Near the beginning of freshman year of high school, Sally slipped me a red as I ambled toward French class. A grin burst across my face when she whispered, "Mellows you out." I waved a thank-you and tossed the capsule back with a long sip from the water fountain. I jiggled my feet under the desk and moved my jaw from left to right. Each time the clock hand progressed forward one minute, I paused to assess my high-ness level.

At the thirty-minute mark, I stretched my legs to their full length as the spasmodic urges eased and my butt melded into the chair. When I attempted to pick up my pen, my fingers sort of skimmed it instead, so I watched it roll off the desk edge. As I closed my eyes, my chin dropped to my chest. My breathing slowed, and I worried I'd nod off and fall deep into the beautiful calm clouds at the center of my mind. I forced my head up but then let it rest on my shoulder.

From this angle, I scanned my classmates' faces. I spent all day with this group, like last year and the year before. I couldn't remember why they weren't all my best friends. Weren't these my people? Smart and friendly, uncomplicated and open. Okay, that differentiated them from me. But still. As a few glanced my way, I looked them right in the eye and nodded. After class, I skated down the hall, or thought I did. When the last bell rang, I murmured, "Bye-bye sweeties, bye-bye."

I began ingesting whatever pills I could lay my hands on. I raided the medicine cabinets in my house and every home I visited, mostly stealing barbiturates and muscle relaxers. I calculated how many pills I could pilfer without them being missed, such as six from almost-full bottles but two if nearly empty. Dusty lids might prompt me to swipe the whole container. With limited pharmaceutical knowledge, I swallowed anything and everything. If I didn't float toward heaven within thirty minutes, I devoured another. Fifteen minutes later, another. If three failed to propel me to the soaring heights I sought, I hurled the remainder down the toilet and put the pills on my "waste of time" list.

The trauma and drama at home, added to my preexisting anxiety, escalated my drug use. As an adult, I realized I suffered from post-traumatic stress disorder due to Allan's assaults and living under constant threat. Getting high shoved my pain into the background. But when I numbed those feelings, I sacrificed my connection to most other emotions. Beyond laughing at something funny, I couldn't experience joy or pleasant sensations. I even lost my sense of taste and smell to the point that Mom took me for testing. The only feelings I noticed were rage, terror, and drug cravings. My friendship bonds also were weak because my ability to understand other people dissipated and I didn't have spare emotional or mental energy to figure out how to improve my relationships despite a hunger for connection.

Drugs were a survival technique because the abuse kept coming. For example, when I was fifteen, Mom insisted I break up with my "bad influence" boyfriend, Will, as punishment for constantly missing curfew. She didn't know it was more my fault than his, since he often had trouble rolling me to the car for the ride home. The next day I hitchhiked to his house. As we listened to Lynyrd Skynyrd in his living room and toked on a joint, we heard gravel fly when a car peeled into the driveway. Footsteps resonated across the porch. The storm door banged open. Three long rings of the doorbell and my mother's "Mary Beth" startled us into action. I jumped up and clutched Will's arm to steady myself.

"I know you're in there! If you don't come out now, I'll call the police."

Will mouthed, "What do you want to do?"

I released my grip and rubbed my brow. He leaned down, I think to kiss the top of my head, but the abrupt movement startled me so I jerked away. I wanted to plead for help but just grunted a "sorry." A few tears filled my eyes before I could stop the flow. As my stomach dropped my brain announced, "It's hopeless, you have to go with her."

I grabbed my coat and rested my hand on the doorknob. As my mother peered into the window, I threw open the oak door and sprinted to her blue-and-white Ford LTD. I sat in the passenger seat and tried to zip my jacket with fingers atremble. She glared at Will and returned to the car.

Mom smoothed the trim of her faux fur coat and checked her lipstick in the mirror. She started the vehicle and adjusted the heating vents. My mother paused, then twisted her upper body in my direction. "Why can't you do what I say?"

Nauseated from terror, I tried to maintain an impassive expression even as I gawked at Will standing in his yard. My mother reached over and clutched the back of my skull with her right hand. She forced my face toward her. Then smashed my forehead into the steering wheel. Twice. "Maybe next time you'll follow orders."

My upper body swayed from side to side. Stars sparkled and swirled around me. I lowered my head and sobbed into my mittens. Anger and frustration threatened to overwhelm me. To prevent further escalation, I swallowed my feelings and my tears. I stared out the window and ignored her "ungrateful bitch, why do you push me to the point I have to do these things" tirade on the drive home.

The ongoing violence compelled me to keep using. In my house, I couldn't control events or even decide what happened to my own body. But I could decide what substances to smoke, drink, or swallow. I mixed various combinations of alcohol, pot, and pills as I tried to find the perfect combination to regulate my mood. I sought happiness, peace, security, and bonding with my peers. And sometimes I achieved my goal for an hour or three.

Mostly, though, I lost that balance because I could not stop. I never drank or used a little, not unless that exhausted the available supply. I sucked down alcohol until I couldn't sit straight, smoked pot until I couldn't understand the conversations around me, and took downers until I couldn't stay awake. The rare times I had uppers, I'd pop several to stay up for the night in an artificial happiness bubble. All this, for a while, Friday through Sunday. Then several more days a week in summer. Then after school, during school, and when skipping school.

Was I already addicted? Probably. In addition to continuing to make risky decisions, I almost overdosed on pills twice. I just didn't use daily yet, at least not quite. I doubt most addicts know when they cross the line. I cannot pinpoint that date. Even had I anticipated the outcome of my drug use, it wouldn't have mattered. I lived in today: how to avoid being abused today, how to feel a smidgen better today, how to numb out today. And the chaos of addiction felt familiar to me. Crazy shit happened, emotions ran high, and everyone lived on the edge. This world felt like home.

People ask if I was born an addict, but I can't answer that either. Gambling addiction runs in my family but not chemical dependence. Environmental? I certainly experienced many of the risk factors: minimal parental supervision or support, emotional neglect and abuse, inconsistent discipline, and nearly constant family conflict. All this changes the brain's stress systems, such that I probably was more prone to substance use disorder. The physical abuse, sexual abuse, and witnessing domestic violence all likely exacerbated this vulnerability. And Mom twice abandoning me to live with others undermined my sense of safety or ability to trust.

Yet it also feels like I used my way into addiction. I knew I couldn't change my parents and their proclivity toward violence. So I prioritized the pain-reduction strategy of increasing drug use. I began young, used to excess, and began to escalate my consumption soon after I took that first drink. So much so, that by the time I started my sophomore year, my life revolved around drugs. ◉

# CHAPTER 17
## *Acid*

IN MY SOPHOMORE AND JUNIOR YEARS of high school, in addition to ongoing use of all the other substances, I dropped a lot of acid. My druggie friends ascribed to the '60s belief that drugs were cool and harmless. We didn't consider alcohol to be a drug, and only old war vets ended up alkies. Junkies shot heroin, so don't fall into that trap. All other drugs could be consumed safely. As to pot, it seemed hypocritical for parents who drank to complain when marijuana caused fewer accidents and didn't lead to as much violence. Many of the pills we consumed we stole from grown-ups. We heard stories about kids who freaked out on LSD and ended up in mental wards, but common lore dismissed such events as limited to those with weak minds who couldn't handle the beautiful introspection and fluidity of an acid trip.

In Bordentown in the mid-'70s, an LSD variant known as four-way windowpane, aka blotter acid, flooded the market. The manufacturer stamped the LSD onto thin paper, in a blue or green pattern, that melted in your mouth. Like a common window configuration, a larger square was subdivided into four perforated squares constituting one dose each.

For our first acid trip, Sally and I each bought a four-way for twenty dollars. We intended to take it at her house and then head to New Heights Inn for a few beers. As I lay on my bed struggling into my skintight maroon jeans, I noticed my drug kit peeking out from my pocketbook. I reached backward and grabbed the phone.

"Sally, I'm thinking we should drop the acid now. I'll be there in a half hour, and it'll probably take that long to kick in. Plus, then we'll have a chance to get used to it before we walk down that dark road to the bar."

"All right, that's fine. But be careful on your way over. Lights from the cars on the highway might look weird."

"Sure, sure. Whatever you say. See you soon." I rammed the phone down onto the receiver and snagged my purse as I swung into a sitting position. I decided to swallow half of the four-way because one hit of anything was never enough, so two should be perfect for my first trip.

I removed the hot rollers, brushed out my curls, and sprayed on just enough Final Net to hold my look while allowing some bounce. I left the garage apartment and, through the house's screen door, I yelled, "Bye, going to Sally's," into the kitchen toward my mother. As I headed up Heiser Avenue toward Route 206, purple and yellow trails followed the luminous orange tip of my cigarette, and I swung my arm to create figure eights and zigzags. The ear-piercing horn blast from Mrs. Fisher's station wagon woke me from my trance. I undulated around the vehicle and began repeating, "Stay away from cars, stay away from cars."

When I arrived, I focused on the ground as I slid past Mrs. Brown, to avoid her seeing what I knew must be gigantic pupils, since the headlights had burst into painful shards of light. Mesmerized by my brown boots moving of their own volition, I tripped and plowed through Sally's bedroom door and across her room. As I reached for the desk to steady myself, she turned to greet me. But it wasn't Sally. A monster with similar hair and shape sat on her bed, with a shiny white face and sparkling red lips.

I turned to run but slammed into the wall. I issued a blood-curdling scream and then another. Sally's mother appeared in the doorway. The monster shook me by the shoulders and spoke in Sally's voice. I eyeballed the beast and realized it was my friend, her face covered in cream.

"Sorry, Mrs. Brown, the Noxzema, the Noxzema."

"It's all right, Mom. You know Mary Beth can be jumpy."

After she closed the door, Sally swiveled toward me. "You broke our agreement. No way you're that high on one hit."

To which I shrugged my shoulders in a "what did you expect" way.

I dropped LSD regularly at school and on many weekends. This psychedelic drug usually created euphoria. My cares melted away, the universe felt softer and safer, and everyday activities became more interesting. Once, when playing solitaire, I became absorbed in watching the patterns on the back of the cards shift and oscillate. During first period gym, if we'd started our day with acid, Sally and I would be too high to participate so we'd sit in the weight room and watch our classmates float their way through volleyball. I'd have deep conversations with people to the point that we'd hold hands and express our admiration and love. However, I twisted my ankle when I jumped off the roof of a van because I thought the ground was rising up to meet me.

I rarely took one dose. Instead, I dropped at least two and some-times all four. Although acid is not considered addictive, my reasons for using it paralleled those that drove me to other mood-altering substances. I enjoyed the high and the novelty of the experience and the resulting distance from my painful life. LSD covered the world with a beautiful shimmer, relaxed me, and entrenched me even further in Bordentown's drug-taking group.

I did feel some compulsion to use it. I craved living in that soft glow, filled with giggles and comradery. When I drifted around my house in an acid bubble, my parent's behavior could not induce the rage and terror that consumed my core being. I stayed in the garage apartment until dinner, then listened to the hum of their voices from a distance. If I realized they spoke to me, I'd respond in half sentences, which they seldom mentioned. And, maybe because fear never washed over me, I didn't feel the need to lash out in response. So they might've just appreciated that I didn't escalate the interaction. And why would I when I could enjoy a few hours' bliss?

Regrettably, shortly after I obtained my driver's license, I drove in the rain on acid, lost control of the car, and slammed into the median so hard I bent the frame. And I destroyed my relationship with Sally because, when high, I prioritized bonding with the people around me over safeguarding relationships with friends not in the room. I told a fellow tripper a personal detail about Sally's family life, Sally then warned me not to share her business, and I did it again anyway. And she cut me off, which surprised and stunned me.

I thought of my mother's refusal to acknowledge the concept of privacy, though not from the perspective that I had behaved like her, because that took me decades to realize. Instead, the concept of setting a boundary and then enforcing it entered my mind for the first time. I wondered how Sally had learned this—and what other important life skills there were that no one had bothered to teach me. ◉

# CHAPTER 18
## First Snort

IN THE MOVIE *Postcards from the Edge*, the main character tells her drug rehab counselor she isn't an addict because she didn't use any specific drug regularly. The counselor responds, "Then you're a *drugs* addict." I consider this an accurate characterization of me at sixteen, if not earlier. Years of abuse had primed my brain to crave more and stronger drugs, a particular danger for those who start young as I did. I felt compelled to consume alcohol and other drugs and used to excess every time, which required larger and larger doses when I developed a tolerance. And I put myself in danger to gain access to my beloved mood-altering chemicals.

Regardless, a month before my seventeenth birthday, any ambiguity about my status as an addict disintegrated when I discovered methamphetamine.

For a year, I had been drinking at the Silver Fox, a dive bar popular with the local criminals and addicts. My ears pricked up at every discussion about crystal meth. Rumor had it that a motorcycle gang in nearby Pennsylvania had engineered a way to mass-produce this speed. Mid-level dealers recounted their efforts to join the distribution chain. They described the powder as easy to snort but also water soluble and thus injectable.

One night, I sucked down three Bacardi 151s with a splash of Coke, seeking solace after Allan twisted my arm for vacuuming too long. As I wobbled toward the bathroom on my platform wedgies with the cork heels, drug dealer Dennis's tattooed arm reached out to steady me. I crunched my eyes open and shut, then watched his blue snake undulate up to the Grim Reaper's luminescent yellow eyes.

"Mary Beth, you gonna make it to the toilet?"

"Don't worry. Fine."

"When you came in, your face was puffy, like you'd been crying. What's up?"

"Aw, Dennis, that's sweet. Just the usual drama at home."

"I've got something that will put your worries in the rearview mirror. Take care of business and meet me at my favorite table."

I careened through the bathroom door and bopped my shoulder against the mounted paper towel holder. I unbuttoned my beige slacks and clung to the commode while they dropped to the ground. After I peed, I struggled to reassemble my clothes and add fresh peach lip gloss. I intended to glide to Dennis, but my ankle buckled and I swayed for a few seconds before I regained my balance. I slid into the seat across from him and tossed onto the floor my brown purse with colorful patchwork tiles.

In the pinball machine's shadow lay a mirror, a short metal cylinder, a razor blade, and a brown vial with a black lid. I broke into a broad grin. "Is that crank?"

"Yep. Got my first eight ball today. Tried it myself, a few lines to my wife, and now you."

For a second, I felt proud to know he chose me to share the meth with after his spouse, although I knew I'd be expected to pay in sex at some point. But my mind skirted over the price for this coup and back to the riveting events at hand.

"Eight ball?"

"Eighth of an ounce. Three and a half grams."

"Ooh, grams. So scientific."

"Well, you're the brain. You would know."

My alcohol fog dissipated as my attention telescoped to the four corners of the table. Dennis scooched his chair forward while he flicked the mirror's edge with two fingers until it skated into position. He unscrewed the lid and tilted the vial. The white powder sparkled like crushed diamonds, despite the low light. As Dennis tapped the rim, a small avalanche of crank escaped and the pile grew. My excitement rose with the mound.

The razor blade glinted a spellbinding silver blue as Dennis smoothed the speed flat and diced the meth to a fine dust. With a graceful motion, he cut a line through the middle, swiped one half left and the other right, then formed two thick lines.

Dennis clacked his teeth, surveyed his work, and rolled the cylinder, a metal straw, back and forth. I considered snatching it from his fingers and vacuuming up both portions before he could react, but my long-term interest in gaining access to free drugs overpowered the impulse. As a reminder, I gripped my chair's front legs.

Flipping his hand palm up, Dennis presented me with the straw. With an index finger, he closed one nostril. My heart palpitated, noticeably, as I copied the gesture. My lungs expanded to their full capacity as I bent toward the mirror.

I'd like to say I paused and considered the risks of using speed. I'm not sure why, exactly, since that analysis wouldn't have deterred me. But anyway, I didn't.

Instead, I shoved my hair back, thrust the straw into my nose, and suctioned up the line. A burning volcano shattered my mind into a thousand pieces. I coughed as the bitter chemicals flowed down my throat. I wondered how the crystals converted to liquid in a matter of seconds. I cracked my jaw open and maneuvered it from side to side. A loud roar ricocheted from ear to ear. My eyes pulsated tears.

Dennis grasped my wrist, lifted my chin, and moved his mouth. Pink Floyd's "your lips move but I can't hear what you're saying" flitted through my brain. Flashing oranges and yellows from the pinball machine expanded into three dimensions. Warmth flowed from my belly button to my neck to my arms and tingled every neuron en route. My heart slammed against my chest and forced me to suck in gallons of air.

"Good God! I feel so alive. It's so bright, so beautiful." I clutched Dennis's hands. "Thank you."

Dennis and I played pool, talked with friends, snorted more speed, drove through nearby dairy farm country after the bar closed, and snorted and snorted and snorted. Around 4:00 a.m., he had to return home, so he dropped me at my car. I walked up and down Farnsworth Avenue, hoping to find someone I could talk to, but no luck.

So I headed home, shook Cindy awake, and begged her to play Rummy 500. I told her all about crank and how Dennis promised boatloads would arrive soon. She made me explain in detail how it felt and watched me talk a mile a minute for two hours. I gesticulated and piled on adjectives.

Madison Avenue couldn't have devised a better sales pitch. ❖

# CHAPTER 19
## Addiction for Sure

"WAKE UP."

I forced myself to trudge to consciousness. "Cindy, Jesus. What?"

"Dennis said come over. Now. He has it. Speed, speed, speed."

I flung off the covers, leapt to my feet, and raced to the bathroom. Cindy hunted for my keys while I threw on some clothes. We giggled when I snagged my toe on the half-open door. I didn't want to spend precious minutes applying makeup, but with only a few hours' sleep after a hard crash, I had no choice.

"Did he say where he got it?"

"No, but I hope it was from Tommy, like last time. That was incredible."

She tapped a Marlboro out of her pack, then had to make three attempts to light it because her hand shook so much.

As I blotted my rose lipstick, I paused. "I wonder if his wife is home. She always looks at me as if I want to steal him."

"Then maybe you shouldn't have gotten all dolled up."

"You never know who you'll run into. Could be a bigwig dealer who'd be useful if impressed. Anyway, did Dennis call us first? I'd hate to have to wait while he handles other customers."

"He didn't say, so we should get our asses in gear and get there before the mob." We sped toward the porch, then fell to the floor in hysterics after we bumped into each other.

As I put the '73 Valiant into gear, my sister jammed Pink Floyd's *The Wall* into the eight-track player. We rolled down the windows and belted out the lyrics to "Comfortably Numb."

"So, Cindy, where do you wanna go after we pick it up? The river?"

"Good idea. After we taste it."

The car fishtailed through the jug handle.

"Watch it. Could you try to get us there alive?"

As we pulled into the driveway, toward the house set far back from the road, we noticed a yellow Corvette parked on the brown grass that passed for a lawn. Cindy jumped up and down in her seat. "Tommy, Tommy."

After we parked, we sauntered to the rear door, yelling "Knock, knock" as we walked in. When we crossed the threshold into the kitchen, we spotted a shimmering pile of crystal meth on the table. And we reached for our wallets.

Days like this blended together as I rode the meth wave that flooded South Jersey. Only crank now satisfied my deepest cravings. All other drugs became second-best replacements, so I used them less and less. The deluge slowed every couple of months, the result of escalating demand or brief supply chain glitches, so I'd be forced to hunt longer or harder, with an occasional failure.

My meth obsession existed from that initial snort at the Silver Fox. At first, speed created a better version of me because it enhanced the intense energy that is my natural metabolism. I felt calm, not in a quiet way, but absorbed in the beauty of the high rather than the misery of my life. I was a dynamic woman with a lot to say. I experienced joy and bonded to my new crankhead friends, partners in this wondrous experience. I shared stories, favorite music, some secrets but never all. My drug buddies described their dreams, planned exotic vacations, and recited arguments in which they incinerated their opponents. They taught me backgammon and cribbage and read from *Lord of the Rings* and *Alice in Wonderland*.

My brain reacted to my drug of choice differently. Meth didn't provide the mellow high of pot or downers, which had some benefits in squashing my rage. But chemically it fit me best. It was the perfect union, a stimulant that made me feel powerful and alive in a bright new world. So I hunted down this drug with true urgency and desperation.

Although I saw people shoot up within a week of using meth and glommed onto the immediate visceral reaction they experienced, the idea had been implanted months earlier when I found Allan's *Hustler* magazines with cartoons about junkies using TV cords or neckties as tourniquets to slam drugs. This appealed to me so much, as an expression of my total commitment to drugs, that sticking a needle in my arm became my back-of-mind plan as the logical next step. I took it the summer before my senior year, when Bubba shot me up that first time.

Prior to meth, I had learned to disassociate from myself and my life, to a degree. But crank better masked uncomfortable emotions. I often did not know what I felt because numbness encased the pain. Crank worked better, as the high was higher and the crash deeper. Sometimes I exploded in rage, but this was rare. Mostly, I lived in a cycle of getting as high as I could, for as long as I could, until I sank into the deep blackness of a sleep without dreams or ruminations. My version of heaven.

The meth benefits came at a steep price, most notably impaired thinking and deteriorating physical health. Loss of sleep increased the penalties. IV use got me higher for a while, but then I required more and more speed to have any hope I'd attain that level. And during a speed run, I needed increasing amounts to delay sleep. If I had enough crank, or access to it, I would stay up for three days, succumbing to my addictive drive to use and use and use. All speed runs end in a crash, but I stopped only when I literally couldn't stay awake or temporarily couldn't locate any. For the semi-alertness phase, I would start to nod off like a baby, my head drooped forward. Then I'd force my eyes open until exhaustion flattened me for ten or twelve hours, wherever I was—on my sofa or in a chair at a dealer's house or with a needle in my arm.

During the night I would twitch and moan, which might rouse me, or, more likely, disturb a cohort who'd shove me with a "quit it." When I woke from this comatose state, I would crawl to alertness. My head ached and my tongue stuck to the roof of my mouth from dehydration and poor dental hygiene. I had to wiggle my lashes loose because dried mascara cemented them to my skin. It often took several attempts to stand straight due to dizziness from lack of food and the general rebellion of my body. Awash with anxiety, I'd search my purse, hoping I'd saved a wake-up hit. Relief if I located a stash, overwhelming horror if I did not.

I lost so much weight you could count the bones in my back, which didn't bother me because superthin was in. My parents didn't notice this, or that I stayed out for days, and accepted my vague explanation about the strange spoons that appeared in the silverware drawer. But other addicts expressed alarm. They commented about my constant drug seeking and nagged me about my loss of control. From the harsh edge of sixty hours awake and sliding toward unconsciousness, I heard several druggie buddies confer on whether to take action, like call my mother, but their fear of being labeled narcs precluded this inclination. I sometimes lied to my meth pals about when I last used, announcing, "Wow, a few days break, and I feel great." This reduced their concern and resulted in access to their crank stash.

I threw up green chunky bile because nothing else remained in my stomach. I hallucinated from the crank and lack of sleep, hearing or seeing things that weren't there. As just one example, I sat with a friend on a store's steps at 2:00 a.m. and sought to prove to him that people hid in the shadows of the church across the street. Many times, I overdosed to the point that my heart pounded so hard and fast I barely could breathe. I'd laugh this off with a "guess I should be a little more careful," and never think about it again.

I picked at my face and arms and gave myself a staph infection. I would sit in the car at night beneath a streetlight and reopen every wound as I scraped out imaginary bugs. At Anthony's Pizzeria, I ran into my fifth grade teacher in the ladies' room after one such session. I bolted out the door, hoping she didn't recognize me, because I could not stand the thought of her seeing me like that. Also at Anthony's, I once felt the vermin, which I believed lived in my mouth, attack my food every time I took a bite. So I kept spitting out the pizza, which astonished my fellow addict dinner companions.

I shocked other friends as well. My car wouldn't start one day and I needed to go to my fast-food job, so I asked Laurie for a ride. I wore a long-sleeve shirt under my short-sleeve uniform on this hot summer day to cover my bruised and needle-hole dappled arms. I pretended not to notice Laurie's stunned look, which I'm confident was her realization that I did so to hide the track marks she'd caught wind of through the high school rumor mill.

My childhood friend Tony saw my car at a local hangout near the river. He walked up to my window and caught me shooting up. He tried to talk to me about it, but I brushed him aside. Will realized the severity of my addiction when I visited unexpectedly, then spent ninety minutes in the bathroom trying to hit a vein, making him wait outside from where he revealed concerns that only partially penetrated my brain. By the time I succeeded, this dose wasn't sufficient, so I had to start the process over again—an increasingly common occurrence.

The winter of my senior year, I contracted bronchitis. I became sicker and sicker as my speed run progressed. I crashed on a table at the Silver Fox. When the bar closed, two regulars, Claus and Claire, let me rest in the back seat of their Cadillac. They headed to New Heights, the same bar Sally and I used to frequent, because it stayed open until 2:00 a.m. Too ill to walk that far, I waved them away, so they tossed me a blanket. "It's twenty degrees, Mary Beth. Cover up."

I drifted in and out of sleep, woken by violent coughing fits or meth-induced muscle spasms. I heard their footsteps on gravel as they returned. Claus held my wrist and checked for a pulse. Claire swatted him. "Can't you hear her wheezing? Although she does sound like she's dying. Let's take her to our place and get some sleep. In the morning we can call Joey. He lives across the street from her."

By 6:00 a.m., my breathing was so labored they did phone Joey. "You've got to come get her. She needs a doctor." Joey took me home, and my mother drove me straight to the emergency room. She asked to be in the room while they treated me, but I didn't want her to see the track marks, so I used the few breaths I could muster to cry out, "Get her out of here, she's making me nervous." The doctors saw the evidence of my intravenous use but uttered not a word. Despite several tries, the nurse couldn't hit any of my overused veins. I offered to do it, but they said it was against policy. So they brought in the nurse from pediatrics, who managed to put the IV into my hand.

A few days later, Mona burst into the garage apartment that Cindy and I shared. "Mary Beth, I need works. You need to give them to me."

"What?"

"Dennis is on his way to get speed from Tommy, but he already said he doesn't have any needles. Give me a set."

"I only have two. Neither of them is new. If I was flush, you know I'd take care of you. But today, I just can't."

"I'm sorry. But if you don't turn over one, I'm going to walk across the porch, into your mother's house, and tell her to check your arms because you've been shooting speed. I hate to threaten you like this, but you leave me no choice."

"Jesus, Mona. That's cold. I wouldn't do that to you."

"Really? Are you sure about that?"

As much as this angered me because it was a betrayal, I got it. Desperation justifies heinous acts. Mona could have snorted the speed, but that's not a satisfactory option for IV junkies.

Once I turned eighteen, and they couldn't call my mom, I missed weeks of school. Because of my strong academic history, and the story I gave about my stepfather beating me so I had to move to my friend's place in Trenton and didn't have a ride, my teachers allowed me to make up the work. I was admitted to several top universities and awarded the most scholarship money but missed the awards ceremony. I also didn't join the senior trip to Disney World because I was too strung out and feared exposing my addiction to roommates.

I missed other fun events, too. Once Bubba and I went to see Pat Travers in nearby Philadelphia. Local rock stations WMMR and WYSP played his "Boom, Boom, Out Go the Lights" often to advertise the event. During the opening act, we went to the car to get high before Pat took the stage. We shot once, twice, three times. When

"Boom, Boom" played in the background, we glanced at each other, and Bubba poured another mound into the spoon.

In other ways as well, insanity often followed when I hung with my peers. One evening, when I drove Dennis to his dealer after a day of shooting drugs at his apartment, he informed me he'd stashed a gun under his seat because a warrant had been issued for him for a parole violation.

"I'm not going back to that fucking jail. If the cops try to pull us over, floor it. I'll hold them off with my magnum. I'll try not to kill them, but if that's what it takes . . ."

I exhaled a stream of smoke from my cigarette and nodded consent. I wondered whether I would be more afraid of him or the police if the blue lights flashed in the rearview mirror.

I hung out with a biker chick for a while because she was generous with her unending supply of crank, even after she bragged about beating a girl to a pulp for looking sideways at her man. She and her boyfriend later tortured an old alcoholic regular of the Silver Fox just for fun.

And, to my eternal regret, I agreed to teach Cindy to shoot up after she begged for weeks. In many ways, she was a younger version of me. We were so close in age and grew up sharing a room and playing together. As a result of all the neglect and insanity, we also have a war-buddy bond that runs deep. Cindy and I had similar reactions to the abuse. Too many drugs, too many boys, skipping school, and staying out all night. Cindy began her drug use at an even younger age than I did. And while I worried about her descending deeper, I understood her motivation and eventually agreed. I justified this as her decision. Plus, I assumed she'd find someone else to initiate her if I refused, and they might not teach her properly. All of this I still believe was true. But that doesn't mean shooting her up was a loving sisterly act. ❧

# CHAPTER 20
# Science of Addiction

PEOPLE OFTEN ASK HOW someone so smart could become an addict. But brain disorders don't discriminate based on intellect. Some experts categorize addiction as a progressive chronic, relapsing brain disease whereas others view substance use disorder as a pathological form of learning. Either way, to me, that I chose to use drugs is not surprising. This decision is consistent with the view that substance use disorder often is an adaptation to a dysfunctional life. Depressed, anxious, and traumatized people face a much higher risk as they seek relief from suffering. Similarly, a person can be vulnerable if they feel isolated, don't have a support network, or cannot deeply connect with others, in part because an active addict can superficially attach to a circle of other addicts although usually not in a harmonious and fulfilling way.

Also, from my point of view, the substance use disorder snuck up on me. The immediate cause is excessive intake of habit-forming substances. Then the addictive chemicals alter the brain by inserting themselves into mainstream processes. Substance use disorder involves numerous changes in brain anatomy, chemistry, and cell-to-cell signaling, including in the molecular machinery for learning. Scientists have developed a detailed picture of how addiction disrupts pathways and processes that underlie desire, habit formation, enjoyment, cognitive functions, and emotional regulation. These brain changes warp many different areas of life: how time is spent, feelings, relationships, thinking, and much more.

Mood-altering drugs cause a surge of the neurotransmitter dopamine. Dopamine creates pleasure, so the brain remembers this feeling and wants it repeated. When drugs flood the brain with dopamine, the brain makes less, so the drug user needs to increase consumption just to feel normal. Altering dopamine production impairs executive functions, which include judgment, decision-making, working memory, and self-control. Dopamine also is needed for the amygdala to function properly, which is responsible for emotions and stimuli reactions. Addictive substances take advantage of the brain's plasticity and remold neural circuits to assign supreme value to the drug at the expense of other interests such as health, work, or family. Drug use becomes compulsive and outweighs everything else, even true survival needs like food and sleep. As a result, substance use disorder alters impulse control and judgment and creates a dysfunctional pursuit of rewards that doesn't stop despite adverse consequences.

This is why, unlike most people, individuals with substance use disorder cannot be counted on to do what benefits them because repeated drug use disrupts well-balanced brain systems and replaces normal needs and desires with a one-track mission to seek and use drugs. Drug cues gain prominence and the field of attention narrows, like a camera that zooms in on one object. Moreover, brain alterations create the perceived lack of willpower, so the inability to make clear decisions is a byproduct of the same disorder from which the addict is trying to escape. This is one reason why addiction is so insidious. It's difficult for the drug-addled brain to make the rational choice to stop using. And, with speed, the lack of sleep exacerbates the impact of the chemicals because to remain healthy a brain requires rest.

In addition, starting at a young age increases addiction risk because early drug use interferes with normal brain development, including risk-taking. Before the child learns how to analyze choices, her brain organizes itself around the core concept that she needs drugs. The benefits of drug use are overvalued and the rest of life undervalued. Short-term rewards win out over long-term harms.

All these impacts hit me. I started young, did not anticipate the impact of constant crank use, and did my best to ignore the consequences. I fell headfirst into a compulsive pursuit of drugs, even when the rewards declined and the costs increased. Plus, when I graduated high school, I hadn't rested properly for two years. I spent less time on previous priorities like academics, although part of me still wanted to go to college and succeed professionally. I ignored my deteriorating health, let friendships lapse, and accepted the chaos. I focused on every reference to drug use, like the cartoons about shooting up. Meanwhile, my brain's ability to control my behavior, when faced with such cues, diminished. Despite initially using drugs to alleviate my pain, I didn't notice I'd accepted new drug-induced misery and chaos.

And tolerance developed, so I required more speed to achieve intoxication. For most of my addiction, I did not use crank for true happiness because that became fleeting. Instead, I hunted down every source and every lead until I ferreted out enough to alleviate my distress. Although speed does not cause the physical withdrawal symptoms of alcohol or heroin, without my favorite drug I felt depressed, anxious, exhausted, and consumed by the compulsion to shoot up speed now. To avoid this misery, I'd try to squirrel away enough for two shots, minimum, to reduce the risk I'd run out. Any hint that my crank sources might run dry caused me to double down on my efforts because little else mattered except shooting speed into my veins every day or even every hour.

On those rare occasions when a consequence scared me enough to consider quitting, I spent two minutes thinking about it and then gave up because I felt unable to stop. But, mostly, I chose not to dream about the impossible. •

# CHAPTER 21
## Arrested

I STARTED HANGING WITH BOBBY, who was easygoing, got along with everyone, and had a clean-cut look of short hair with slightly long bangs, though his sad eyes supported the rumor he'd been raped in jail. His former cellmate was a high-level dealer, so Bobby always had speed. When the Silver Fox closed at midnight, we would walk around town for an hour, then sneak into his attic bedroom at his mother's to have sex. I enjoyed my time with Bobby. It was simple, without problematic demands or drama.

In early August, in the middle of the night, high on meth, Bobby and I parked my Valiant behind a baseball field in an isolated area. I'd stored my crank vial and hypodermics in a wraparound leather pouch under the driver's seat. After shooting up with Bobby's stash, he stowed it in the glove compartment. We sprawled on the hood of the car, gazed at the stars, talked, and smoked.

A cop car drove down the only road into the park, turned on a spotlight, and headed in our direction.

"Shit, Bobby, there's no way out."

"Stay calm. Your car's shut tight and we're just sitting here. They might just question us and move on."

"Can't believe this. Never arrested as a juvenile. Now I'm an adult. Plus, I'm supposed to leave for college in a month."

"Smile and look mellow. Although you'd better throw my shirt on to hide your tracks. It's kinda lucky you're such a hard stick. With the bruises in different spots, sort of looks like you're clumsy."

The police prowler pulled up, and Officer Smickely, who I knew by appearance, rolled down his window. "Bobby, what are you doing here?"

"Just chatting with my girl, sir. It's out of the way, so we won't disturb anyone."

Officer Smickely scrutinized me, then stepped out of the car. "Mary Beth, right? I've seen you in town a lot, young lady. And not with the best of company."

I rubbed my neck. Sweat leaked from the pores of my forehead, underarms, and where my butt met my back. "True enough, Officer. I don't always have the best taste in boys. But Bobby is a sweetie pie."

"Didn't I see your picture in the paper last month?"

I lifted my face and beamed, for his benefit, while I snuck my shaking hand underneath my thigh. "You did, you did. Highest SAT score in my class."

Officer Smickely's partner, a cop I didn't recognize, walked a circuit around the car.

Smickely continued, "So, Princeton?"

"No, Officer. UCLA. I leave in a month. I've never been to California, so I'm excited. And it's a great school."

"Mary Beth, I need to check your vehicle."

My eyes darted from one cop to the other. I considered falling to my knees and begging for mercy, but with a faint suggestion of offering sexual favors.

Bobby turned toward the unknown cop, who stood tapping the trunk. "I know it's after hours. But, as you can see, we aren't causing any trouble. How about we head home and call it a night?"

"The thing is, Bobby, before you slammed the trunk, I thought I saw a motorcycle. And it so happens, a Honda '70 was stolen from a nearby house."

"We didn't have the trunk open tonight, sir."

"I think you did."

The other cop yanked on the back door and started the search.

I clenched my arms across my chest, then rubbed my hot skin before floating skyward. The earth drifted beneath me and I choked from the lack of oxygen. I rejoined my body, stared at the stars twinkling above, and wished I could dissolve into my atomic particles and float away.

"Mary Beth. Mary Beth. Can you hear me?"

As I hurtled back to Earth, Officer Smickely snapped his fingers twice. "Recognize these?"

He brandished both drug kits. I remembered Dennis's parole violation and Bobby's traumatic incarceration history. I figured I'd be in the same trouble whether I claimed just my speed or Bobby's, too, so I swore both were mine. They took him into custody anyway, but they didn't end up arresting him.

At the police station, they interrogated me about where I got the meth. I'd complained to Bobby that a middle-aged pervert had been following me in a black sedan. I wasn't positive because I knew sometimes my speed-saturated mind played tricks on me although I didn't share my uncertainty with him. Regardless, confident they'd never locate this possibly imaginary guy, and to protect my true drug connections, I fingered him as my dealer.

They booked me and drove me to the women's pretrial jail ten miles away. The facility was half full, so I had my own room with walls, not a cell, but a large window so staff could watch me. I crashed hard and, for the first time in months, slept three nights in a row. After, that is, I spent the first few hours agonizing about the ramifications of my arrest and, I was sure, conviction. Could I get probation, or would I spend months or years in jail? Could I delay college? Or would they revoke my admission? Would my parents kick me out? Would I be able to get a job? How would I avoid future arrests now that I was a verified criminal? If a probation officer searched my house, I'd be screwed. If I had to take drug tests, I'd be screwed. If an authority even saw me during a typical day, looking like the druggie I was, I'd be screwed. The one thought that didn't cross my mind was "Maybe I should use this as a push to clean up."

On the fourth day, I reached Shirley, from my high-academic group in high school. We weren't close, but she was the only person I could think of with a checking account, at least one with money in it. I cried that my family wouldn't help, even though the drugs weren't mine, and swore I'd repay her. She bailed me out, and I even paid her back a few weeks later.

By the time I was released, counting my pre-arrest drug run, I hadn't been home in ten days. I had Shirley drop me in the center of Bordentown. Relieved to be free and intent on banishing my "Will I end up in jail?" anxiety, I hightailed it toward the Silver Fox, where I hoped to find speed but at a minimum could pour some Bacardi down my throat. I also wanted to spread the word that I'd kept my mouth shut and protected my friends. Lo and behold, Bobby had preserved my reputation already by singing my praises for covering for him.

As I approached the main intersection, my mother screeched to a halt in her Ford LTD, parked in the middle of Farnsworth Avenue, and jumped out. "Where the fuck have you been? I've been hunting for you for two days. We thought you were dead. I'm taking you home. Now."

"I just got released from jail. I'm not going anywhere with you."

My mother froze in place, despite a car whipping by with a "get out of the road, idiot." I twirled toward the Fox and marched on. When I swung the door open to enter, I glanced up the street in time to catch Mom's blue-and-white behemoth turn toward home.

After a quick two-day meth run, I returned to the house, intending to grab some clothes and head back to town. Bobby waited at the corner in a car borrowed from Dennis. My Valiant occupied its usual position, which meant my parents had talked to the police and paid to get it out of impound. I checked my watch. Almost 8:00 a.m., so they might be awake. I squatted between the LTD and Allan's truck, which was parked in the driveway, and maneuvered my way forward.

The kitchen lights were on, but the room appeared empty. I swiveled toward the garage apartment while I dug for my keys, then I spotted my mother rounding the corner. She broke into a run as I plowed through the apartment door and slammed it behind me. Locked out, my mother banged and banged against the wooden barricade. "Don't make me get my key. You will regret it."

Cindy rolled out of bed. "What's going on? They said you were arrested for crank."

I shrugged. "What should I do?"

"She's been ranting for days. Get it over with."

I stretched out my arm, released the bolt, and backed into the wall. My mother burst through the entry, emitting a sort of howl. She lurched across the coffee table and grabbed the pink hairbrush, the hard molded plastic kind. I spun toward my bedroom, but the gleaming silver kitchenette table and matching chair blocked my way.

Mom gripped my arm and dragged me backward. As I clutched the edge of the stereo console to steady myself, she swung the brush and made contact with my forehead. My neck careened to the right and I fell to one knee.

My high-pitched yelp failed to deter her. Now behind me, Mom pummeled my back with her pastel weapon. The assault continued as I struggled to rise, so I crawled to the sofa. When I planted my hands on the cushions and pushed my body upright, my mother clobbered my neck with such force that the bristle head broke from the handle and flew across the room.

I sagged to my knees. Icy coldness pierced my chest. I felt disoriented as my mind drifted out the window and over the trees. My mother's shouts grew louder in my ears, although I knew she'd been shrieking without relenting.

Cindy's tear-streaked face came into view. "MB. Can you hear me? Are you all right?"

I pursed my lips into a thin smile and rose. I stared straight into my mother's eyes. "Get the fuck out of my way." I slung my purse over my shoulder and headed out the door. As I strode up the drive, I heard her bare feet slap onto the concrete porch and race toward me, so I exploded into a sprint.

Mom chased me up the street. Her robe flapped and exposed her sheer negligee. "If you leave, don't think you're ever coming back. You stupid bitch. You motherfucking whore junkie."

Bobby started the car, turned it around, and flung open the passenger door. I hopped in and we peeled out.

"What the hell? Was that your mom?"

I stuck my head out the window to cool myself down. I tried to recall what my mother had said. But, although she'd shrieked insults throughout the entire attack, only a few words permeated my fear firewall. My focus was on my efforts to escape. Later that day, I did wonder why she was livid. I remembered the warnings that one mistake can derail your life, usually shared when she was in hysterics after an incident with Allan, so that might've been the motivation. But I also doubted she had a conscious reason. This response to my arrest would not help me, and I didn't believe that was her goal. I also realized that, despite the beating, I wasn't that upset with her. The rage I used to feel when treated like this had evaporated. I just wanted to flee from the maniac's blows.

Several days later I went to my high school to speak to the counselor about putting off college. Mr. Eck, my two time English teacher and college recommendation writer, flagged me down in the hall. "Miss us already?"

"Hey, Mr. Eck. I ran into a little hiccup and need to delay college."

He paused while I continued to walk forward. Since it was summer, I wore a skimpy cream top with embroidered flowers. Mr. Eck sputtered behind me, so I rotated around.

"Your back! What happened?"

I glanced over my shoulder and spotted the mosaic of purple and green bruises.

"Oh, I forgot. I upset my mother."

Mr. Eck examined me from head to toe, now noticing the track marks and red splotches that covered my arms.

"My God. What's going on? I knew something was off with all the school you missed. But I had no idea you were in this kind of trouble."

Mr. Eck's concern seared into my heart. Tears spurted from my eyes. His shock trumpeted the depths to which I had sunk. The stunned look on his face reminded me that most mothers don't bludgeon their daughters with pink hairbrushes. And most college-bound students don't spend the summer shooting powerful drugs into their veins.

I brushed past him and exited the building. Mr. Eck followed. "Wait, please, talk to me."

I leaned against the trunk of my car and lit a cigarette. Certain that the midday glare enhanced the evidence of my disintegration, I folded my arms and donned oversized sunglasses.

"Can't go to college. I was arrested. For methamphetamine."

"Mary Beth, you are skin and bones. You look like you're dying. Why don't you just stop?"

Hunching my shoulders, I hugged myself in a futile effort to stave off the shivers running up and down my spine. My chin quivered as a soft moan slipped out. "I don't know. I just can't."

I bent my leg and crushed my cigarette out with the sole of my sandal, then flicked it near the yellow school buses. "Sorry, Mr. Eck."

He reached toward me, but I slid past and planted myself inside the roiling hot Valiant. As I backed up, I watched Mr. Eck move out of my path. And I drove off.

The reality of having devolved from ace student to drug addict hit me hard, and I sobbed for a few blocks. Then I pulled into a far corner of the Acme parking lot and shot up.

My mother did allow me back into the house a week later and she hired a lawyer. The attorney recommended that I go into therapy to show the judge I was addressing the issue. To be fair to Mom, the psychiatrist was at Princeton University, so she did try to find someone with the requisite expertise. But he knew little about addiction. He diagnosed anhedonia and gave me antidepressants. He never suggested a drug treatment facility, even though I admitted to a significant drug history and looked like a depraved addict.

I had to delay college for a year because I could not leave New Jersey until after my October court date. Since I didn't have a prior record and had been accepted to a prestigious university, the judge reduced the charges to a disorderly person offense, which I believe was a level below misdemeanor. He sentenced me to one-year probation at which point the charges would be dismissed. If I wasn't arrested over the next few years, he would expunge my record.

The judge asked me if I understood. I repeated the details about probation and clearing my record if I adhered to the terms. The judge noted that most defendants do not use words like "adhere." My probation officer allowed me to attend UCLA the following year if I submitted a monthly report. I later did file to expunge my record. The order states that my arrest and conviction "shall be deemed not to have occurred." •

# CHAPTER 22
## Promiscuity

BETWEEN CHET AND BOBBY, I'd racked up a prodigious number of sexual partners. When I was fourteen, I slept with three friends, one after the other, in the neighborhood fort. By sixteen, I'd had sexual encounters with at least six men in their mid-twenties or thirties. They all expressed astonishment at my prowess but otherwise never mentioned the age implications. The greater the number of boys, and adults, who desired me, the more value I felt I had. This abuse of my own body also arose from my general dissociative reaction to the physical and sexual abuse at home.

As my substance use disorder progressed, so did my promiscuity statistics. I earned the approval of men at the top of the local drug dealer tier because of my sexual skills and attractiveness. If they weren't available, I'd fuck or suck almost anyone who filled my spoon with meth. I accommodated them to reinforce the friendship bond or in an unstated exchange for speed. If someone had bigger tits or got the best guy, meaning the one with the most crank, I felt alarmed. Maybe I'd lose access to an endless supply of free drugs, particularly since my looks began to deteriorate as I sank deeper into my meth addiction.

I stole speed from many of the men I slept with. I wouldn't snag their whole stash. We were pals, to some degree, so I had to avoid alienating them. More important, a "drug thief" label would undermine my long-term interest. But if they fell asleep, I would evaluate how much I could pilfer without them noticing. Once a friend, when he suggested I blow him, handed me a half-ounce bag of speed and told me to take as much as I wanted. This instruction confused me. I hungered for it all but couldn't say that. I slammed a giant shot, another one after he came, and pocketed two grams before I snuck out of his house when his wife's alarm went off.

I never required condom use, although somehow avoided STDs. And though I shared needles, too, AIDS didn't hit my communities for another two years. I did get pregnant twice. First at fifteen, a couple years after my mother's miscarriage. I thought, *If Allan beat her like that when she carried his child, what will he do to me?* Too terrified to face him with this news, I had an abortion, which I might've done anyway once Sally informed me you didn't need parental consent. My boyfriend, Will, arranged for a guidance counselor to cover for us at school that day, but she forgot, and the vice principal called my house. Allan drove to Will's, so we hid while he ran from door to door and hammered on the windows. I warned Will, "He really might kill us if he gets inside."

When I was eighteen, caught up in daily meth use, I often forgot to take my birth control pills, so became pregnant again. The doctor didn't seem thrilled by my return visit, particularly when I told him I used meth daily. "That is so irresponsible! You've almost certainly damaged this baby. Let's schedule the abortion." His tone irritated me, but I knew he was right on all counts. I couldn't pinpoint the father, so I asked the three possibilities to pay a fair share for the procedure, but all refused.

Despite sometimes feeling pressured to have sex when I didn't want to, and occasionally giving in because I was afraid to say no, I failed to appreciate the extent to which my choices exposed me to danger. One of the extreme episodes occurred when we took a family vacation to Las Vegas. I'd overheard Allan mention that drinks were free when you gambled. At seventeen, I was underage for both activities, so I donned a pair of navy slacks, a tight silk top, and three-inch wedge sandals. With full makeup and my hair curled, I hit the Keno lounge, an easy game like Bingo. The waitress didn't bat an eye when I handed her my betting slip and drink order. My drink, though, had more Coke than rum. And senior citizens dominated the Keno crowd, so there were no cute guys to flirt with. So I headed out to the Strip to ensnare some company, using my best imitation Marilyn Monroe walk.

Within five minutes, two guys appeared, one on each side. "Ooh, baby, you are something else. Visiting?"

"Yes, just taking a stroll after a bit of gambling."

The auburn-haired hunk wearing the almost-disco polyester pants and blazing blue satin shirt identified himself as Tim and his short friend in blue jeans as Frank. I pegged them as mid-twenties. We smoked pot in their car and drank in a dive where the bartender filled my glass with Bacardi 151 and added just a dollop of Coke. I remember speaking with enthusiasm but can't tell you about what. Tim kept close and nuzzled my neck a few times while Frank struck out with a cute brunette.

Two hours and three drinks later, Tim suggested we all go to their apartment to listen to music and smoke another doobie. When I tried to leap to my feet, my ankle gave out and I grabbed Tim to steady myself. As we ambled to the car, I had to put considerable effort into keeping my head upright. I hesitated when Frank headed up the stairs to the apartment, so Tim spooned me from behind as I ascended.

"Don't worry darlin'. I've got you. You won't fall."

"So sweet. It's these heels. Higher than I'm used to."

Tim steered me to the sofa and I slumped into the cushions. Frank disappeared after we smoked the joint. Waves of dizziness swept over me until I put my head between my knees.

"You look like you'd do better on my bed."

I let him put my arms around his neck, so he could pull me to my feet. Then we sort of danced down the hall to his room. Tim turned me around until my butt rested on the bed. I lay on my side and he pulled off my shoes, then pushed me to my back so he could take off my slacks. I knew he intended to have sex with me. Although not particularly interested, I wasn't going to argue. He stripped off the rest of my clothes. Tim tried to get me to suck his dick, but I couldn't manage it, so he fucked me, which hurt at first because the lack of foreplay meant I was dry.

"That was great, babe. Great. Listen, I know Frank likes you, too. You don't mind, do you, having sex with him?"

My stomach clenched and I felt light-headed again. "No. No. Tired. Need to go to the hotel."

Tim towered over me and grabbed my chin. "I promised Frank, plus my other roommate, Greg. I'll drive you back, but not until you keep my word. I'm taking your clothes. But don't worry. I'll give them back. After."

When Tim left to get Frank, I sighed and hugged myself. I could feel the urge to burst into sobs, but the feeling was far away. I turned to the window and thought about jumping. But I was on the third floor. I'd probably break something. Plus, I was naked, and not certain

I could walk to the window, much less figure out how to open it and squeeze out. So I gave up and gave in.

Frank and Greg acted as if I wanted to have sex with them, and I didn't say anything to the contrary. However, Greg gave me a concerned look and, after he finished, asked if I was okay. I just nodded. Tim brought my clothes and I dressed, which took a while because I fumbled with my bra hook and buttons. Frank and Greg ignored me as I trod through the living room to the front door.

On the ride to the hotel's back entrance, Tim pointed out neon signs with the names of famous singers and asked if I planned to see a show. A sour taste filled my mouth, so I just nodded yes. He dropped me right at the glass doors and left with a "have fun." As I tried to reach the elevator, I hugged the wall and took baby steps until an employee noticed and helped me to my room. I crawled into bed next to my grandmother and passed out. I didn't mention this to anyone in my family, or anyone else, not on the trip or after we returned home.

Over the next months, I did, however, consider this event a few times for a few minutes. I decided this was not rape because I did not crawl out the window naked and jump to the ground, did not scream, and they did not hit me. The modern concept of consent either did not exist or at least had not reached me. I thought rape required violence. Since I decided not to try to escape, I, in my mind, allowed the sex. So I wasn't raped. I just fucked guys I didn't want to fuck. While I never forgot what happened, for the next couple years I refused to think about it further.

I previously enjoyed sex to a degree, but after this I didn't feel any pleasure. Usually, I impersonated a sex kitten because that's what the men craved. Once, though, a guy licked my breasts while we stood on a sidewalk in the middle of the night waiting for our connection. He looked up and said, "This doesn't affect you at all, does it," to which I just shrugged. I had disconnected from my physical body and most emotions before I began using, but the chemicals made this easier to maintain. At times, the promiscuity caused me to feel disappointed in myself, but I shoved aside such thoughts. I wasn't thrilled when someone mentioned that, behind my back, people said I was easy or called me a meth whore. But I did not care enough about my reputation to change.

The chaos from all this was epitomized by my couple of months relationship with mid-level meth dealer Pfeiffer. Because he had crank, I told him I loved him, even though I didn't like him much. He left his pregnant wife for me, or so he said. I hadn't asked for that and hadn't wanted it. He used this purported declaration of commitment to insist on constant attention. I complied with his sexual demands, such as dressing up in high heels and skimpy outfits and letting him watch me masturbate, which I did to the point of pain although I never complained to him.

In return, he kept me high and lent me his wife's red Mustang. I felt powerful and in control driving that car, a sign of my desirability. But this accolade created chaos when I drove to school because his sister-in-law was in my class. When she found out, his wife was furious, so she paid someone to beat me up. The thug, someone I'd had sex with, took the money but relayed the plan to me. He said he liked me better than her, so not to worry.

If not for my need for crank, I would have eschewed Pfeiffer and others like him. I broke it off after he bragged that I occasionally bought our drugs. I was willing to demean myself sexually for a large quantity of free drugs. But I was livid to learn he told others I sometimes spent my own money. This undermined my need to believe I was winning the game and enthralling every speed connection in town.

Despite developing relationships with all these dealers, being with them involved risk. It was always possible their place would get raided when I was there. The bigger concern, which began to bother me, was that sometimes these "friends" would become aggressive if I said no to sex. For example, my first snort donor, Dennis, and I slept together at times. One afternoon, in my car, he tried to convince me to give him oral sex, which I politely refused since I needed to crash. He pushed my head down repeatedly, trying to force me. I cried and after a while he left. Later, when I ran into him at the bar, he bought me a drink and gave me a speed vial. I interpreted this as an apology. Afterward, I'd hang out with him in a group but never alone.

Or the dealers would use me in other ways. Tommy, Bordentown's primary wholesale drug dealer, was a frequent sex partner. I also spent a lot of time with him at his restaurant. The guy selling him a new freezer saw me and offered Tommy a significant discount if I had sex with him. I acquiesced as a favor to Tommy and because I knew he would compensate me with drugs. Though I agreed, a part of me believed I had no choice. Or, rather, I was afraid of upsetting Tommy, a primary connection and source of many free highs. In general, it just was easier to say yes, which resulted in overflowing spoonfuls of meth. I gave people the message that I was open to doing these things for them or their friends, but I actually did not want any of it. And I felt betrayed and violated by the only friends I had at this point. I believed Tommy liked me, but I also was a commodity to be used for his personal gain.

In a way, it's odd I was upset by these events since, more than anyone, I exploited my body. When I was nineteen, I took the next step when I visited Las Vegas with my mother. While she gambled the night away, I trolled the prostitute strip outside the hotel. As I laid out a form-fitting white summer dress, hoping the dainty eyelets wouldn't announce my lack of experience, my stomach fluttered. I imagined a limousine pulling up and the chauffeur escorting me to the vehicle as my competitors turned green with envy.

Instead, as I hit the street, two women approached. "Honey, you don't belong here. These men will think you're one of us and you'll get into trouble." I smiled and walked away. A few honking cars and catcalls reinforced my confidence. Luckily, within five minutes a nice older man picked me up. I didn't know the going rate, so I asked for $50. We went to his room and had sex. He commented on how I seemed like a college girl, not a hooker. But from stories in the sensationalistic *Trentonian* newspaper, I believed I was more similar to the other ladies than he realized because I shared their addiction, abuse histories, and willingness to trade my body for money or drugs.

The "sex and drugs and rock and roll" motto of the day provided me some cover. But that slogan's fun aspect didn't apply. The appeal of this behavior wasn't limited to the access to drugs or the power of being sexy. Being in dangerous situations, trapped and forced to comply with an abuser, felt familiar. All this related to Allan's molestation and ongoing sexual comments, the only positive attention I received from him, and the abuse more generally.

Still, once in a while, when I acted in self-harmful ways, including high-risk activities like sex with strangers, I would think, *I've lost my mind* or *I'm bat-shit crazy*. This message also came from others, mostly through their expressions when they heard what I'd done.

What I, and my drug cohorts, should have thought was, *What happened to you that you're driven to act this way?* ●

# CHAPTER 23
## College and Two Muggings

AFTER THE ONE-YEAR DELAY CAUSED BY MY ARREST, I moved to Los Angeles for college. Bordentown Regional's guidance counselors could advise about only New Jersey and Pennsylvania schools. I struggled with bronchitis each winter, so wanted a good college in a warmer climate. Mom brought home a fat guide, called something like *The Best Colleges in America*, which described each university in two pages and provided a grid of the acceptance rate by GPA and SAT score. I applied before my mid–senior year absenteeism binge and had the highest SAT score in my class, so was accepted to multiple colleges. UCLA won because of its strong academics, warm weather, and distance from home. My friends envied my unusual path from our working-class high school to a California university. None of us ever had visited LA but envisioned a glamorous and exciting city.

When I applied at the beginning of my senior year, I experienced the usual concerns: Will I succeed academically, will I make friends, where will I live, how will I handle everything on my own, what will I eat since I can't cook, and how do I do laundry? Still, I giggled with glee whenever I visualized moving across the country to a famous university in a huge city with interesting people and opportunity for new adventures. I also hoped for a less anxious life, safe from Mom and Allan, but struggled to imagine I could break free of the agony inside me.

As my departure neared two years later, I still wanted to succeed, and part of me believed I had the intellectual ability. Nevertheless, I debated putting off college indefinitely. I quaked in terror at the thought of relocating to a strange locale where I did not have a dealer because I did not foresee controlling my meth use, despite a desire to cut back so I could ace my classes. I knew I was strung out and facing a major crash when I depleted my speed supply. And I was well aware that two years of shooting crank and not sleeping had diminished my brain function and stressed my body.

I didn't know what the professors would demand of me, but I predicted I'd fail. I just couldn't picture myself as a student rather than a meth head and doubted I could conjure up the focus, intellect, and discipline required just to eke out passing grades. I assumed smarter and better-prepared students would make me look like an incompetent moron. Plus, I felt exhausted at the thought of signing up for classes and buying books and navigating the city and figuring out the campus and locating an apartment and interviewing roommates. But I could not think of a good excuse to stay home, so I boarded the flight to LA.

On the plane ride to California, Mom relayed my early history: Don was my biological father; the Catholic unwed mothers' home; and living with the nuns. She also claimed she'd phoned Don when I was in my early teens to ask for his assistance in dealing with my erratic behavior. According to her, he'd said he couldn't talk and promised to call back, but never did. For the first time ever, she announced that she loved me. I smiled and nodded but didn't believe her. Maybe she had feelings for me but not real love or any actual interest in my life.

Her lack of effort to prepare me to live on my own three thousand miles from home exemplified this. Teachers and family all had assumed I would attend college, yet neither of my parents saved any money. I learned about the financial aid application by chance, and no one suggested I compare tuition and living expenses at different universities to ensure I had enough capital to complete my education. Scholarship money and grants helped but didn't cover all expenses.

Then my mother left Allan in the middle of my freshman year, which cut off most of the family income. On top of this, while Mom obtained a court order for John to pay enough for half my rent, she kept most of this support, although she pretended she mailed me a check every month and just could not understand the incompetence of the post office. By pure chance, UCLA was a premier public university with reasonable fees once I became a California resident my sophomore year. Still, though I'd planned to get a job for spending money, I had to work fifteen to twenty hours per week because I needed cash for basic living expenses like rent and food.

Plus, I'd only seen UCLA in pictures from the catalog. I had no idea how LA was laid out or where in that sprawling city the university was located. Mom traveled with me to Los Angeles because I'd lost the dorm room lottery. I needed her to assist my apartment search and sign the lease. With late recognition of my financial challenges, we selected a studio in a cheap, rundown building in Hollywood. Mom assumed the bus traveled straight to UCLA, through Beverly Hills, but it instead took a circuitous path, which cost me ninety minutes a day in commute time.

More noteworthy, I'd hoped to escape from a life filled with danger. For this first apartment, which I shared with Ramona, another student from New Jersey, my mother didn't bother to visit the area at night or check the crime rate. The building manager suffered severe injuries from a beating in the lobby. Young prostitutes strolled my block, and one crawled into the stairwell and died. When we left the apartment after dark I would say, "Hope we don't become another senseless killing tonight."

We shared the building with hordes of cockroaches, but I didn't know how to force the owner to resolve the issue. When I mentioned the skittering creatures, Mom responded, "There's nothing I can do from here." So I lived with roaches that crawled over the kitchen counters, in the bathtub and sink, and sometimes crept on the living room walls. The landlord told us we needed to be cleaner, but we weren't filthy and didn't leave food out. True, we also didn't keep the garbage covered, so part of the blame rests on our shoulders. Mostly, though, the building was infested.

On the positive side, I managed my cash flow. I calculated the monthly amount available from my scholarships, financial aid, and job, and stuck to that budget. I ate cereal, sloppy joes, and spaghetti due to my minimal cooking skills. The ladies at KFC across the street could tell I struggled when I counted out pennies for a small order, so they'd always stuff the box with extra chicken. But at the end of the month, I often ate discount peanut butter with a spoon or off-label pasta with margarine.

On top of feeling relieved to be away from my parents, I did enjoy many aspects of college. I dove deep into my early American history major and took classes in the politics, economics, and social aspects of the era. I relished my exposure to literature, anthropology, and psychology. I developed my reasoning and writing expertise. I listened to friends discuss physics and engineering and social issues.

And religion. Although I'd been raised Catholic, half-heartedly, my high school boyfriend, Will, had introduced me to the concept of agnosticism, which I followed for a while. By college, my belief in hell had fizzled, and blind faith contradicted the rational analysis I valued. Due to exposure to other creeds, it now seemed ridiculous to believe the correct theology was the one into which I happened to be born. I realized I didn't ascribe to a supernatural being who intervened in human's lives, in part because the deity made irrational decisions, like when he purportedly saved a few from a catastrophe while he allowed millions to die from famine. I soon accepted that I didn't believe in God at all. Everything could be explained by science, or would be once humankind expanded its knowledge.

I earned excellent grades and was admitted to the honors program. Despite this, dread of certain failure overcame me before each exam. I attributed my success to luck, which was about to run out. By the time grades arrived in the mail, the next quarter had started, so the joy from my achievements dissipated within seconds as I already lived in the foreboding phase for my new classes. "Sure, these grades are great, but these new subjects will kick my ass." My friends were astonished at my anticipation of imminent doom because I excelled yet acted as if I hung on by my fingernails. They commented on my great grades, that I didn't miss class, kept up with the work, no all-nighter study sessions, and achieved this while I held down a job. But I couldn't see it or feel it and thought they exaggerated. I should've been proud of my accomplishments but never could muster that confidence.

Still, a big plus was that I managed to keep my addiction under moderate control. Even though at first my brain remained foggy and my body slogged through withdrawal fatigue, I began to feel human again. When I did imbibe, drugs were fun, mostly, like the time the twenty-somethings in my building shared their mushrooms one Halloween. A neighbor played the Psychedelic Furs' "Pretty in Pink" in honor of a costumed ballerina. When she returned three hours later, that same song happened to be booming from the cassette player. "Have you guys been listening to this all night?" To this we rolled on the floor in hysterics. Because we were so high, we might've done that.

Paul, a guy in our building, would visit and we'd have a beer or two, play cards, listen to music, then walk to the Thrifty and get ice cream cones. However, I soon escalated to excessive alcohol consumption most weekends. During one drunken haze on a sunny Saturday afternoon, I sat on the ledge of our second story window and waved and chatted as people strolled by below. I wondered what the passersby would think if I jumped down. On impulse, in one motion, I twisted around and hung from the window, my body against the wall, as I gripped the ledge. Only then did I realize how far my feet were above the ground, so I couldn't just let go and touch down softly. I didn't have the strength to pull myself in and was losing my grip. Just as horror roiled my mind, I heard, "Oh my God," then felt Ramona and Paul each grab a shoulder and pull me in. Ramona grilled me for weeks afterward. "What were you thinking? You could've died or broken a lot of bones. I just don't understand you. Why did you do it?" I didn't have an answer to that because I never stopped to evaluate my behavior or feelings. I just plowed ahead, focused on keeping my grades up and not running out of money.

I sometimes did succumb to the urge to use other drugs. Before an economics final, we took black beauties and stayed up all night playing hearts. I'd swallow lodes, a combination that provided a heroin-like high, popular in Hollywood at the time. During one of these nights, I left my friends in a seedy part of LA and walked around in a stupor. I found my way back just as they were about to initiate a search.

In these first California years, though, I only used speed when I visited New Jersey. I didn't have easy access in LA, but I didn't pursue meth either. For summer break, I thought about shooting crank for much of the plane ride home. I stared out the window, remembering the warmth and power of the adrenaline rush of the first shot. I checked my watch about every ten minutes, and the old lady in the middle seat twice asked me to stop jiggling my leg. As I paid the taxi because Mom didn't show up at the airport, I hauled ass into the garage apartment, threw down my suitcase, and queried Cindy about who was holding crank. I felt giddy as we drove off to hit up my dealer buddies. We chattered in the car, my face flushed, my mind euphoric. That summer, I used every weekend but managed to stay clean most of the week for my job. One of my coworkers commented on how much thinner I was every Monday, but then I would gain a few pounds by Friday. Still, until the middle of my senior year of college, I significantly reduced the amount of poison I put into my body and fell back into the abuser category.

Violence followed me to California, though. I walked home after class one day, immersed as my mind outlined a paper on Chaucer's *Canterbury Tales*. Backpack slung over my shoulder, I carried a bag of bread and milk in the other arm. As I crossed the street, a teenage boy on a bike rode behind me, extended an arm, and ripped off my bookbag with such force that I spun around, then he hightailed it around the corner. I dropped the bread and milk to chase him, thinking more of my textbooks and notes than my wallet, but he sped out of sight. In tears and near panic from the certainty I would fail without my class materials, I trudged back to pick up my groceries, but they were gone. I shook myself straight and raced home to call the cops. Instead of concern, they acted like I was a rich girl too stupid to know she shouldn't live in that neighborhood.

"You know, this is practically the ghetto. College kids live near campus."

"I can't afford that. I'm poor, trying my best to finance my education with limited funds."

"C'mon. Your parents or someone could help you. Or maybe don't waste your money on spring break vacations or shopping trips."

"You don't know what you're talking about." I bit the inside of my cheek so I didn't snap at them further.

I couldn't sleep at all that night because I couldn't afford to buy new books and didn't trust anyone else's notes, even if I could convince a classmate to let me copy. I obsessed over thoughts like *This is it, I'm finally going to fail out. No one will help me*, and *I'm gonna be stuck in some low-end job and have to live in this pit forever*. I tossed and turned, got up to pace, and sat on the sofa in the dark, staring at the wall. The next day, the history department secretary called. After he removed my wallet, the thief had tossed the backpack into the rear of a truck, whose owner was nice enough to look for my name in a notebook and contact the secretary.

One Friday night a couple months later, at a college bar, Ramona and I drank and smoked pot. Even though various men bought us drinks, I'd drained my cash reserve so, instead of going straight home, we took a side trip to a bank in a moderately bad neighborhood. My drugged brain didn't consider that I could wait until morning and walk to the bank a few blocks from the apartment. I did leave my purse in the car, as a safety measure, and carried just my debit card so I could withdraw spending money for a few days. As the ATM spit out a twenty dollar bill, an adolescent boy rushed over, spooned behind me, clutched my hand, and tried to force me to release the cash. I attempted to stomp on his feet to get him to back away, but this failed to deter him. Ramona saw the mugging but couldn't get the car door to open, so she honked the horn. The boy brought my hand to his mouth and bit me, breaking the skin. I let go of my hard-earned dollars and he ran off.

I knew I needed a tetanus shot but didn't have insurance and emergency room visits were costly. I phoned a girlfriend enrolled in medical school, who told me no cure existed for deadly tetanus, but I had seventy-two hours to get the shot. "Good, then I can go to the clinic Monday." In retrospect, I failed to appreciate the danger of waiting so long, but poverty sometimes leads to poor decisions. Plus, I'd long ago developed inferior risk assessment skills.

I felt angry about these events, but just briefly immediately there-after. I'd describe my attitude as resignation mingled with a belief that I was a magnet for violence. Even with my contributory imper-fect choices, the likelihood I would suffer some new assault seemed inordinately high. I'd improved my life when I'd moved to California, attended college, and reduced my drug use. But I somehow still ended up victimized. ◉

# CHAPTER 24
## Yet Another Kidnapping

SPRING OF MY FRESHMAN YEAR, done studying for my next final, I threw on a gauzy white shirt with blue embroidered trim, Levi's 501s, and Earth shoes—remnants of my New Jersey wardrobe but outdated for Los Angeles in 1981. I decided to commiserate with Paul at his new apartment, so I sprinted to the corner of Sunset and Fairfax and plopped onto the bus stop bench.

As I craned my neck to search for the overdue bus, a dilapidated van screeched to a halt. A brown-haired guy leaned out the passenger window. "Hey doll, my name's Vincent, what's yours?"

Several other women stood nearby, but Vincent fixated on me. I sat up straight and peeked through my lashes. The driver tossed me a glance but focused on traffic. Vincent appeared to be barely twenty with a wavy shoulder-length mane, shiny hazel eyes, and a radiant smile.

"Where ya headed?"

"To my friend's, on the other side of Hollywood."

"Want a ride?" Vincent tapped the door in time with the music and pointed to the driver. "Doug won't care."

"No thanks. The bus will be here soon."

Vincent started to reply, but the light turned green, so he waved as they swung right.

Five minutes later, the van again stopped at the corner. The noise from the engine and fumes from the exhaust overwhelmed my senses. I did manage to decipher Vincent's renewed overture. "Still here? Sure you don't want us to drop you off?"

"I'm fine. But thank you very much."

"Come on. A babe like you shouldn't take the bus. You deserve two chauffeurs, and we're offering our services." The signal changed and they rounded the corner again.

Another few minutes passed. I checked my watch and huffed in frustration. The old lady next to me grumbled that the transit company lacked respect for people's schedules.

And then the van returned. Vincent smiled. "I don't think that bus is coming, darling. Why don't you let us give you a lift?"

I shielded my eyes from the sun and scoped out Sunset—just the usual mix of Mercedes and beaters. I took a gander at the old lady, expecting to find admiration. Instead, she cleared her throat and uttered a soft tsk. I mentally waved her off as I stood and strolled toward Vincent, who hopped out so I could climb in. I knelt between the two front bucket seats and my long legs stretched into the rear compartment. Pointing ahead, I explained where Paul lived.

After we drove one block, two strong hands grabbed my waist from behind. Someone dragged me backward and thrust me down with such force my temple bounced off the floor. The assailant shoved my right arm against my spine, sat on my calves, and stuck something hard into my back.

Vincent's order resonated in my ears. "Don't you fucking move.

He'll shoot you." We picked up speed. "Harry, do you have her?"

In that moment, in every molecule, I knew they would rape and murder me. My heart pounded so hard that the sound of blood roared in my ears. I winced from the arm wrenched behind me and Harry's weight on my legs. The rough worn carpet chafed my left cheek. I scanned a pile of blankets and wondered if he had hidden there.

I felt terror but not complete surprise. For a long while, part of me had expected to die like this. The daily fear of living with Allan resurfaced, as did my high school chemistry teacher's lecture when he caught me hitchhiking. Bobby's voice echoed in my brain as he warned me not to get into cars with guys I'd just met. I remembered Nanny reading from the scandal rag newspaper, which taught that men murdered and raped women every day. The *Trentonian* described these crimes in graphic detail, like "the intruder crept through Bonnie's window and put a gun to her temple," or "they found sweet Betty's naked body in the bushes, beaten to a bloody pulp." Cindy and I even acted out these stories when we tortured our dolls by pulling off their limbs and sticking them with pins.

I'm sure all these thoughts flittered through my memory in seconds. Vincent's voice brought me back to the present. "We'll let you up if you'll remain calm."

I managed to blurt out, "Okay, okay."

Harry freed my arm and paused, then raised himself into a stoop. Released, I crawled to the rear of the van, my skin sticky from the flood of cold sweat. I absorbed every detail of the vehicle: green color, two upholstered seats, and a six-pack of Bud.

I turned my attention to my captors. Harry smoothed his golden locks into place as he gawked at me. When he met my gaze, he averted his baby blue eyes. Doug laughed and yelled, "Asshole," when a Corvette cut us off. Vincent twisted in his seat to verify my cooperation.

I heard the horns of nearby cars and sensed even slight turns of the wheel. I controlled my breathing. I shrugged my shoulders twice to loosen my muscles. I sat against the back doors and looked past my kidnappers to track our path. As we passed Paul's street, I fought the urge to curl into the fetal position. Since I'd lived in Los Angeles for only six months, a few blocks later we left familiar territory.

Doug said we needed gas. Vincent snarled, "Jesus Christ," as we pulled into a service station. Doug and Harry stood outside directly behind me. One of them removed the fuel cap and gas flowed into the tank. Harry muttered something about not wanting to do this. Remnants of Doug's reassuring and then dismissive response floated over me.

Vincent moved from the passenger seat to Harry's spot and sat in the shadows. "Swear to God, one sound and I'll blow your brains out! I don't care about the fucking mess." He ranted about the stupidity of forgetting to fill up. He bent forward and narrowed his eyes. "Just sit there."

I fixated on the closest exit, which was nearer to me than to Vincent. I recognized the silver L-shaped handle on the cumbersome sliding door, from similar vans owned by Bordentown boys. I calculated the time it would take to reach it, engage the lever, and propel it to the right. My mind shifted to the door behind me and assessed the long seconds required to rise on my knees, turn, and push it open, which I could attempt only after Doug and Harry filled the tank. I heard people outside and tried to determine how close they were. I deliberated cracking a door partway and screaming for help. I estimated the distance between Vincent and me. I pondered the likelihood that he had a gun because I had not seen it. I considered his rage if I failed to escape and imagined an excruciating death.

I weighed the probabilities of success and failure. Maybe there would be another chance, or maybe I could manage my kidnappers well enough that they would set me free, but the odds did not favor either possibility.

Ultimately, I did not believe I would make it out before Vincent shot or tackled me. It was unlikely I could thrust a door wide to yell for help. I did not trust that the strangers outside would react even if they heard me. The pummeling from this three-minute debate drained me. Sick with foreboding, I struggled to suppress my tears. I decided not to try.

Doug and Harry returned and settled into the front seats. Harry squinted at me and began to organize his wallet. Before we drove off, Doug adjusted the rearview mirror. "Vincent, we'll be there soon."

Vincent now behaved as if we were en route to a party. "Harry, turn up the Zeppelin." He gave me a beer and let me smoke a cigarette. He told me I was Harry's birthday present, who was too old to remain a virgin. "Isn't that right? You've been too afraid to screw a girl."

I remained calm and interacted with Vincent as if we were new acquaintances getting to know each other. I'd read it was important to make your kidnappers see you as an individual. So I assessed ideas, jettisoned some, and selected others, with the goal of creating a bond and convincing them of my humanity. I chose a gentle but engaged tone and relayed information I surmised might be meaningful to them.

For the next thirty minutes, I talked about various innocuous subjects. I babbled about my part-time job typing orders for personalized pencils and matchbooks. To amuse them, I maligned my rich classmates at UCLA. I mentioned I'd recently moved to LA for college from a small working-class town. I listened to their conversations and watched their interactions. Vincent said I was pretty and that all would be well. I beamed and nodded.

He took out his drug kit and we snorted cocaine. The white powder burned, then a wave of euphoria. I uttered an involuntary, "Wow." But after this burst of positive energy, the coke further heightened my level of distress. I took a few seconds to recalibrate my breath.

"Do you have anything this good in New Jersey?"

I never had used coke. Still, I grinned. My "nothing like this" evoked a satisfied smile from my captor.

Vincent and Doug reminisced about a party they'd attended. They compared me to a hot blond who'd ignored them both. Harry gaped at the blinding streetlights, sipped a beer, and chain-smoked. Vincent chided him for being a wet blanket, so he began to sing along to the radio.

I glimpsed a sign with the words "Long Beach" printed on it as we hauled ass off the highway. From a newspaper story I had read, I recalled that the iconic Queen Mary ocean liner docked there, but this exhausted my knowledge. I saw bright lights in the distance. We parked in a dark isolated spot near a marina. As he departed with Doug, Vincent advised, "Treat my bro right."

Birthday boy Harry shuffled toward me. "Sorry about all this."

I contemplated asking for help, but, based on Vincent's clear dominance and Harry's capitulation, I knew he didn't have the guts to upend the plan. A primal scream pressed against my throat, but I allowed myself just one silent sigh. "It's okay, honey. Everything's fine." I smiled and caressed Harry's neck. We kissed and talked and kissed and talked. Today he turned eighteen. His family had surprised him with a barbeque. And his sister still owed him a gift.

As he spoke, I listened to Vincent and Doug in deep discussion near the front of the van. I couldn't make out the words, but the intensity of their tone concerned me. I needed to balance making Harry feel special with my apprehension about leaving his buddies together too long. When I thought he felt comfortable, I discarded my shirt and bra. I crouched before him and offered my bare breasts. While Harry had his dick inside me, I fought the urge to vomit—not because of this rape but as a result of visions of being strangled or stabbed or bludgeoned to death.

After Harry finished his perfunctory bumbling, he slowly dressed. I strained to hear Vincent and Doug but detected only the muffled crunch of feet on gravel. My anxiety escalated and my heart thumped as each second passed. With one foot out the door, Harry swiveled his neck around. "Vincent says girls can't get enough of his pecker." I clasped his arm and squeezed, in thanks.

Once outside, Vincent ribbed him. "How's it feel to be a man? Well, at least not a cherry boy."

Driver Doug joined me. This surprised and concerned me to the point of panic. As the leader, Vincent should not go last unless he planned to murder me immediately afterward. Dizziness enveloped me as blood rushed to my head. I slowed my heart rate, swallowed my horror, and focused on the task at hand.

Doug sat close, reeking of pot, and offered me a toke off his joint. I opened my jaw twice, trying to start a conversation. But my mind would not cooperate. Clamping my teeth onto my lip shocked me into action. I unbuckled his pants. Doug pounded me from behind. "I know you like it. Getting fucked by a real man." Doug came, flashed me a smirk, and left.

When I heard them all laugh, I assumed because Doug made a funny gesture about having just had sex, I half believed I might survive the night. Yet, at the same time, I considered drawing this last rape out to extend my life another thirty minutes. I tried to pump myself up. *You can do it. Just one more. But don't forget, he's the most dangerous, so the most important. Treat him like a boyfriend. Show no fear. You survived Allan. You can survive this.*

Vincent flung open the door and leapt to a squat. Sparks flew as my cigarette tip swiped his jeans when I scurried out of his way, to make room. He fondled my leg, snatched my Salem, took the last drag, and crushed the butt into the wheel well. "Apologies for spoiling your plans. Had to help Harry. He's like a little brother."

With one hand, Vincent slithered out of his black T-shirt, which exposed his bare chest. He kicked off his grungy work boots and wiggled out of his navy corduroys. His half-erect penis glowed in the light. "I never wear underwear." Vincent French-kissed me and twirled my nipples. "Relax, honey. This can be fun for you, too."

"With that beautiful cock, I'm sure it will, baby." I lowered my mouth, began sucking his dick, and moaned. On the verge of ejaculating, Vincent thrust my face away.

"I knew you were a whore. Waiting for the bus, my ass. Admit it. You swallow cock for money."

My jowl clenched and I squeezed my lids shut. I jiggled the muscles loose, then peered into his eyes. "No baby, no. You got me so hot, I could go down on you all night." Vincent hoisted me on top and I rode him until my thighs ached.

Afterward, he told me to get dressed. I wondered if they were preparing to lead me to a better killing spot. "Don't worry, darling. You've been a good sport. We'll drop you at your friend's place."

As we left the marina, I imagined this might be true. Doug and Vincent appeared happy as they discussed the best route to take. Harry seemed relieved. I oscillated from giddiness and hope to fear and trepidation. If they planned to murder me in an even more desolate spot than the marina, I had little chance of escape. For a few moments, it seemed I floated above the van, almost like my soul wanted to escape before the final horrors. This was odd since I didn't believe in a literal soul. Maybe I envisioned this because I'd disengaged from my throbbing body so I could concentrate better. Or perhaps I was practicing how to dissociate my mind from the torment they'd inflict.

Harry resumed his original position in the van's empty center. He lay on his side, propped up by his left elbow. He closed his eyes and sipped his beer. Generic neon-lit fast-food restaurants punctured the midnight sky. I watched the freeway signs. Were we circling back to Hollywood? I did not recognize any street names, but that meant little. When we exited on Sunset, I exhaled slowly.

Vincent turned to me. "Almost there."

We pulled up to Paul's building. Vincent slipped out of his seat and into the dark interior. And he opened that heavy sliding door. Adrenaline surged and my heart raced.

I stepped out of the van. My brain said, "License plate, license plate." But my body shrieked, "RUN, RUN, before they shoot you in the back."

My feet hit the ground hard.

And I ran.

I charged through the black metal gate, bolted up the concrete stairs, banged on Paul's door, and flew into his apartment.

"What's up? It's past one o'clock. You were supposed to be here hours ago."

I collapsed onto the cracked yellow kitchen tile, one leg bent underneath and the other sprawled toward the open sofa bed. Tears burst from my eyes and poured down my face. My chest heaved and sobs echoed in my ears. The white heat of anguish washed the numbness from my body.

"Paul, oh my God, oh my God."

He pressed the door shut and kneeled before me, lifted my chin, and kissed my forehead. "What happened?"

The warmth of his touch and his concern transformed my taut muscles into drooping noodles that could no longer hold me erect. I fell backward and sprawled across the floor as if about to make a snow angel. I let myself bawl for five minutes, then told Paul the tale of the past six hours.

I never reported this rape. I thought filing a report would be fruitless because I'd failed to get the license plate number. And I didn't think the police would credit my claims since I voluntarily joined my rapists in the van. I used drugs with them and participated in the sex. I didn't scream or fight back. A few bruises showed later and my shoulder hurt for weeks, but they didn't beat me. Plus, I anticipated defense attorneys would use my extensive sexual history to undercut my credibility. In my worldview, only perfect women with clean hands have the right to be free from sexual assault.

Similarly, though they didn't suggest this, I speculated about whether Paul or Ramona blamed me. I tried to justify myself, repeating phrases like they planned this, they targeted me, they hunted me. But even in those moments, shame erupted over my failure to see the warning signs. I had thought I'd adapted to Los Angeles. I knew I lived in a high-crime neighborhood and had learned to protect my purse and hurry through dark streets. And yet I'd walked straight into a trap when I climbed into that van.

I should've realized these men were predators when they came around the second and third time. Instead, I'd responded to Vincent as he presented himself rather than as the threat he was because he resembled and behaved like Bordentown's nice guys. He'd flirted and charmed me, and I'd felt flattered that he chose me. I'd let down my guard and nearly died. I berated myself as an idiot, responsible for her own gang rape. My brain churned these ideas and regrets, obsessively, in the months after, and intermittently for two decades.

This kidnapping occurred the Friday before finals. Ramona says she remembers me sitting in a chair, very quiet, after the initial explanation burst. I did study for much of the weekend, with intermittent breakdowns. My first exam was on Monday, also my twentieth birthday. As the proctor distributed the tests, I wanted to scream, "I was kidnapped and raped." Instead, I choked back my tears and spent the next three hours riveted on the exam. The rest of the week is a blur, but I earned several As and one B. I believe I was able to study for and take finals because I was inured to violence and pain. My agonies and damage impacted me in the long run, but in the short-term I knew how to handle trauma.

Within weeks, I revisited the Las Vegas episode. The Los Angeles abduction more clearly fell into the kidnapping and rape category because of the violence when Harry overpowered me and threatened to kill me. Now, though, I contemplated the similarities: There were three men, I was not allowed to leave, and I was forced to have sex. I began referring to the events as the "LA rape" and the "Las Vegas rape." This terminology disturbed me because it referenced my long trauma history. Who has so many sexual assaults that they need to distinguish them geographically? Why was I the unusual person who gets kidnapped three times and gang-raped twice?

I didn't know then that my adverse childhood experiences primed me for future assaults because, while hypervigilant in some ways, I was so numb I couldn't recognize danger at times. This applied to what I viewed as maybe rapes. I couldn't count how often I'd had sex when I didn't want to because I'd felt pressured or perceived a risk of physical consequences if I refused. I recalled when I'd lacked the ability to agree because I was too wasted. Although I thought about these situations, I brushed them off until decades later, with the emergence of the modern concept of rape as including lack of consent.

All this contributed to my belief that safety did not exist, whether I played in my front yard, met two guys taking a walk, took a ride from seemingly nice boys, or made too much noise in my house. My brain repeated and repeated that my life was just one horror after another. I waited for the next torture because I lost hope that any other future was possible for me.

After finals, I reverted to a familiar pattern. Overwhelmed by this deep sense that I would never escape abuse, which sickened my heart, I only mentioned this rape to a few people. Bordentown Claus asked if I'd had sex with all three simultaneously because he wanted to suggest a three-way with Dennis and him. My alcohol consumption increased, and I'd take any drug available. On visits home, I used as much crank as I could get my hands on. I threw glasses against the wall to watch them shatter. I began to pull out my eye lashes, which continued for years, because forcibly removing the hair hurt but somehow felt satisfying.

Only in my late thirties did I become proud of my younger self for having survived such perilous situations. I thought a lot about how

I'd guided myself through a complex dynamic and three different personalities during the LA rape. At the time, I'd felt concerned about my acquiescence and, for inordinate hours, reviewed every detail of my gas station decision. I'd mused on whether I'd made these choices because childhood abuse had taught me to accept violence. But now I wondered if that trauma had trained me to control my fear and evaluate the proper course.

At home, I'd become attuned to the adults' emotions and intentions, analyzed degrees of risk, and formulated appropriate responses. Were they happy or on the verge of exploding? What were the odds that their rage would be directed at me? Could I tamp down the threat, or should I brace myself for the unavoidable onslaught? In the van, also, I'd understood I could not control the situation. Instead, I'd focused on reducing my risk. Although I did what my rapists wanted, I was not passive. I'd listened and watched and evaluated my kidnappers to discern their objectives and personalities. I'd chosen a reaction that lessened their concerns and increased their positive feelings toward me.

I came to realize that, rather than being submissive, I'd fought for my life by navigating this life-threatening situation. I finally trusted my contemporaneous decisions because, in those moments, I understood all the nuances and the probabilities better than I ever could in hindsight. I became grateful to my younger self. I do believe my actions had an impact and probably saved me. I was savvy and able to think on my feet. I'd controlled my fear to do what needed to be done to increase my odds of getting out alive.

And that is why I am still here today. ❧

# CHAPTER 25
## *Martin*

SHORTLY AFTER THE LA RAPE, Ramona moved out, and rail-thin and pale-skinned Victor moved in down the hall. A suburban Northern California transplant who yearned for big-city excitement, Victor exposed me to punk rock: the music, the look, and the lifestyle. I bought a mini-skirt and fishnet stockings to fit in at the Whisky a Go Go and the Roxie, venues that featured LA punk bands, including my fave, X, whose pain and despair lyrics resonated. I even attended the New Year's Eve 1981 show when Fear and Black Flag headlined. Although this now-famous event turned violent, I stayed in back and just watched the melee.

Victor introduced me to his friend Martin, my kindred spirit and immediate boyfriend. Charismatic, damaged, and addicted to alcohol, although he'd consume any substance, he was an odd mate for Victor, who hated conflict and enjoyed bonding with his companions. Martin moved with frenetic energy, often dancing on his feet from side to side, like a boxer. Despite short legs, covered in worn corduroys or faded jeans, with his long torso he overshadowed me by two inches. He dyed his hair blowsy blond, which he cut with any random pair of scissors, and rolled his own cigarettes with cheap liquor-store tobacco. An extravagant smile would burst across his narrow face at an odd phrase or unexpected joke.

But chaos and violence attached to Martin like a second skin. When his temper flared, he resorted to verbal aggression, physical intimidation, or outright assault. After he finished a six-pack of Olde English malt liquor, which he preferred for the high alcohol content and to remind him of his British heritage, he'd broadcast his opinions about white racial superiority and governmental oppression, ideas absorbed from his "nothing's my fault and the world is against me" father. Martin retaliated for any hint that someone thought they were better than he was, and any minor disagreement could flash into a major brawl. Going to a bar with Martin meant accepting a fifty-fifty risk he would fight with a stranger, or even a friend, by night's end. Despite the frequency of such events, he wasn't skilled and frequently ended up bruised and bloodied.

All this energized me and shook me out of my academic life. I believed another horrible event would happen soon regardless, so attempts to avoid misery seemed futile. Martin embraced and pursued intensity and risk. From abuse and neglect stories dropped here and there, I understood that his rage and confrontation seeking stemmed from a desire to overcome the numbness and feel more alive. I enjoyed watching him act out the way I felt, his self-destruct impulse barely thwarted by a glint of hope for the future. Victor said we were two peas in a pod, except one went to college.

I left Martin and LA to go home for the summer. I shot a lot of speed and slept with too many guys but quit both again when I returned for my sophomore year. Still despondent from the rapes, I managed to function. I attended class, studied, and continued to earn good grades. I worked in the microbiology department, where they taught me to use a Wang word processor, brand-new technology at the time.

For a few weeks, I crashed at the small house on the Hollywood Hills periphery where Victor rented a room. He lived close to the estate of swashbuckler movie star Erroll Flynn, the purported site of 1920s cocaine-fueled parties and starlet seductions. A fire had incinerated Erroll's villa long ago, but the property offered a great city view.

One night Victor's sister Lisa suggested we head to Erroll's. We all dressed in punk rocker black. Lisa's love, Sid, added a spiked dog collar. The siblings sported matching short cuts with their brown hair dyed ebony. In contrast, I matched Martin's golden blond, his hair now shaved short and mine with pink Krazy Kolor highlights.

"Lisa, I can't believe how much you look like Victor. You're the punk Donnie and Marie."

Relishing the balmy September breeze, we hiked the mile to Erroll's. We laughed and chatted during the trek. Martin walked backward, facing us, smoking a hand-rolled cigarette. "Did I tell you about the time I made boatloads of money smuggling trucks in the Middle East with a gang of outlaws?"

We sauntered through the large wrought-iron gate and into a tiny forest. After just a few steps, shrubbery obscured the neighborhood homes. We stopped talking so we could experience the quiet, broken only by chirping crickets. We marched up the hill and deeper into the woods. I inhaled the pungent smell of oak and eucalyptus. Sid pointed to intermittent pieces of concrete foundation and blackened wooden walls. "Damn. Erroll did good. Built himself a mansion."

A few minutes later as we neared the top, we heard voices. We soon reached a batch of high school students, about twenty kids altogether. The guys wore khakis and Izod shirts with the signature alligator. The girls flaunted pastel blouses and designer jeans. It was clear they, too, planned to spend a pleasant evening at Erroll's, enjoying the seclusion and the company of friends.

We placed our jackets on the ground and sat near the edge of the incline. Martin handed each of us a beer, and Sid passed around a joint. We spoke in hushed tones. I told them which classes I would take that quarter. Victor and Martin engaged in the familiar Sex Pistols versus Dead Kennedys debate. Lisa and Sid snuggled and whispered endearments.

From a distance, I heard a loud whir. I glanced up, irritated by the invasion, then scanned our temporary community. Several girls giggled as two boys chased each other near a decrepit fountain. I turned to my right. Below us, houses clung to the steep hillside. Before us, the expansive and shimmering Los Angeles.

The sound of an approaching helicopter intruded into the serenity of my thoughts. I tilted my head and watched the chopper hover above. The underbelly read LAPD. Perplexed, I peered at my friends, but they just stared into the sky, apparently enthralled. The high school students gasped concern as searchlights scanned the area. A voice boomed from the heavens. "Pick up your belongings and proceed to the entrance at the bottom of the hill." The kids mumbled anxieties about going to jail while they complied with the order. The helicopter repositioned the beacon to illuminate the path.

Martin rose, gathered the beers, and tossed them down the hill. Sid rushed to a nearby tree and stowed the Altoids tin that held his pot stash. Both returned to our circle and leaned back on their haunches.

Victor asked me, "Do you think they can arrest us?"

"Trespassing? Why would they bother?"

Martin lifted his arm, extended his finger, and poked each of us in turn. "Fuck the pigs. Stay where you are. We're not criminals. We're just lounging on a hill." Victor started to rise, but Martin's glare forced him to the ground. We looked at the view and waited to see what, if anything, would happen. Not a wise choice in 1981, I knew. Although it was ten years before the Rodney King beating, the Los Angeles Police Department already had a well-deserved reputation for excessive force.

The trees changed from dark to light as the beam from the helicopter swept over Erroll's estate. The spotlight skimmed us a few times, then settled into that position. My heart raced and I consciously had to force my body to remain seated.

Four officers approached from the shadows with guns drawn. "Hands in the air. Stay where you are." They encircled us. "All right, all of you, stand." Victor bent at the waist to grab his jacket. "Hands up. You don't need that piece of crap." Victor snapped back, fully erect. "Okay, now pick it up."

The officers maintained their perimeter and herded us to the gate. I snuck glances at my friends, hoping to see their eyes as wide and excited as mine felt, but they seemed absorbed in grim thoughts. I, on the other hand, breathless, waited for my life to explode. In front of the gate, the high school kids sat in the dirt, with the girls huddled in clumps. Patrol cars blocked them from the street. The policemen had separated the girls from the boys and signaled us to join our group. I waved Lisa over. "Make sure we stick together."

All the officers wore full police regalia—guns, handcuffs, and billy clubs evident in their utility belts. Several paced back and forth. The sound of their heavy boots echoed with each step. A young buff cop scowled. One of his colleagues spoke on a walkie-talkie.

Martin leapt up. "Let us go. Now. Private property and Erroll didn't complain. This is bullshit."

One cop approached him from behind, placed his right arm across Martin's throat, and braced the hold with his left. Martin rotated his shoulders in an effort to shake free. The policeman squeezed so hard I could see an engorged vein on Martin's forehead. I watched, mesmerized, as Martin's legs gave out and he hit the ground. I wanted to race to his side to check if he was hurt but feared I'd attract the cops' attention. Two officers dragged him to a police cruiser and shoved him into the back seat. Martin's head wobbled as they forced him to sit. When they slammed the car door shut, his temple banged against the window.

I heard several boys' sharp intake of breath. Victor's furrowed brow indicated distress, but Sid feigned a cool attitude. A few of the high school girls choked back tears. Lisa and I murmured comforting words when we could. "Don't worry. We weren't doing anything."

I wiggled my mouth to release the tension and hide my apprehension from the kids. I recalled months earlier when two policemen had beaten Victor over an open container of beer. When I'd bailed him out, the desk officer had laughed. "Wait until you see the skid marks on your friend's face."

After about twenty minutes, a paddy wagon arrived. "We're going to take everyone to the station. Ladies first." The police van maneuvered into position. The rear doors swung out and a female officer situated herself three feet behind. "You, in the peach, stand up and walk to me." The policewoman frisked the girl and pushed her forward. She disappeared into the paddy wagon. One by one, the procedure continued.

My turn arrived near the end. As she searched me, the officer muttered a warning. "Go ahead, punk, just make a move." Confused, I didn't dare respond. *What is she talking about? Why would I ever do that?* I stepped into the paddy wagon and sat on one of the benches that lined the walls. I saved a seat for Lisa, who soon joined me.

After they crammed the last girl inside, two male officers locked the portal. The kids stammered their concerns, especially as to whether the police would call their parents. As I surveyed the group, the small rectangular window at the top of the door slid open. A cop tossed something silver inside and closed it.

As my mind tried to analyze this event, a dense noxious fog filled the enclosed back of the paddy wagon. My eyes burned, my throat restricted, and my chest ached. I bent my head, crossed my arms, and rammed my face into the square they created. I tried to inhale through my shirt. My brain caught up and I shrieked, "Tear gas!" The high school girls choked. My neighbor managed to yell, "We're suffocating."

When the fumes began to dissipate, I scrutinized the teenagers. Some held one another, but mostly they sobbed to themselves. It seemed to me they'd just lost their innocent belief in a reasonable world. Lisa rubbed the shoulder of the girl next to her. I swallowed my fury. "Everyone okay? Stay calm. I don't think they'll do that again." I nodded toward the high schooler across from me and put my hand on her knee. "Are you all friends?"

"Yes. Homecoming game celebration." I spoke to a couple more and then we all sat and pondered what the cops might do next.

The officers drove us around Hollywood for about an hour, pausing to harass prostitutes. As they engaged the loudspeaker attached to the vehicle, it emitted a sharp warning screech. "Ladies, ladies, I don't see any johns looking for the cheap ass you're selling tonight.

Get out of my face, or I'll drag you to the back and throw you in with the rest of the trash."

After we pulled into the police station, new orders issued. "Out. Out. Line up single file." We took turns at the counter inside and provided our names and addresses so they'd release us. I didn't have my identification, so I used the fake name I'd prepared when shoplifting as a teenager. Lisa and I spotted Victor and Sid on the other side of the room, being similarly processed. Once they rejoined us, we asked for Martin. The officer cracked a door and we glimpsed a row of cells. They freed Martin and we trudged toward Victor's place.

As we swung onto Highland Avenue, Sid broke our silence. "Those bastards. I can't believe they gassed you girls. For what? Sitting on a hill? We ought to sue them."

I shook my head. "They'll deny the whole thing. Maybe if we had some of the high school kids' names. But no court would take five punks seriously. Heck, I can't even prove I was there."

Afterward, Martin leaned into the choke hold as proof of his bad-ass status. He'd regale every person he met with the story of how he'd challenged the cops and they were so afraid they had to sneak up behind to incapacitate him. I'd chime in about the tear gas to try to establish myself as a true punk rocker and overcome the suspicion I faced whenever my UCLA student status came up. Plus, I added this to my litany of bad acts by cops, like handling Allan with kid gloves, illegally searching my car, and beating Victor. I don't think I realized it at the time, but this fit in with my parents' abuse and neglect. I long ago had concluded I couldn't rely on the people charged with my safety. In fact, they often were threats rather than saviors. To this day, when I see a movie where someone helps an endangered person, my eyes flood with tears. This indicates I must've once wanted protection and suffered at the loss of this fantasy.

One afternoon a week after the Erroll incident, Victor and I swallowed a combination of codeine and doriden known as "loads," which provided a heroin-like high. We didn't tell Martin because he couldn't handle strong drugs. Instead, we barely sipped on the two quarts of Olde English he passed around. As I played solitaire in slow motion, Martin smacked his forehead.

"Yo, Victor, I just remembered. Sid told me about a furniture warehouse near his storage unit. Easy peasy to break in. We could grab some new stuff for you. Sell the rest."

"What? No. Anyway no truck."

"We can borrow your roommate's."

"He won't let you."

"He's not here. I can hot-wire it."

The import of this conversation almost had registered when Martin tapped me on the shoulder, then barged out of the house. I pulled myself up and paused to watch him race across the street to the truck, slide his arm through the window frame, and pop the lock. Victor must've had an adrenaline rush because he leapt to his feet and raced through the living room. I could hear Victor's "No, goddammit!" and "Martin, what the fuck?" as I inched my way outside, focused on not tripping. Martin lay across the driver's seat, I assumed to connect the wires needed to start the truck.

Victor careened back and forth between Martin and me and begged each of us in turn to abandon this plan. I just dipped my head in Victor's general direction and forged on. As Martin muttered, "Fucking piece of shit," from underneath the dash, I slung open the passenger door and crawled in. Victor sidled around the truck bed, then fell to his knees before me, in the grass strip that bordered the sidewalk. He clasped his hands as if in prayer.

"You know this is insane. He's gonna get caught. You'll both go to jail. You'll get kicked out of UCLA. And Martin's so drunk you might not even make it. He'll get pulled over and lose his license. Please, Mary Beth. Make him stop."

The engine sputtered into action and Martin straightened up in the seat beside me. His eyes aglow, he pecked me on the cheek. "Don't worry, baby. We'll be fine." He turned to Victor. "Bet you don't refuse the cool new furniture." I nudged Victor backward, gripped the door handle, and pulled it shut. I waved as we drove off.

I wasn't sure why I sided with Martin when I knew Victor was right. I didn't want to challenge Martin since I wasn't certain I was immune from his violent tendencies. But the danger also exhilarated me. The many ways this could go wrong, the multitude of chaotic scenarios, left me short of breath as my mind blazed through each possibility. As Martin hunched over the wheel and concentrated on piloting us through hectic LA traffic, my cheeks almost split open from the grin of all grins. Three times I burst into laughter, until Martin punched my shoulder. Well, closer to a love tap. "Knock it off, crazy bitch. I'm driving here."

Martin actually located the warehouse, which looked more like an armory than a piece of cake. We walked around it twice, and he managed to wrench one door out an inch. After each circuit, he complained about Sid giving us bad advice and chugged another can of Olde English. For whatever reason, he didn't succumb to anger or frustration. So I held his hand and exclaimed "Stupid Sid" and "Mean building" a couple times.

Another Olde English for Martin and then we beelined back to

Hollywood. Since I'd used up my "I took strong downers" limited energy, I sank into oblivion. I jerked awake when the truck swerved, three blocks from Victor's. Martin's arm was stretched out toward the windshield with a finger pointed. I saw two cops propel a hippie girl toward their cruiser.

"Didn't that asshole choke hold me?"

I stared at the policemen and wracked my brain. Before I could respond, a booming crunch resonated as we sideswiped the patrol car. Martin bounced in his seat, like a kid gawking at a high-wire act. He kept driving, so I twisted my head and watched one policeman shove the prisoner to the ground. Then both cops jumped into their vehicle.

We sped around the corner and flew toward Victor's. As Martin slammed the truck into park, I hopped out the passenger side and crossed the street. Martin's second foot hadn't touched down when the cops fishtailed into sight. The choke holding cop tackled him on the lawn, which Victor and I witnessed from the shadows created by the front door's overhang. After the police arrested Martin, Victor fell to the floor and covered his face with his hands, his pale visage now alabaster white. "Told you so." ◉

# CHAPTER 26
## Northern California

MARTIN DECIDED TO ATTEND A STATE COLLEGE in northern California and asked me to do the same. I refused to reduce the value of my
degree to trail after him but did agree to transfer to the University
of California, Berkeley, an hour south of his school. I moved with
Martin to his father's house for the summer and then relocated near
campus in the fall.

Mr. Williams lived in Cotati, a mix of suburban houses and family
farms. He worked odd jobs as a painter or handyman, with Martin's
assistance on occasion. Mr. Williams owned a house he'd converted
into a duplex and lived downstairs so he could rent the larger upstairs.
The plumbing he'd installed in his unit didn't work properly, so he
emptied buckets of water into the toilet to force a flush. To avoid him
seeing my poop, I made every effort to hold my bowel movements
until elsewhere.

Victor returned to Sonoma County, too. Invited by his high school
friend, one night we all attended a party at an upscale home. Martin
parked his Toyota truck between a Porsche and Mercedes. Inside the
house were lovely dark wood, chestnut brick, and recessed lighting

to showcase the art. Some in the crowd dressed punk-ish but fell into the poser category. Conversation centered on career prospects and the marketability of an MBA degree. I sipped my first-ever scotch at the bar while Martin chugged two cans of Olde English from a bag.

To reduce the risk that Martin would embarrass him, Victor slipped me a couple hallucinogenic mushrooms, swallowed some himself, and then presented the bag to Martin to split three ways. An hour later, during a music lull, as I floated through the room on a pink cloud of peace and love, Martin's voice echoed in my brain. "Get over here. I need a cigarette. Take care of your man." I managed to find his face in the crowd and saw him pretend to slug the guy next to him, who scowled and stepped away. I moseyed in that direction but paused to thank Victor for his wondrous gift. When I reached Martin, I tried to locate my Salems, in the green pack, but colors melded together or dispersed into overlapping prisms. As I plunged my hand deeper into the seemingly endless depths of my pocketbook, Martin grabbed it with such force that half the contents plummeted to the floor. To my ears, each object shattered upon impact. I swayed toward him, swatted his forehead, and bent down to recover my belongings.

When I straightened up, Martin punched me hard in the face. Well, actually, I experienced a remote pain and put a hand to my nose, which felt wet. As I wiped downward, it occurred to me my lip might be fat. But I wasn't sure. Maybe it was the shrooms. I squinted at my fingers and marveled at the glowing patches of rosy paint. From afar, Victor said, "Mary Beth, bloody nose." To stanch the flow, I tilted back my head, an instinct developed in childhood. Someone handed me tissues, which I pressed against my nostrils. I heard arguing and turned in that direction. A few guys surrounded Martin and seemed to give him the ultimatum "leave or else."

Wide-eyed Victor came into view. I asserted control over my tongue. "Make them stop. My fault. Hit him first." A part of me would like to say I didn't mean this, but I did. I knew I sometimes instigated the chaos, like when I mouthed off to Allan. Since I struck Martin, albeit lightly, I deserved what I got. In my mind, he reacted as anyone would. Or at least how I should've known he would. So it wasn't fair to blame him. I also stuck up for him out of an allegiance, our broken people bond. Victor and those other boys couldn't understand because they grew up in normal households. I think I even apologized to Martin on the ride back to the house. Pretty sure he didn't reciprocate.

For several days, we fell back into our normal routine. To transfer to Berkeley, I needed two summer classes, so I spent three days a week on campus. The average student IQ exceeded even that at UCLA, which thrilled me. The academic discussions proved more interesting and challenging. To beat this competition required concentrated effort. So that Saturday, as usual, I stacked my books next to the bed, which lay on the floor, and hunkered down for a study session. Before I slipped into total immersion, I glanced out the patio door window and noted that Martin sat on a lawn chair in the yard. Olde English in hand, unopened schoolwork on the ground.

A loud clang against that window woke me from my trance. Martin stood outside, chair at his feet. I assumed he'd thrown it, which raised alarm bells. As he barreled toward me as fast as his short legs would take him, I closed Marlowe's *Dr. Faustus* and stowed it behind me to keep it safe and to free up my hands. I pondered rising to stand tall but hesitated to initiate a confrontation. I realized I was gritting my teeth but ignored this so I could focus on analyzing Martin's every move. He'd barely crossed the threshold when he opened his mouth.

"You think I'm a loser because you go to a better college. Rub it in, frigging Shakespeare. Flipping pages. Impossible to read that fast. Just to irritate me."

I wanted to smile, but my tense mouth precluded any such effort. Rather than correct his Shakespeare error, I tried to de-escalate the tension in the room. "Martin, I'm glad you decided to go to Sonoma State. You're taking math and physics. I'm just a history major."

A slight blush spread across his cheeks and he cleared his throat. "Don't lie to me. Miss Hoity-toity. Miss La-di-da. You look at me like I'm rotten meat, gum on the bottom of your shoe." As he said this, my eyes darted to the bedroom door and then to the sunny day outside. I thought of Mr. Williams, who watched soccer in the nearby living room. The memory of being trapped in the van swept over me. And my decision to stay put. I just couldn't do that again. Plus, if I could get to my feet, I'd be able to defend myself better. So I stood in the corner between the bed and the wall while Martin carried on. "You wouldn't have a roof over your head if it wasn't for me. I could toss you out. You'd be living in the street in Berkeley with the other lowlifes."

I rubbed my wrists and stared at the ground, although I could see his lower half. When his left leg twitched, I scrambled across the bed, Martin two steps behind. As I circled back toward the patio door, he pummeled my head and I lost my footing. I thudded across the grass, palms first, and managed to regain my balance, but Martin rammed into me from behind, then grabbed my shoulders and swung me to the ground. "Stay down" rang in my ears as I scooched toward the driveway. He planted both hands on my butt and pressed so hard that my belly and head hit the dirt. For a second, damp grass cooled my hot, tear-stained face. I tried to crawl away, but with another "stay down," he kicked me twice. Martin seized the back of my hair and dragged me toward the house. Part of me wanted to plead for mercy, but I just couldn't. I did, though, scream for help. From the other side of the fence, a neighbor shouted that he'd called the cops.

Mr. Williams, who I'd known could hear all this, appeared and told Martin to back off, then suggested he let me leave since the police wouldn't arrest him if I didn't press charges. I said, "Good idea." As soon as he released me, I ran to the phone to call Victor, to get him to pick me up nearby. I made this choice for multiple reasons. In my worldview, Martin's behavior, while wrong and unfair, was only borderline outrageous. I did think I was smarter, and maybe he'd picked up on that. I sympathized with his emotional damage and knew the violence arose from his distress. I also considered that an assault charge would push him deeper into his descent. And I needed to live there because I didn't have any money to move until my financial aid came through in August.

After that beating, Martin often berated me for hours, so angry that spit would fly from his mouth as he bellowed. He'd block the bedroom door so I couldn't leave or tower over me as I sat on the floor. Sometimes he forced me to lie back, straddled me, and pinned my wrists above my head, then, just inches from my face, spouted his complaints against me and life in general. Or he'd threaten to burn me with a cigarette held near my cheek. Several times, he emptied a can of Olde English over my head and wondered aloud if the alcohol would catch fire. I hollered "help" and "let me go" because, due to the heat and no air conditioner, the sliding door always remained open. But no one came to my rescue again, so I abandoned this strategy and, instead, fought him off when I could and complied when I couldn't.

All this did change my perception of Martin. I saw him more clearly as an Allan variant. Neither was stupid, but they weren't bright either. They didn't read or follow the news or enjoy intellectual conversations. Both had superficial charm but drank too much and reveled in their drunken anger. Both liked to show off their mate but felt intimidated by her relative sophistication and intellectual superiority. They felt compelled to control us, so they had to dominate physically since that was their primary advantage. They battered our souls to reinforce our preexisting belief that we didn't deserve better. And both had beaten me in a backyard.

Martin was happy only when he drummed for the punk band Soldiers of Fortune, after Victor invited him to join, because he excelled and this music comported with his renegade self-image. The Soldiers practiced in a warehouse and I often watched. I would sit in the rafters and drink beer. Once, Martin gave a ride to his bandmate Duff, a mellow guy who just wanted to perfect his guitar skills and horse around with his buddies. Duff sat between Martin and me in the truck. We argued so Martin leaned over and smacked me across the head and then my face. Duff looked stunned and sputtered a "what the fuck." A cop happened to witness this, pulled us over, and yelled at Martin for hitting a woman. The officer demanded to know if I was hurt and I said no, which I thought was the truth because I wasn't bleeding and had no broken bones. The cop sent us on our way, just like when I was a girl and the police came but didn't arrest Allan, except that one time when he was about to murder my mother.

One day, a few hours after one of his tirades, rage welled up as Martin played drums at band practice. He looked sublime, as if life was wonderful. He poured alcohol down his throat, and I worried about what he'd do after he worked himself into a drunken fit. I went outside to the parking lot with a bottle of malt liquor and dropped to the gravel next to his truck. Overwhelming sadness and loneliness and fear consumed me in waves. Sobs shook my body, which I tried to quell so he wouldn't hear me if the music stopped.

I rolled the bottle between my palms, grabbed it by the neck, and smashed it on the curb. I watched the slivers glisten as the sun hit the liquid puddles. I clutched a triangular shard, held up my left hand, and sliced my wrist. Not to commit suicide, but for the pain and the blood. With the searing ache, I felt joy and relief. A bright red line appeared and tiny drops trickled down my arm. I laughed so hard I buckled over and bashed my head into my knees. I swiveled my hand to encourage the flow, then cut myself again, a half inch lower. I inhaled a deep breath, for the first time in months, maybe years, as if I was back in a body I'd fled. I wet my finger and swirled the blood, before I wiped it on the truck and giggled at the red contrasting with the baby blue. I lay on my side and smoked a cigarette. Dizzy from the alcohol and stimulated by this new experience, I muttered to the vivid blue sky, "Fuck you, Martin, sick son of a bitch."

As trepidation crawled under my skin at the thought of returning to his father's with him, I threw myself forward, snagged a larger piece of glass, and slit my wrist in the same spot. My skin split and blood spurted out. "Oh shit!" I put pressure on it, which slowed the rushing river but failed to stop it. I staggered to my feet, dug in the glove compartment, and wrapped my wrist with napkins. I sprawled back to the ground, then felt the sticky wetness spread. I considered getting up, but that seemed too hard. My eyelids drooped shut, and I wondered how much blood you can lose before you die. I heard footsteps approach, then someone paused, bent down, and raised my arm.

"Oh my God, Mary Beth. What have you done?" Duff had wandered out, maybe to look for me. He lifted me up, slid his arm around my waist, and walked me inside. "Aw honey, why did you do this?" I glanced at him and saw tears, which confused me since I barely knew him. Duff maneuvered me through the band equipment and to the bathroom, where he washed the blood from my wrist. He went to his car and grabbed a T-shirt, which he tore to make strips. Victor approached as Duff bandaged me up. "Cut herself. Bleeding like a pig. If this doesn't stop it, hospital."

Victor examined me and then turned to Martin. "What the hell?"

Martin trudged over and snorted. "She's a loon, Victor. You know she is."

Duff moved Victor out of the way and poked Martin in the chest. "Something's wrong. You're her boyfriend. If she needs help, it's your job to make sure she gets it." I perused Duff, surprised this mild-mannered sweetie would risk Martin's wrath. The depth of his concern astounded me, and I contemplated whether this is how loving people reacted to self-destructive behavior. I felt seen for a few moments, which contrasted with my past history when important adults didn't notice when I didn't shower or used a ton of drugs or missed school or lost weight or fell asleep in class or picked my skin raw.

I now understand the cutting was a post-traumatic stress reaction to prior abuse and the escalating situation with Martin. I started this relationship shortly after the LA rape, and I think those two events were connected. Martin attracted me because his raw energy and love of chaos reflected my feelings, and made it easier to ignore the kidnapping and sexual assaults. And I didn't want to be alone and needed the emotional attachment. The cutting, which I thought I invented until years later when I read an article about self-mutilation, arose because I couldn't repress all the agony. The slicing released pain in the moment, and for days afterward when my wrists throbbed, I experienced it as proof that all was as it should be in the world.

I continued the self-harm in my junior year and still have scars. While sober, I intentionally purchased beer in glass bottles to smash when inebriated. Once my supervisor at my job on campus noticed the self-applied dressings on my wrists. Concerned, she asked if I'd intended to hurt myself. Like with Duff, I had a flood of euphoria that she'd noticed although I told her I'd had an accident when drunk. One night, with warm blood on my arms, I called a rape hotline because I guessed maybe I'd been impacted by those traumas. I tried therapy again but had no money, so I went to a clinic with unskilled student counselors. We discussed mostly family issues. I laid all the blame on Allan and the sexual assaults but didn't mention Martin. And I defended my mother when the counselor pointed out some deficiencies because I wasn't ready to face her neglect and abuse.

And then I moved in with Martin my senior year when he transferred to San Francisco State to be closer to me. He'd throw everything off my dresser and fling books and shampoo bottles at me. Martin would back me into a corner and beat me over the head and shoulders. Sometimes he wouldn't let me study or talk on the phone. He'd call me names and threaten to kill me if I didn't hang up, although in a harsh whisper so the person on the other end couldn't hear. As the months passed, his attacks escalated such that I never knew how far he would go. Eventually, I convinced Martin to move into the other bedroom. But we still shared the rest of the apartment and he continued to harass me. He punched me several times and gave me black eyes that I covered with makeup.

As I later reflected on sticking with Martin, I thought about how, when he moved north, I could've let him drift away. But I didn't. I followed him. True, I didn't live with him my junior year, except for the summer. This was another opportunity to break it off, since I wasn't trapped in his house once I left for Berkeley. But then I moved in with him, which put me in a vulnerable position. His behavior in our apartment didn't surprise me because a part of me anticipated continued abuse. I didn't like being beaten, but I stayed with him for another year. I would provoke Martin because the energy escalation felt familiar and excited me. And because I needed to stand up for myself, just like with Allan. I even convinced him we should get married, had him announce it to our friends, but luckily didn't go through with it.

Perhaps that's the biggest surprise, that I don't have to refer to Martin as my first husband. The damage I brought with me to California prevented me from feeling like a typical college kid. I managed to reduce my drug use, but then replaced that insanity with an abusive boyfriend and cutting myself. I remember saying that a good man wouldn't stay with me once he realized how bat-shit crazy I was. Martin was on my level in that way. We both bled emotionally and spewed our anguish around every room we entered. •

# CHAPTER 27
## Speed Again

IN JANUARY OF MY SENIOR YEAR, I became a regular at the Bear's Lair Pub on campus, which I would characterize as a dark hovel, except it was clean. Deep brown wooden walls, benches, and table-tops, and dimmed lights. During the day, students watched the soap opera *All My Children* and ate grilled sandwiches or mediocre pizza. A few even drank beers before class.

The first time I peered into the Bear's Lair, I recognized it as my kind of place. A cloud of smoke drifted through the room. The bartender beckoned me over and handed me a beer, gratis. I turned to sip it and saw a woman sitting in a corner booth, with a textbook, burning cigarette, and empty mug. She was beautiful, with shiny black hair, bright blue eyes rimmed with thick lashes, and a rocking body beneath her lace Stevie Nicks–ish dress. She peered at me and smiled, so I took a couple steps closer.

"Hey, darling, what a pretty thing you are. I'm Gina."

I stood taller in my snug white corduroys and form-fitting red sweater and tossed my shoulder-length blond curls. "Aiming for a dressed-down Marilyn Monroe." Gina laughed, in a soft breathless way, as I slid into the bench across from her. I poured half my beer into her mug and she offered me a Marlboro. "No thanks, I'm a menthol girl." I fished around for my pack, and Gina flipped open her gold lighter as I bent toward her.

We talked for the hour before class and shared the basics. Same age, both liberal arts majors, both working twenty hours per week. Gina was unattached, and I briefly mentioned my charismatic but troubled boyfriend. We discussed the men in our past and complained about our coursework. From then on, Monday through Thursday we met for lunch and the soap, then headed back to class or our jobs. On Fridays, we would drink beer at noon because we had a two-hour gap until our next class, and then were free for the weekend.

Several mugs into a lazy afternoon, we giggled about punk rocker Heather dating football player Mark as they parked themselves at a table catty-corner from us, then we returned to our conversation about balancing work and school. Gina and I snapped to attention when Mark pounded the table. "I said no!" We could see Heather's forehead scrunched in fear as she cowered in her seat.

When Mark grabbed her wrist, Gina leapt to her feet. "Darling, calm down. You're scaring us." His dark eyes glowered at her, but Gina caressed his arm with one hand while she gestured for me to stay seated with the other. "It's okay. You want to take a walk and cool off? We'll sit with your girl." As we watched him march toward Sproul Plaza, we scurried out with Heather and shepherded her to the dorms. She hugged us, then fled to her roommates for safety.

We straddled a frosty concrete bench and I searched my backpack for my gloves. Gina's face crumbled. "My last boyfriend punched me because I put too much mayonnaise on his sandwich."

I clutched her hands in mine. "My stepfather beat me for spilling milk." As she pressed her cheek against mine, the ice that encased my soul, my truest self, melted just a touch.

Gina muttered, "Bastards." I nodded and pulled her up. She slipped her arm around my waist and we strolled through campus.

The following month, Gina and I fell headfirst into sisterly love. We shared our life stories and bonded over the numerous similarities. Like me, Gina excelled at school, and her family financially helped her less than they could have. We both had to figure out how to navigate the university system to get what we needed to finance our education and graduate in four years with all our requirements satisfied. Like me, Gina did not receive love, attention, or guidance from her parents. While they did not abuse her physically, they did emotionally. Gina, too, had been raped and became promiscuous at an early age. And like me, Gina struggled with drug addiction by her mid-teens. We understood each other at the deepest levels because her story was my story, and mine was hers. Since I'd lost Sally, I hadn't had this powerful a connection with a girlfriend, so this was a big deal for me.

As Martin's beatings increased, which motivated me to be home as little as possible, on Fridays Gina and I started to remain at the pub through the afternoon and into the night. On those days, for the first time in college, I missed some classes. Around 5:00, a group of men who delivered the campus mail would show up. They'd send us a pitcher of beer and stop by to say a few words. Once we all shared a joint on the patio. After a couple weeks of this, Rick, the tall graying brunet with a mustache and warm brown eyes, carried over three mugs of beer. Neither his cheap cologne nor the Camel cigarette dangling from his lips could overcome the strong smell of alcohol on his breath. He gestured for me to move farther into the booth so he could join us. I glanced at Gina, and she signaled okay with a slight shrug.

"I hoped to see you girls since it's Friday." Rick rolled up the sleeves to his persimmon button-down shirt. "Ever snort crystal meth?"

Gina spun toward me and slapped my shoulder. I would have preferred we appear less eager, but my brain booted up the memory of inhaling that exquisite white powder and the rush of adrenalin forced my eyes wide. "Yeah, we've done speed. Not in a while though."

Rick unlatched the clasp to a chain attached to his belt and extracted a black leather zippered pouch. My mouth watered, fingers tingled, and ears twitched. As I crushed my Salem into the heavy glass ashtray, I glanced at the bartender, who gave me a thumbs-up. Rick opened his drug kit and shook out a clear vial and razor blade. He tossed a twenty-dollar bill to me and I rolled it into a tight cylinder. He tapped out a mound of speed onto the table, about a third of a gram, with grains so fine he chopped the crank just once. My heart pounded in my chest and blood banged my ear drums. Rick cut three equal lines and leaned back so I could lean in.

I crushed one nostril closed and vacuumed up my portion. The searing pain left a trail of ecstasy in its path. My head slammed itself into the wood behind. The lights sparkled in rhythm with the roar of crank racing through my body and into my brain. I coughed and took a deep breath as the meth triggered a dopamine surge in every neuron. *Oh my God. How I've missed you. My soul mate. My perfect partner.*

As Gina and Rick snorted their lines, a friend of Rick's, Doc, strolled into the bar. A white T-shirt, emblazoned with Berkeley's radio station call letters KALX, exposed his skinny arms. A slight paunch protruded above the worn black belt that held frayed jeans a half inch too high at the waist and the hem. He combed his hair neatly, which surprised me since he had an uneven Supercut. His eyes were a pleasant gray-green and his nose slightly too prominent above thin lips. There was a softness to his face and a nerdy sweetness to him, so I drew him into the conversation.

"Do you deliver the campus mail, too?"

"No. In '68, I came here because it was a great school with a radio station. I was a DJ, then ran KALX. Now I supervise KFJC in Silicon Valley."

Rick added, "Doc was on the front page of the *Wall Street Journal* last year for this big 'Louie Louie' marathon."

I put my beer down and studied Doc. "Wow. Impressive."

Rick and Doc described the music and Berkeley protests of the '60s. Gina and I flirted a bit because they were nice and to garner more beers and more lines. With each snort, my eyes expanded upward and outward, and I giggled when my well-mascaraed lashes flicked just under my brow. Gina threaded her fingers into mine, comingling our sweat, and we bounced our forearms in time to the Grateful Dead's "Casey Jones." The four of us shared funny or outrageous drug stories, each trying to outdo the other, although neither Gina nor I mentioned our addiction or the sicker parts of our history.

Rick and Doc suggested we move to Larry Blake's Rathskeller, a local hangout with sawdust on the floor, live music, beer, and burgers, although none of us even browsed the menu. Around 2:00 a.m., we relocated to Rick's apartment, snorted another two lines each, taught Doc to play spades, and surfed through various topics until dawn. I thought about Martin pacing with an Olde English in one hand and a fist accentuating his raging tirade as he waited for me. But, for a little while, I didn't care. I felt exhilarated and enthusiastic about life. I revealed my high Law School Admission Test score, my hope I'd be admitted to Berkeley's law school, and dreams of fighting for justice. In glowing terms and at length, I explained my senior thesis, "Keeping Women in Their Place: Ideology and the Status of Women in Eighteenth-Century New York." Then Gina said she needed to head home. And the bubble burst.

Staying up all night had allowed me to avoid Martin although I knew pushing him off meant he'd be more pissed once I faced him. As Gina drove me to my apartment, fear welled up and her voice dissolved into incomprehensible murmurs. I didn't want her to know that Martin beat me because I thought she'd pressure me to leave. She couldn't take me in because she lived with her parents, so I had nowhere to go. I gazed at my furrowed brow reflected in the passenger window and pinched the inside of my arm to squelch my tears. I slipped out just as Gina came to a stop.

I held onto the metal rail as I climbed the concrete stairs. Martin flung open the door, gripped the back of my neck, and yanked me into the apartment. My ankle scraped the coffee table as I stumbled to the floor. I curled into a ball when I saw Martin extend his leg backward to increase the velocity of his kick. "Where the fuck have you been? Sucking someone's dick? Taking it in the ass? You whore."

"No, no, I swear. I went to Gina's. I called, but you didn't answer."

"I've been here for hours."

"Leave me alone. I didn't do anything."

Martin hovered over me, grabbed me under my armpits, dragged me into the bedroom, and slammed the door. I tried to believe the attack had ended but, based on past history, couldn't convince myself. Although still wired from the speed, I crawled into bed and listened to him mutter to himself for an hour. Once he quieted down, I cracked the door open, and verified he was asleep. I carried the phone into the bedroom, slid the door shut with the cord underneath, and called several New Jersey friends since it was morning there and they'd be awake. I didn't mention the abuse, but connecting to friends quelled my anxiety until I drifted off in a fitful sleep.

I spent many hours over the next few months with Gina, Doc, and other Bear's Lair pals. The negative result was my increased meth use. The positive outcome was I felt supported enough to leave Martin. In April, Rick, Gina, and I packed up my belongings and put them in storage. I slept on an acquaintance's sofa until graduation, relieved to be free of Martin's abuse, and focused on finishing my thesis and my last round of finals.

In early recovery I wondered whether college, without Martin, would have been a turning point in my substance use disorder. Recovery groups often don't believe that geographic changes solve addiction, which I'm sure is mostly true. Plus, if not Martin, I might well have chosen someone else like him. He provided chaos and danger, and I don't think I knew how to live without that energy. But I did control my drug use to a notable degree for three years, likely because I didn't use meth. Not to minimize the drinking and swallowing other drugs or related insanities, but these were limited to the weekend or episodic.

My speed use started again when I moved in with Martin and faced a daily risk of violence. Plus, I felt debilitated by the LA rapes, which amplified my childhood anguish. Those beautiful shining crystals offered a way back to fun and camaraderie—a way to cover over the trauma-created brain scars and pull me out of a depression I didn't even know I had. The intensity of snorting crank also provided a stimulus similar to living with Martin, without the bruises.

So, as it turned out, I created a new life with Martin that mirrored my New Jersey childhood, then reached for the same escape. ●

# CHAPTER 28
## Law School

THROUGH MY BEAR'S LAIR FRIENDS, I gained easy access to speed. We'd run from the pub to the club to Rick's apartment, play cards through the night, and converse for hours, all of which I enjoyed. Above all else, though, I craved the intensity of snorting line after line after line until exhaustion forced me into the deep oblivion of the crash. Which I loved. No nightmares, or at least I didn't recall them. No tossing and turning with worries or fears. Only darkness until I crawled back to the light ten hours later.

I maintained enough control that spring to graduate without tarnishing my academic record. I was even accepted at Berkeley's top ten law school. But over the summer, I plunged deep into the crank rabbit hole for the second time. I snorted speed almost every day, usually in large quantities. When I started law school in the fall, I struggled to make it to class because I was too high to pull myself together or too low to stand on my feet. I soon missed consecutive weeks and didn't read half the assignments. I once remembered that I had a major paper due in two days for a class I had been to twice. My avoidance skills dominated such that fear about the impact of all this only hit me when I sat down for finals. Instead, once every couple of weeks, I'd stay up for days to catch up, yet wasted a lot of time tweaking or doing crosswords. In another effort to compensate, I prepared for many tests with study guides I bought at the bookstore.

During first semester finals, my body rebelled against running so hard and I developed a severe case of bronchitis. The morning before my first exam, the university hospital wanted to admit me. I insisted on taking the test since I'd studied and lacked confidence that I could repeat my efforts. So they pumped me full of adrenalin to ease my breathing, which produced a speed-like high but more ethereal. I sang to myself all the way to the law school, where I took the exam, then returned to the hospital and checked myself in. My veins were so bad from my prior shooting days, they had to tape my arm to a board for the IV. A guy I'd had sex with at Berkeley, one of just a few, came to visit and I didn't recognize him. Gina reminded me, and we thought it hilarious I'd been so high he didn't make an impression.

For the next two years, I would stay up for three days, then sleep two nights, then begin again. I acquired a horrible habit of rubbing my eyes raw, then I'd dig into them to remove the resulting mucus. I often had to peel my eyelids open in the morning because the gunk glued them shut. Sometimes I wore an eye patch to law school to cover whichever eye was worse and claim infection or injury. In my contracts class, I looked down at my book and a large, cold, wet, itchy lump of goo slid over my eyeball. I had to use my fingers to get it out. The student next to me choked back a gag. A week later, as I smoked a cigarette on the law school patio when I should have been in class, a huge blood clot slipped from my upper sinuses into my nose. I ran to the restroom to clean up the mess and stop the bleeding as I tried to ignore the strange looks and people moving away from me.

I did pass all my classes, with mediocre grades and minimal post-exam retention of the material. In my third, and last, year, I sat in tax class for the first time in a month. I realized I would fail this course and probably others. And I wouldn't be able to muster the discipline needed to pass the bar exam. I went to the dean, said I had financial problems, and withdrew. I returned the following fall, continued the same pattern, and withdrew again. The dean warned me my credits would expire in a few years, which didn't matter to me since I had no hope I'd ever make it back.

I knew I had allowed an amazing opportunity to slip away. This loss saddened and disgusted me. During much of college my intellect and ambitions outweighed my addiction, but I found I couldn't hang on. I told myself I was ill and on the verge of collapse, which was true. I believed I was headed toward a nervous breakdown, maybe also true. However, I did not acknowledge that I was sick and exhausted—physically, intellectually, and emotionally—because of my substance use disorder.

The life of the addict is not fun, not exciting, not glamorous. It's a miserable, all-consuming, agonizing, chaotic existence. My world revolved around getting and using more speed. Everything else was tangential, including food, sleep, and health. And law school. •

# CHAPTER 29
## Doc

I STARTED DATING DOC after I ditched Martin, which provided some joy. When I'd meet him at the Bear's Lair, his face would brighten, and his eyes would sweep over me as if he couldn't believe how beautiful I was. Whenever I said something smart, he'd jump in so we could pursue the topic. He looked proud when introducing me to his friends and bragged about me getting into Berkeley's law school. He'd take me out to see bands and go to nice restaurants. He found a Philly cheesesteak place so I could have a taste of home. We'd lie in bed, snuggle close, and talk for hours. Plus, as I told Gina, "He's dynamite at sex. Proficient, yes. But it's also that I feel connected to him. I can relax into the sensations. I've never had orgasms like this."

Doc's normal approach to life was kind and mellow, a welcome relief after Martin. I don't think I realized it then, but his personality was similar to the first father I'd ever known, John. On the other hand, John had abandoned me. And Doc announced, repeatedly, that he wasn't interested in commitment. I thought, and think, the depth of his aversion arose from his father's debilitating illness, which dragged on for decades beginning when Doc was a child. As a result, Doc was hyperaware of the potential downside of finding yourself trapped with a needy partner. So I tried to talk to him about his upbringing.

"What was it like for you, as a kid, when the family had to prioritize your dad's needs?"

Doc scratched his head for a moment. "That's the way it had to be. He was in pain and sick, and we had to care for him."

I interlinked my fingers with his. "Were you afraid? That he might die?"

"My mother told me the doctors were doing everything they could. Trying all the treatments."

"Okay, but did you have any feelings about the situation?"

Doc seemed puzzled, with his forehead scrunched and his mouth agape. "I wanted to help."

Since this tactic failed to resolve his fears, to prove to myself he was devoted to me, I'd push for a compliment or flirt with the nearest guy in hopes of triggering jealousy. But it was like Doc had radar that honed in on any attempt to force a reaction. He'd either ignore me, which might cause me to lash out in anger, or he'd utter a few harsh words and disappear for a while. Afterward, I'd use all my charms to get him to smile at me or hold my hand. Then I'd stick to my best behavior for a few weeks. When he didn't break up with me after I kept repeating this pattern, I used this as proof of his deep love and hidden bond to me. I convinced myself Doc just couldn't admit we were a full-fledged couple.

Probably related to his commitment issues, Doc limited his visits to the weekends, even though he lived only forty-five minutes away. We both used speed on Fridays, but he always stopped to sleep. Certain he abstained on workdays, I dropped lies about being a weekend imbiber, too. I tried to rest Thursday nights and would shower and fix up my face to hide the severity of my addiction. The summer of 1987, after months of effort, I convinced him to buy a house so we could live together, although he signed a mortgage he could afford if we broke up. I wasn't sure if this reflected general self-care or that he wasn't oblivious to the risk of becoming entangled with me.

After I quit law school the second time and relocated to Silicon Valley with Doc, I had to get a job and behave like a grown-up. My crank use focused on trying to perform basic life activities, even if not particularly well. Get up, get dressed, go to work, grocery shop, clean the house. And interact with Doc. This became more difficult to synthesize with my "conceal the extent of my meth use" goal. Luckily, I thought then, he managed the college radio station on a sort of swing shift. When he left in the afternoon, I was at work. I could get high until he came home around midnight, and pretend I'd waited up. I'd lie down with him until he fell asleep, then get up and snort crank until morning.

I typically stayed up for seventy-two hours, slept one or two nights, on those days consuming just 25 percent of my usual amount of speed, then started anew. For a while, I forced myself to take a week break after each run. I could perform some normal activities, but every day I counted down to my target crank date. That light enabled me to make it through the drug-free tunnel, but I was able to maintain this pattern just a couple months.

Over time, Doc grew increasingly anxious and angry. He occasionally woke and found me playing solitaire or filling out crosswords. And he started commenting on my appearance. "Are you feeling all right?" Or even "You look like shit. You need to take a break from the drugs." He grew frustrated when I canceled plans or didn't want to go out to eat. "Jesus Christ, not again."

But he never sat me down to talk about my drug use or have an actual discussion about his concerns. Instead, we had long-winded disputes regarding tangential issues, like me ordering him around in front of his friends or calling in sick to work too often. As a result of my intense approach to such discussions, whether flying on speed or crashing, Doc said he felt interrogated and had no hope I'd ever hear his point, which caused him to avoid me. If I anticipated a challenge to my drug use, I'd cross my arms and lash out about some minor flaw of his to redirect the conversation. All this negatively impacted our relationship. I never asked Doc what he wanted but wasn't getting, and I should have. But I did not have any more to give anyway.

One day, a year after I moved in with him, I went for a medical checkup. When the doctor left to get her prescription pad, a drawer remained open. I noticed a batch of plastic bundles, about six inches long. For a second, that's all I could see, like the room vanished. As I stepped forward, I glanced at the door to confirm it was shut. Then slid the drawer toward me. The doctor's hypodermic needles, my favorite type, the ones used for insulin, displayed with the orange caps aligned. I seized a handful and thrust them deep into my purse. As the doctor returned to the room, I stifled a giggle. *If she took my blood pressure now, I'd be wheeled to the ER.*

Adrenaline surged and super pumped my heart during the race home as I envisioned slamming crank. I blasted past the door, gathered the paraphernalia of spoon and water and cotton, then hovered on the toilet's edge to catch my breath. My hand trembled as I assembled a strong dose and I flushed hot when the red geyser entered the clear barrel. My temperature jumped three degrees as the meth careened from my arm to my neck, then face, and down to my belly. I coughed as the ether rose in my throat, which precipitated an icy chill up my back. My pulsing eyes tracked a thin red spray as I withdrew the needle. My skin felt the exquisite warmth of the blood as it landed on my arm. I released a deep gasp, then whispered, "Welcome home."

Six months later, before I prepared my morning shot, I drained an abscess by poking it with a syringe. As I pressed the blood and pus out, I upchucked a bit of vomit, then heard a low moan escape my lips. After I poured peroxide over the wound, I scrutinized the veins in my arms and hands, aggravated they were so tiny. All of them already were covered in bruises from overuse, which took weeks to fade from purple to green to gone, so I faced a tough day. I stared at the floor, shrugged my shoulders, and allowed myself to feel dejected for a minute. Then I spent the next hour trying to get a hit anywhere I thought might be viable. Several times, a bit of blood appeared in the hypo's barrel, but then the flow stopped.

As I looked down at my lap in defeat, I spotted a superb vein, twice as thick as anything on my arms. I scanned both thighs and located another and another and another. I dug into my memory to see if drug lore cautioned against shooting up in your legs, since I'd never observed anyone do it, but couldn't recall any warnings. Breathless at the image of weeks of quick and easy injections, I lifted my head toward the ceiling and expelled a "whoo, whoo." As I prepared to pop this cherry, I checked the syringe because, I thought as a sign my body was dying, my blood had turned nearly black and was so thick it clotted easily. Since the needle had clogged, I removed the plunger, tapped the clot and the meth into the spoon, diluted the mixture, then stabbed myself in my thigh, to no avail. To avoid wasting the speed, I again eased out the plunger, put the hypodermic inside my mouth and shook it so the glutinous emulsion slid into my throat. Between gags, I swallowed some Pepsi and choked down the crank. Roiled by a powerful amalgam of contempt and disgust and shame and sadness, it took me a full five minutes to cap off the feelings.

Drinking bloody meth and lancing abscesses did gross me out, but I accepted all this as an unavoidable consequence of being an IV drug addict. In contrast, I nose-dived into horror anytime my crank supply ran low. Once my dealer couldn't provide meth for two days, even though I'd cracked open my last gram. Confusion and self-loathing rushed through me because I always refilled my backup vial as soon as my stockpile dropped to an eighth of an ounce. How had I made this mistake? Didn't my dealer know I needed the drugs? How could he let this happen? What was I going to do? Any other sources I could tap? All this and more sledgehammered my brain, over and over.

Having failed at my replenishment efforts, I had to ration my stash, so I slept that night. The next day I struggled to wake, weighed down by the heavy blankets and cold sweat. I hauled my body into a sitting position, gripped the bed's edge, raised my head, extended my palm until it rested on the wall, and straightened my body in three stages. I shuffled up the hall and peeked at Doc as he paused to glare at me before he slammed the front door on his way out. Worried he was near the end of his rope, I peered into the mirror: dark circles, deep hollows, gray alabaster skin, and dead eyes. *You're killing yourself. Shooting poison.* Since my vial neared empty anyway, I decided not to use, just for that day.

I reheated a McDonald's cheeseburger, grabbed a Pepsi and my Salems, melted into the sofa, and flicked on the TV. I nodded in and out, absorbing segments of soap operas and game shows. Around 4:00, I microwaved popcorn and settled back in. "Doing good, just a few more hours." I flipped to a wildlife show and saw men wrangle a rhinoceros to the ground. The camera moved close as a veterinarian pushed off the cap to a large syringe, punctured the tough skin, and drew blood. As the gorgeous red liquid flooded the barrel, I bolted to my stash and shot up. Afterward, while the glory of the meth washed over me, I laughed. "You can't even watch PBS."

I remembered this as proof of the depth of my sickness and inability to control myself. *You should stop* flittered across my mind every couple of months, but getting clean seemed as likely as jumping to the moon. I didn't think I had the emotional or physical strength to make a real attempt. I couldn't picture life beyond the upcoming days or imagine any positive change, not even when the haze cleared for a second and I saw the steep downward trajectory behind me and before me.

One day, in summer 1992, we were supposed to meet Gina and her cousin at the beach at Santa Cruz. Doc came into the kitchen as I swigged a Pepsi. "So, we're not going, right?"

"What? No. Going. Can't disappoint Gina."

"You're a frazzled wreck. And it's her family. They'll wonder what Gina's up to with a drugged-out friend."

"Don't exaggerate. I'm fine. It's breezy there, so let me throw on some shorts and a light top, and I'll be ready. I can fix my makeup in the car."

Doc spun around and stomped into the kitchen. The door to the olive-green refrigerator slammed against the wall and the Heineken bottles clanged almost to the shattering point. My eyes flitted across the full-length mirror such that I registered only my outline. I dragged the brush through my overly bleached hair and tossed my drug kit into my oversized purse. The seat belt clicked into place seconds before Doc peeled out of the driveway. Five minutes into the ride, I nodded off, waking to the squeal of brakes as we avoided a guy carrying a surfboard a block from the boardwalk. Doc's tight grip on the steering wheel reminded me of the thin ice beneath my feet. I pressed my forehead to the cool window, although it was warmer than the look Doc shot my way.

During the walk from the car, he quickened his pace until he was a half block ahead. Then he turned and charged toward me. I was so surprised, I stopped in my tracks. As he neared, I watched his Adam's apple bob up and down as if keeping time with his footfalls. He pushed me backward, another shocker.

"Why did I let you argue me into this? Everyone on that beach will see the bruises. Your sleeves ride up and your track marks show." As I tried to grasp this attack, direct and loud, and in front of strangers no less, Doc shoved his hands into his pockets. "Don't count on me letting this go on forever. It may be too late already."

My knees wobbled and the world turned dark for a second. I believed him. My time was running out. "Okay, I hear you. Let's talk tomorrow."

Doc clutched my arm and sort of towed me to the beach. I expect it was a sunny day, blue sky, wisps of clouds. But such details eluded me. Doc made polite conversation for an hour, said he needed a beer, and left. Gina and I took this opportunity to go to the restroom to shoot up. When we returned, Doc was nowhere in sight. We chatted with her cousin, dipped our toes in the water, and did another speed/restroom run. Doc never came back, so I headed to the car and found him sitting on the trunk. On the trip home, I didn't dare speak, afraid he'd announce his decision to kick me out. Doc dropped me at the house with an "I'm going to the radio station for a while."

I did a shot of crank and called Gina. "I'm worried he's about to throw in the towel."

"Mary Beth, hon. Sorry to say this, but you should give it a rest—for a while. When you left, my cousin asked if Doc beat you. Because of all the bruises."

"Really? Man, oh man. I'll try to cut back."

To be honest, I didn't believe this even as the words came out of my mouth. I did try to cut back, for a few weeks. And, then I back-tracked when the meth compulsion overpowered my fear of losing Doc.

After I got clean, I asked Doc why he'd moved in with a meth head, especially after refusing to commit for years. He said he saw potential and trusted I would get my act together. My recovery successes seem to validate that theory, but I'm not confident it's 100 percent accurate. I don't think it explains why, six years later, he still waited for the long odds that this frog would turn into his princess.

It seems to me anyone who prioritized self-preservation would've kicked me to the curb within a year or two. I'm pretty sure, in Berkeley, he didn't realize the depth of my addiction. Even when my behavior brought this to light, he didn't understand substance use disorder. As he has acknowledged, Doc believed my meth use was a choice, so he thought I could quit anytime. This gave him some hope I'd see the destruction soon and give it up, or at least tone it down. Plus, he isn't skilled at accessing his feelings, so couldn't process all the emotions triggered by my speed addiction.

After years of effort, I did morph into a better version of myself. Nevertheless, just because his theory proved correct doesn't mean he made a good decision although I'm grateful he stuck by me. •

# CHAPTER 30
## Down the Corporate Ladder

AFTER I WITHDREW FROM LAW SCHOOL, I worked my way down the corporate ladder, from law clerk to office manager to basic administration. Although always technically "laid off," I lost all these jobs due to my addiction. The more disjointed my work history, the more difficult it was to get hired. My top-tier education resulted in some people selecting me while others probably recognized something must be awry.

A month after Santa Cruz, as I readied for an interview at ATEL, I forced myself to take a close look in the mirror. White linen pants appeared oversized, navy jacket seemed to swallow me up, and heavy foundation didn't quite cover the pick marks. The day before, I'd crashed hard, so I hadn't touched up my hair color, and the dark roots extended almost an inch. I tried to reassure myself. *This is word processing. They should be thrilled with my Berkeley degree and some law school.* But the knowledge that my resume evidenced my deterioration nagged me into anxiety. Plus, I felt discombobulated since I'd just withdrawn an application when I'd learned my desk would be in the lobby so they'd notice my lengthy breaks to get high.

When I arrived, I checked in at reception, then headed to the bathroom. I did a jig when I realized each stall had a shelf where I could rest my spoon to mix a meth shot. I managed to get just the right amount of intoxification to land this job. And I performed well during the training because my veins cooperated for a quick robust hit every ninety minutes. But within the month I struggled and spent two hours each day in the restroom. Even the great tie-off from the emergency medical kit didn't help. Sometimes I'd go into my favorite stall, with just one shared wall, and realize I'd forgotten to clean up the blood droplets. Once my water vial rolled across the floor and I had to race to the handicap unit to grab it before my neighbors got a close look. Three months into the job, I dropped a syringe on the elevator floor, next to the hiring manager, and mumbled "insulin." Once a week, I took a long lunch to run to the needle exchange to trade dirty needles for fresh, the only addict in a suit.

Getting up and dressed expended my work preparation energy, so I didn't bother with hair or makeup. When late or absent, both frequent, I used the litany of excuses I'd developed over the years. Glasses broke, grandmother died, new antidepressant made me groggy. I muddled tasks and missed deadlines. And I could be aggressive, particularly with people I viewed as incompetent, as I was when a customer service representative told me she was trying hard. I replied, "That's what's so pathetic." As usual, when the slide toward termination began, in the depths of my addiction, I couldn't resolve the issues. I just did my best to delay the consequence. This time, I hung on for nine months.

Twenty years into abusing substances and sixteen into meth I found shooting speed a necessary evil, not a fun excursion. My goal was rudimentary functionality. The compulsion to consume speed was entrenched. And I did not believe I could survive without drugs since the anguish would annihilate me if allowed to surface. Due to the weighty baggage, the addict life was the optimum I could accomplish. If I had to feel the searing pain of the many traumas, I wouldn't just self-mutilate or take extreme risks. Next time, I'd kill myself or wind up in a mental institution. So, while addiction was an imperfect solution, I feared it less than the alternatives.

Still, a desire to shake off the misery and hopelessness would bleed through my mind's reeling chaos. But I was conflicted. In the superior position, my substance use disorder. No surprise, considering I had been an addict my entire adulthood and a chunk of my childhood. The torment was even older, originating in the abuse and neglect that had made drugs attractive. Yet, although I didn't say this aloud as it seemed ludicrous based on my actions, I wanted to be happy and successful. I yearned to be a supportive partner to Doc, improve my health, get and keep a good job, go to the beach without track marks, and just engage with the world.

Thus, to summarize, substance use disorder is not fun. It is a horrible, demoralizing, life-threatening, and life-altering experience. I was ruining my life and destroying my body. Sometimes I could not see this, other times I did not care, but mostly I did not know how to crawl out of this deep, dark hole. I'd continued on this self-destructive downward path for two decades. I'd ruined the academic and career opportunities I had worked for and wanted, and maybe demolished my relationship with Doc. For the last few years, I knew I was a junkie but did not believe I could live any other way and did not have the energy to pursue recovery.

At least I didn't until I did. •

# CHAPTER 31
## Recovery Begins

THE FIRST TIME I ADMITTED my crank abuse to a medical professional was to the psychiatrist after my arrest, the summer after high school, who just gave me antidepressants. Along the way, various doctors saw track marks and abscesses and occasionally mentioned treatment but did not pursue the topic after I brushed them off. I tried therapy several times to address the trauma but made little progress because I didn't mention my substance use disorder and wasn't willing to delve into my pain. I always had meth in my system in therapy anyway, which impacted my understanding in the moment, and my addiction numbed out my true feelings and thoughts over the long haul.

A few months after the confrontation at the beach, I sat in the dining room, where I'd been for two days except when I shot up in the bathroom. I pulled the Living section from my tall newspaper stack and perused the "Winter Weddings" story. As I read, my eyes narrowed and my blood pressure rose. *Seven years and Doc hasn't proposed. Last Valentine's Day he gave me Costco cinnamon rolls with some bullshit story about how I once said I liked them.*

Doc happened to enter the house from the garage at that moment. I heaved myself up, which bashed the chair into the wall, stomped to the kitchen, and blocked the doorway, my lips pulled back, like when a wolf bares her teeth.

"You're fucking using me. We should've been married years ago. But you're too chicken."

Doc flinched, then shook his head, slowly. He looked me right in the eyes. "No way I'll let you drag me down with you."

I pounded the countertop with my fist. "What are you talking about? I've held this job for months."

Doc's voice boomed in my ears. "I will never marry you. I'm not that stupid." He turned on his heels, flung open the kitchen door, and bulldozed his way into the garage.

As his Volvo started up, I wanted to pursue him, but the rare explosion stunned me. Plus, this confrontation, or maybe its import, depleted my energy to the point where I felt so disoriented I crumpled to the floor. Apprehensions swirled through my brain: *Why was he so angry? What was going to happen now?* Then, from accumulated hints, plus that Santa Cruz incident, I concluded he meant my addiction. Not only that, but his reaction tapped into my suspicion that he might break up with me and soon.

A few days later, I convinced Doc to go to couples therapy by acknowledging we had problems and some responsibility lay at my feet. Dr. Lincoln counseled us on numerous issues but also recommended inpatient drug treatment for me. By then I'd half forgotten my realization that my meth abuse might snuff out his love, so I informed an incredulous Doc that Dr. Lincoln was barking up the wrong tree. "We need to get him off his drug obsession so we can address the real problems. Like your refusal to commit and my abuse history."

A year later, when I was working at ATEL and four years into round two of my intravenous use, after another flare-up with Doc, I offered to see a psychiatrist to resolve my substance use disorder. I confessed to Dr. Smith my drug history and current daily use. Although he held himself out as an addiction specialist, Dr. Smith then asked how many milliliters I shot at a time. I explained the question was meaningless because the strength depended on the speed quality and how much water I put in the spoon.

Dr. Smith categorized my methamphetamine abuse as a depression symptom and a form of self-medication. He claimed that, with antidepressants, the urge to use speed would vanish and my addiction would fade away. I latched onto this, perhaps because this paradigm fit my long-held opinion that my drug problem simply evidenced the agonies of my past. I didn't realize he did not have the relevant expertise or any scientific support for this theory. Dr. Smith kept increasing my antidepressant dosage to the point that I suffered severe side effects, yet my addiction continued uninterrupted, so I terminated treatment. While I agree that trauma-induced damage made drugs attractive, Dr. Smith failed to appreciate that my brain had been altered by my substance use disorder, such that addressing just the precursor factors would not cure me.

In 1993, the day ATEL terminated me, I sat in the dining room, struggling to shoot enough meth to stay awake, a compulsion that's just another example of my short-term thinking, as it would've been more logical to go to sleep and save my stash for the morning when the speed might get me high rather than just barely keep my eyes open.

The clang of the Volvo's parking brake, which signaled Doc's return home, snapped me awake. I slid my meth and shooting-up paraphernalia into my drug kit, ran a brush through my hair, and slipped into a long-sleeve shirt. As Doc entered the back door, I turned the corner into the kitchen and rushed him for a hug.

"Hey, baby. Good day?"

Doc leaned back on his heels and looked me over from head to toe. "Fine. What about you?"

"Well, I hate to tell you this, but ATEL laid me off. They're restructuring the departments and I'm redundant."

Doc's face transformed from his normal placid paleness to a beet-red, furrow-browed, clenched-jawed epitome of frustrated anger. "Again! I don't give a fuck what they said. They fired you. Because you're a drug addict. I can't take this anymore. I—will—not let you take me down. Not financially. Not any way. You need to pack your shit and hit the road."

The power of his commitment to those words floored me. I know it's hard to believe, but for the first time in weeks, I recalled Santa Cruz and all the other "he's at the end of his rope" indicators. I did love Doc and wanted to be with him. But I didn't believe I could stop using. Not because I loved meth, not at this point. But because I couldn't imagine such a massive change. Nevertheless, I craved a break and thought maybe I could find a way to consume less so I could function better. With Doc about to kick me to the curb, plus my depleted mental and emotional reserves, and a body on the verge of giving out, I played my last card.

"What if I go to rehab?" ●

# CHAPTER 32
## Chrysalis

TWO MONTHS LATER, I finally located an affordable program that would admit me. The Yellow Pages included just a few options. Many facilities were limited to men, and those for women required a dual addiction, but I used only meth. So I asked for referrals and called those facilities and so on. After numerous rejections, I lied and claimed a secondary alcohol dependence, at which point Chrysalis, a women's program an hour away in Oakland, accepted me.

Chrysalis had a waiting list, so I had to call every Monday until I moved to the head of the line and a spot opened. A major challenge for an addict to follow through, but I complied for three months, at which point the coordinator instructed me to report on Friday. During the interim, my fear and anxiety escalated because I was convinced that, if I stopped using, stopped running, stopped denying, the pain and ugliness inside would be unbearable, my mind would snap, and I'd spend the rest of my life locked up in a psych ward or commit suicide. I recollected therapists promising they wouldn't push me until I was ready to dig into the tough issues, but I never trusted them to know what I could handle. I had strong defenses for a reason.

Chrysalis required seventy-two hours of sobriety because they did

241

not have detox facilities, but I found that impossible and felt proud I had managed twenty-four by sleeping the last day before check-in. They never told me what time to arrive, so, I packed at noon. I didn't take any meth with me because I assumed they would search my bags. But I hid crank around our home in the hope that if Doc hunted, he wouldn't find everything. As we headed to Chrysalis, my apprehension escalated with each mile. I twisted in my seat toward Doc. "I don't remember deciding to do this." His glare allowed no room for discussion, however.

Chrysalis owned two adjacent homes in a lower-income neighborhood. As I lumbered up the steps to the neat house with fading taupe paint, I smoothed my floral top's long sleeves to hide my track mark–speckled flesh although I expected the residents would guess since it was August and too hot for a light sweater. Doc hovered close behind as I rang the doorbell, presumably to ensure I didn't flee. When I walked into the primary residence, it resembled a typical home—living room, dining room, stairs to the right, and a hallway to the left. Near the door, a sheet to sign in and out. Several women meandered about, and one found the house mother. She made me say goodbye to Doc and escorted me down the hall, past the kitchen, and to the offices to complete the paperwork. When she searched my bags but not my person, I regretted my decision to leave my drugs at home.

Most of the women lived upstairs, but I shared the downstairs bedroom with Kate. The next morning, she shook me awake. "Mary Beth, this is rehab, not a frigging vacation." She tossed a bright blue paper onto the bed. "Here's the schedule. Next up, AA/NA study group."

I struggled into my striped jumpsuit and stumbled to Chrysalis's kitchen. From a bag marked FOOD BANK, Kate handed me a bagel. "First rehab?"

I stood tall. "Yup. I've never tried to quit."

"Not to be rude, girl, but you look like you shoulda."

I grabbed a coffee and made my way to the parlor, with its mish-mash of furniture: golden couch with white cushions that almost fit, one blue armchair and one red, and eight folding chairs. The dozen residents ranged in age from barely adult to fifty. At thirty-two, I was a bit older than the median and was the most newly sober, with the women's time running up to three months.

Kate recited the third step: We made a decision to turn our will and our lives over to the care of God as we understood Him. Then my comrades took turns reading the explanation in Alcoholics Anonymous's Big Book. Lorraine, a ten years sober ex-nun, asked us to identify our higher power. I raised my hand. "What if you're an atheist?"

Lorraine leaned back and arched her eyebrows. "A lot of people don't have religion in the beginning. And some people never develop faith in a traditional God. But you need to find a higher power."

"Um, I don't believe in any supernatural force."

"A doorknob. Anything outside yourself."

I puzzled over this for a second. "That's ridiculous."

"Mary Beth, I hear you're a Berkeley grad and think you're smarter than the average bear. But your best thinking got you here."

"Lorraine, I promise you, it wasn't my best thinking."

She sputtered as she rose partway out of her chair. "Higher power or relapse."

Despite a deep intake of breath, I managed to spit out, "You just said it's impossible for me to stay clean."

I asked all the counselors for data that proved only one path to recovery existed and this entailed some variant of God. They told me I was fighting the program. I grumbled to the other women about paying good money for treatment that wouldn't work, and that rehab counselors should be educated enough to assist everyone. How could it be that no atheist ever got clean and sober? Why didn't they research alternative approaches?

Luckily, my logical mind functioned well enough to convince me they must be wrong. Since there is no God, I reasoned, sobriety's bedrock must lie elsewhere. I decided to look for the parts of the 12-step programs and rehab classes that might contribute to my success and ignore the rest. After all, though I didn't think Chrysalis and Narcotics Anonymous grasped everything about recovery, they knew more than I did. I even agreed with my counselor to stay at Chrysalis for five months because, as they said in my day, I was tore up from the floor up. This appealed to me because taking more time to heal my body and brain enabled me to avoid the world for a while longer, like finding a job and dealing with Doc's concerns.

We attended classes about addiction, recovery, family issues, anger management, abuse, and interpersonal skills. Student interns led group, individual, and family therapy sessions. All this afforded some useful insights. Chrysalis emphasized addiction as the source of the ongoing insanity, as well as our mental and physical deterioration. Staff taught that we were addicts who could not consume any drug, including alcohol, and provided guidance about how to maneuver through triggers. NA's "one day at a time" mantra helped me because I could achieve one day even though I still lacked confidence in attaining long-term sobriety. I scrutinized other addicts' headway in rebuilding their lives, benefited from mutual support, and categorized the group as a guide toward sanity.

At thirty days clean, I needed documents from the house so I could apply for state disability. Staff let me take the subway alone once Doc promised to pick me up and drive me home to gather the paperwork. For most of the ride, I felt excited about being on my own and seeing him. I could feel his arms around me in a strong hug and thought we might have time to have sex after lunch at the taqueria. I thought about how I'd kept using for years because I thought the agony would be unbearable if allowed to surface. But maybe I was wrong. Perhaps recovery might reduce my pain. So far, I'd endured much less stress than I'd feared and less than what I had suffered from meth. And already my mental processing had improved as the fog and confusion had begun to dissipate.

I made a list of the good reasons to get sober and the positives that might increase my odds. Assuming Doc would let me return, I lived in a safe environment and he offered stability and a long-term partnership. I'd just taken an IQ test and, much to my relief, obtained results similar to my high school scores. So maybe my lengthy addiction hadn't permanently damaged my brain, at least as to this aspect. I still had my degree and probably could work partway back up the corporate ladder.

But then I broke out in a sweat as the opportunities I'd thrown away rolled through my head. Berkeley law school, legal jobs at good firms, and mid-level administrative jobs at high-tech companies. I'd even blown the word processing position at ATEL. I hadn't held onto a job for longer than eighteen months, ever. So now, instead of being a lawyer, I'd be stuck forever in low-end jobs because I was in my thirties with no references and the choppiest of work histories. I hyperventilated over remorse and guilt and humiliation, then settled down into regret and resignation.

Until my mind swerved to my speed stash. My pulse picked up and joyful giddiness swept over me. I became engrossed in the idea of sticking a crank-filled needle in my arm. I visualized the blood filling the syringe barrel and pushing off. I could feel the warm glow spread through my body. I exhaled an "aah" and looked up.

Shit! We'd reached my stop. I leapt through the doors right before they closed and headed to the exit. I let Doc hug me, for a second, then turned him toward the car.

At the house while I dug through my files, Doc went to the garage. I dashed to a meth cache and into the bathroom and shot up, easily, in a partly recovered vein. I returned half the remainder of the crank to my hiding spot and shoved the rest into my purse along with one hypodermic. I waited three weeks to use the speed I took back to Chrysalis, which I considered progress. Although staff didn't catch me, I realized I risked being booted out and thought about Doc's possible reaction to this. But using twice in five months was the best I could do.

As the weeks went by, I was mostly clean and slept more regularly, so I regained sufficient concentration to read books and blasted through the recovery materials and Chrysalis's small library. At my request, Doc brought the crossword puzzles magazines from my tweak stack. I journaled and began to evaluate my trauma history, my addiction, the turmoil, my recovery thoughts, and future hopes. I actively participated in classes and completed all the assignments, which reminded me of prior academic accomplishments.

And I cultivated connections with the women. I bonded and shared, attempted to be honest as we explored our lives, tried to give useful advice, and supported them as together we clawed our way out of addiction. Almost all had abuse histories, physical and sexual, and most had abused drugs by high school. As a group, we felt confused by our deterioration and extensive losses. The familiar outlets to handle our feelings—drugs and chaos—were not available, and we floundered with normal interactions and activities, reasonable rules, and treating one another with courtesy and concern rather than lashing out. Still, at Chrysalis I was with my people, women who understood my agony and my struggles. It was a relief to be in a group where I didn't have to hide who I was or all my mistakes, which helped me feel less alone and less of a unique fuckup.

And, like the other women, I wanted to be fixed in a few months and found it hard to accept the counselors' warnings that it would take years to reconstruct my life. ◉

# CHAPTER 33
## Atheist Challenges

BEING AN ATHEIST proved one of my biggest and most frustrating recovery challenges. After all, what was the point of seeking assistance if the supposed experts didn't try to find a viable option for me? Sometimes I was angry, faced with the familiar letdown by people who had an obligation to help. I thought about my mother, her general lack of concern and her marriage to Allan, and the police who downplayed the violence. I equated Chrysalis with the Princeton psychiatrist who ignored my substance use disorder and Dr. Smith with his pretense of addiction expertise.

The idea that some people would be better served by other approaches did not exist at my rehab. Chrysalis staff and NA members at meetings, too, expressed antipathy whenever I challenged 12-step orthodoxy. Whenever I asked why the cure would be spiritual if addiction is a disease, the verbatim response from both was we would not "debate the book." They also maintained that if someone in a 12-step program relapsed, the sole explanation was she failed to do everything she'd been advised. If we all buckled under and swallowed the program whole, we'd be fine. It also concerned me that attributing victory to faith prevented the women from experiencing deserved pride. If success results from turning over your will and your life, how can you feel the concomitant sense of accomplishment?

Still, I don't imagine that the Chrysalis counselors badgered me to relinquish my power to God out of a lack of concern. They'd recovered under the 12-step model and had been told this was the only way. These women had rehabilitation counselor certificates, but that education apparently did not include training about secular recovery programs. Instead, I think in an honest effort to address the problem, Chrysalis staff pointed me to the agnostic chapter of the Big Book as the way an atheist could recover through the 12-steps. Excited at this solution, I raced to my room and read that section, to no avail because the authors just provided weak arguments against agnosticism and mandated belief in a higher power.

Despite my objections, Chrysalis forced me to work the steps. For Step 1, "We admitted we were powerless over our addiction, that our lives had become unmanageable." I agreed my life was tumultuous and I couldn't calm it while abusing meth. When I also wrote, though, that while in active addiction I did feel powerless, this was a false perception. I acknowledged it probably was true I'd never be able to use in moderation. But if addicts were powerless over their drug use, they could never stop. The counselor told me I was focused on "semantics." She added, "I'm warning you, if you don't accept Step 1 without qualification, you are doomed to fail."

The next two steps require God or a higher power. Step 2 claims that only a higher power can restore you to sanity, and Step 3 insists you turn your will and your life over to the God of your understanding. I explained my atheism and confidence that supernatural beings belonged to the world of fantasy and wishful thinking. I reviewed the negative aspects of relinquishing your will or your life to anyone or anything, such as undermining confidence in your own ability to navigate the world. I suggested Chrysalis teach us how to set goals and develop realistic plans to achieve them. I thought we'd benefit from more emphasis on the impact of our efforts on our odds of success.

For Steps 4 and 8, I did my best to write a "moral inventory" and a list of people I had harmed although I complained about the negative focus and wished we'd evaluate our positive attributes and how these could help build a solid recovery. Many of the remaining steps don't bother to use higher power terminology but instead reference God. I didn't admit the nature of my wrongs to God or ask Him to remove my shortcomings or defects of character or have a spiritual awakening or any of the rest of it. I wrote "not applicable" or "I'll strive to do this for myself."

Even separate from the higher power and powerlessness issues, I distrusted the premise at Chrysalis and in NA that one treatment approach would rescue everyone. It seemed to me that each person needed treatment tailored to their personal circumstances. For example, I agreed that a thirty-day program would not be sufficient for me considering my twenty-year drug history, the severity of my addiction, and the need to address the abuse and trauma. My rehab colleagues struggled with unique blends of a variety of issues: mental health, physical health, marital, parental, other family, employment, housing, and financial, as well as different personalities, learning styles, problem-solving approaches, and religious beliefs. I found it difficult to presume that the same solution applied to them all.

For all these reasons, I pushed back on staff efforts to force me to comply with the powerless and faith aspects of 12-steps. I chose to assume that atheists could obtain long-term recovery, despite the resistance I faced every time I suggested this. I did worry, though, that perhaps I was arrogant to conclude I knew better than my teachers what would work for me—a particular concern because I knew my brain hadn't operated properly for years and I'd made many poor decisions during that time. This created a gnawing unease and sometimes panic when the "maybe they're right and it's impossible for me" message pushed to the forefront of my brain. I'd take a few deep breaths, smoke a few cigarettes, and return to my decision to keep an open mind and find the ideas that would benefit me. I also decided not to argue with the other women because I didn't want to undermine their efforts. If a belief in God or a higher power bolstered their recovery, I was happy for them.

Although I succeeded in defiance of the mandates to accept an incompatible faith-based system, I did resent the danger created by the purported experts. If I had accepted that a higher power was necessary to attain sobriety, I would have given up because I could not satisfy that prerequisite. Instead, since the 12-step model wasn't a viable path for me, I analyzed that program and applied the parts I found valuable. ●

## CHAPTER 34
# NA Year One

I GRADUATED CHRYSALIS in January 1994 and moved back in with Doc. While in rehab, I'd tried to mend our relationship. For thirty days we weren't allowed visitors. He only wrote once, which terrified me. Afterward, Doc did participate in couples counseling, which provided some optimism. Still, he sometimes yelled in frustration and pain about how he couldn't trust me, I was a burden, I'd forced him to care for me, I wasn't a partner but more like a dying sister, and he wasn't certain he could get over the damage.

Once home, although I knew relapse might be the last straw, the desire to use crank competed with my slight hope that I might be able to maintain sobriety. My brain often became absorbed with nostalgic memories of powerful shots after I'd had a break. Even when I studied my scar-mottled arms and envisioned jabbing myself for hours as I hunted for a good vein, the drive to flood my body with speed overwhelmed me. I'd tell myself I'd entered rehab with the goal to use less, not stop, because that wasn't realistic. Or I only had enough meth stashed for a two-day run, so I could deplete that and not resupply. And I'd used just twice in five months in rehab, though I'd had access during a Christmas visit, which proved I'd progressed. But then I'd remember the occasional peace of my new calmer self and my hopes to make forward strides in my life—and Doc's anger-twisted face. And back-and-forth and back-and-forth.

On the ninth day, I drafted a resume to send to temp agencies that offered part-time jobs, which Doc agreed was sufficient as a start. We ate at our favorite Chinese restaurant and watched television. In the background, though, the debate raged.

After Doc fell asleep, I slid out of bed, tiptoed to the door, and pulled it shut. Heart thumping, I sort of raced with soft steps to my drug kit. My hands shook as I prepared the shot. I tied off my arm and paused to quell my excitement, so I could get a hit on the first try, which I did. When a beautiful gush of blood spurted into the syringe, I had to go through the "settle down, Mary Beth" process again before I pushed the meth into my vein. I closed my eyes to focus on the sublime and divine chemicals that flooded my body. I forgot about Doc for a second and, in an outburst of happiness, drummed the wall with my palms. I jumped up and had to grab the towel rack as a swoon threatened to drop me to my knees. I collapsed on the toilet and waited fifteen minutes until my breathing slowed to a non-life-threatening rate.

Then I headed to my usual spot in the dining room to smoke, play solitaire, and work crosswords. I shot up twice more before the clock ordered me back to bed, before Doc's alarm would go off. A task of utmost importance.

*You just need to lie there for two hours. Pretend to wake up with him. Keep your shit together until he leaves for work.*

I did another crossword puzzle.

*It's okay. You can sneak into bed with him now. He'll be up in an hour and out the door in two. Then you can get high again.*

I glanced down into the mirror and noticed a pimple on my nose, which I popped. Then did a close survey of my face and squeezed a few blackheads.

*Stop! Stop. You still have time.*

As I rose from my chair, I heard the bedroom door open. I wondered if I'd put away the crank and syringes in my bathroom. Doc's quick steps up the hall, toward me, triggered a heart rate surge, on top of its meth-induced pace. I noticed the full ashtray, a dead giveaway, then covered it with a newspaper. Doc stopped three feet away. I didn't dare look in his eyes.

"Hey, baby. Your snoring woke me about an hour ago."

"Show me your arms."

As the cliché goes, an accurate cliché it turns out, my stomach dropped to the floor. "Look, I just . . ."

At three times his normal volume, Doc assaulted me with a barrage of words. He couldn't do this anymore. Our counselor told him if I used, he should confront me and leave. He didn't know if he would demand I return to rehab or throw me out. Then he slammed the door behind him as he left.

For a few moments, I felt as if he'd beaten me with his fists rather than with vehemence and threats. I circled the table several times, muttering, "It will be okay. He's just upset. He'll change his mind." Then grabbed my speed and paraphernalia from the bathroom and shot up again.

But I did notice that, despite knowing the consequences and despite the minimal effort needed to avoid this catastrophe, I could not leave my crank. Not even for an hour, not even to hide my relapse, not even to save my relationship with Doc.

Afterward, I convinced him to let me find an NA sponsor and

promised to attend meetings and locate a therapist. And I decided recovery must be my primary priority. Each week, I went to individual therapy one night, couples therapy another, and attended five NA meetings, the latter because I'd been told that's all there was. My favorite was a smaller women's meeting, denigrated as a coffee klatch by others because it operated more as a support group. I appreciated the NA chips that recognized clean time as a symbol of my achievement, which increased my confidence, like when I attempted to use crank again a few more times. My connection would be unavailable or I didn't have enough cash. When I realized this, the urge already had subsided to the point I could implement the "just not today" approach. And I reminded myself I'd been through this before and had come out the other side.

For me, though, foremost, NA instilled hope I could recover. When hard-core addicts shared their stories, they modeled methods to build a better future. While they all struggled, and many relapsed, some, as sick as I was, prevailed, which encouraged me during the tough days. I watched some members progress in incremental steps, whereas others flamed out when they pushed toward immediate major change. I chose to take it slow, to be satisfied with an upward trajectory to increase my odds of success. Since I'd succumbed to full-fledged addiction as a teenager, I had to construct a healthy life from scratch. As I witnessed success, I began to dream, then plan, then implement a course of action.

In addition to sobriety, I decided my top priorities were Doc, work, and debt reduction. I targeted changes that would improve multiple fronts. For example, my emotions undermined my job performance and my relationship with Doc because I reverted to aggressive self-defense at the first sign of even mild conflict. We tackled this in couples counseling, and I began to evaluate my work interactions. I'd give my therapist examples and she'd help me address the underlying anxiety. I began to hear my harsh tone and learned to apologize for my part when conversations went off the rails. Of course, all this was a process or, in NA terms, progress not perfection.

Also, since I attended NA, I'd joined a society and could have human contact almost any time, whether at meetings, various events, or by phone. I later learned recovery support groups in general provide value because they offer an avenue to bond with others. Recovery friends reinforce the sobriety goal, are a reality check for nostalgic drug stories, and provide peer pressure to stay on track. Instead of struggling alone, support meetings are a fellowship that can help guide you forward.

I tried not to let my misfit status undermine my recovery, but it was a struggle. I respected that NA aided some and appreciated when a couple of members said, "Take what you need and leave the rest." But that caveat was limited. Everyone insisted that failure to accept a higher power and work the steps meant I was running on self-will and would relapse. Since I'd promised Doc, I zeroed in on a more flexible sponsor. Nevertheless, when we couldn't overcome my objections to the initial steps, we agreed to part ways. After this, I stopped broadcasting my lack of faith and, when I spoke at meetings, limited myself to NA concepts I found useful. When I accrued months, then years of sobriety, I received the usual accolades at NA meetings. But no one who knew I was an atheist ever congratulated me for finding my own path or used my success to revisit the "must" of accepting a higher power.

Members often claimed no other approach had 12-step's success rate. However, when I asked for the names of these other options, they clarified that they really meant doing it on your own. When I asked for evidence, no one could point to any. I am sure in pure numbers this was true because NA and AA are huge. But in percentage terms, it was clear from the constant churn of newcomers that the relapse rate was high. The 12-steppers I knew refused to recognize that the success of some, but the failure of many, at least signified this program might not be perfect.

I continued to analyze the ideas underlying the steps. As to Step 1's powerlessness, I concurred that addiction could overtake me again if I did not build a strong recovery and pay attention to this risk. I also gleaned that I'd severed my connection to my true self when I ingested chemicals for two decades that altered my brain and harmed my body. My substance use disorder had diminished my capacity to understand and interact with the world. I had always assumed my intelligence and innate abilities would define my future. Instead, my addiction held control. This was a painful realization, including the agony of lost potential and missed opportunities.

I reinterpreted the Step 3 command to turn my will and my life over to a higher power as teaching that I had limited control, even over my own life. I should take steps to reach my goals but could not determine the ultimate outcome. For example, I could search for a job, create a great resume, respond to want ads, and prepare for the interview, but I might not land the position. My efforts impacted the likelihood of the desired outcome, but other factors contributed to the result. This interpretation released some of the pressure I felt, with every decision and action, to be perfect or face doom.

Also, NA emphasizes the need to avoid situations that may trigger relapse: the people, places, and things that remind the addict of the drug. I've since learned that science backs this up. When someone with substance use disorder encounters a trigger, or cue, the "go" system can overwhelm the part of the brain that's telling them "no, this is a bad idea" because of the consequences. For innumerable individuals with substance use disorder, time, practice, and reinforcement are required to stop this sequence of events.

The good news is that, with experience, healthy choices also can become automatic, which is why it gets easier to maintain sobriety over time. It sounds trite to say you stay clean by staying clean, but that is one recovery truth. Days turn into weeks turn into months turn into years. At that point, you're likely to stay sober. ❧

# CHAPTER 35
## Secular Year One

I VACILLATED BETWEEN CERTAINTY I COULD RECOVER without God and apprehension when faced with the universal consensus I could not. At six months clean I wondered if, perhaps, contrary to everything I'd been told, an alternative program existed that might fit better.

In 1994, before the home computer revolution, the research proved challenging. I'd asked around at NA, to no avail. So one day I grabbed the Yellow Pages, flipped to "Libraries," and jumped into my car. I scoured the stacks for recovery resources but unearthed only AA materials. Having gained seventy pounds since I'd quit meth, I perused a weight-management manual. In the appendix, I glommed onto the entry for Women for Sobriety, described as a secular counterpoint to AA. I burst into an immense smile and inhaled my first deep breath since I'd trudged up Chrysalis's stairs.

WFS founder Jean Kirkpatrick developed an alternate philosophy for female alcoholics, the original modern option to faith-based recovery. Addiction was a life-threatening problem, but empowered females could let go of the past and take control of their lives. Kirkpatrick described the dangers of forcing women to concentrate on weakness, such as the 12-step programs ideas about powerlessness and surrender to an external higher power. Women's egos are not too big but rather too small, so those newly sober didn't benefit from deflation. They need to be built up, to develop their competency, because this provides a strong foundation for recovery. WFS incorporates positive thinking, their version of the cognitive behavioral belief that, if you think differently, you behave and feel different. Focused on emotional and spiritual growth, WFS does not provide specific answers but rather encourages each woman to find the individual path right for her since she is responsible for every aspect of her life. WFS meetings emphasize nonjudgmental sharing and positive self-talk to reinforce that its members are capable, caring, and compassionate women.

As I drove to a WFS meeting for the first time, Tom Petty's "Refugee" came on the radio, my favorite song, with references to being kidnapped and kicked around some. Tom then provides encouragement because, even with these traumas, "you don't have to live like a refugee." At this moment, the song also fit with the steps I was taking to build a recovery approach that worked for me. I rolled down the window and sang loud.

When I arrived, I explained to the meeting leader that I'd been a methamphetamine addict. "Am I welcome here since WFS is for alcohol addiction?"

"Absolutely. You are our sister in recovery."

I took another deep breath, relieved I could participate. When it was my turn to introduce myself the WFS way, I hesitated for a second as I feared my voice would tremble. Shivers raced up my spine when I announced, "I'm Mary Beth and I'm a competent woman."

I replaced a large NA meeting with this group of about a dozen women because of the program's philosophy and the benefit of the smaller number. Everyone spoke, which allowed us to keep tabs on one another's progress and challenges. Instead of fixating on drug histories, we discussed WFS principles, how to find enthusiasm for our lives, and provided feedback on sobriety obstacles.

WFS fit well with my evolving concept of myself. I did not mind identifying as an addict initially because it seemed important to drill that into my consciousness, but I grew less comfortable. I no longer was an active addict but rather had an addiction history. In modern terms, my substance use disorder was in early remission. At the time, I would've said the addict label did not capture my essence whereas "competent woman" empowered me. I also felt comfortable with these women in a way I couldn't with 12-steppers since I didn't have to hide my truth or justify my disagreements with the program.

At WFS, I learned of Rational Recovery, from which today's SMART Recovery evolved, which maintained that substance use disorder is the pursuit of intoxicating pleasure despite the turmoil that results. And it taught that free will sufficed to overcome addiction. RR highlighted that, once solidly established, recovery does not require ongoing attention, which contrasted with NA's insistence we attend meetings forever. RR literature emphasized lifetime abstinence and relapse prevention. But the meetings I attended mostly bashed the 12-steps, which I found reassuring, then tiresome. The RR leader told me I didn't belong there anyway because I had been clean for nine months and had my addiction under control. So I stopped attending.

In RR, I learned of Secular Organization for Sobriety, now overtaken by its child LifeRing Secular Recovery, which focused on each addict's responsibility for her own recovery, rational decision-making, and the power of mutual support. SOS explained the science of substance use disorder and emphasized replacing drug experiences with sober experiences. SOS agreed with 12-step programs that the first year is best used for reentry into the world and cautioned against major decisions, to let the mental cobwebs clear. SOS philosophy included that newly sober addicts often do struggle and challenges arise, but it's a winnable fight if you commit to remaining sober no matter what, known as the sobriety priority. Life is a series of decisions, large and small, and you attain recovery when you make choices that encourage sobriety. Current science supports this idea in that cognitive and behavioral changes rewire the brain and the sober patterns become habitual. The result of neural plasticity, this rewiring begins within weeks of abstinence and continues for several years.

With exposure to all these ideas, I became confident I could find a path out of addiction without God. I synthesized pieces from these programs, added to what I pulled from 12-steps, and built what LifeRing calls a personal recovery plan. As foundational concepts, I would take charge of my own recovery, use my intellect and analytical skills, apply my newfound knowledge, and seek support as needed. When faced with a choice, I tried to pause and consider which option best met my goals, with sobriety at the top of the list. I congratulated myself on my progress because this motivated and sustained me on my journey. With each success, my prowess and determination grew. My recovery also benefited from a change in outlook as I moved from hopeless to somewhat hopeful to cautiously optimistic. These positive experiences provided a critical counterweight to the relapse-risky feelings around my loss of meth, loss of the bizarrely familiar addict life, and loss of addict friends and our shared misery and camaraderie. As I thrived, I began to value my new world more than the old, which enabled me to shove away the "wouldn't it be great to get high" thoughts.

Near the end of my first year as I cleaned out my filing cabinet as part of getting organized, I found my college transcripts. I turned the envelope over and over, then placed it on the ground. I ran to Doc, dragged him to our office, and pointed. "I'm afraid to open it."

"Why? You did well, right? These aren't your law school grades."

"It's been ten years. I can't quite remember. It's like I think I did, but I'm not sure. I mean, I worked half-time. Even during my better drug years, I used too much, too often. The chaos, the LA rape, Martin—I was in such pain. And these are hard schools. Maybe college success is just a story I've told myself."

"I don't think so. Why don't you look?"

I picked up the packet and pulled out two sheets, one with my UCLA grades and the other Berkeley, both a fifty-fifty split between As and Bs. I jumped up and threw my arms around Doc. I felt like I grew a foot taller. Memories flooded my mind, and I remembered who I used to be: the special attention I'd received from teachers when young, permission to read any book in the library in second grade, and my high SAT score. As I pondered all this over the next months, sometimes the pain ripped through me because I'd lost so much. But these accomplishments also encouraged me. I began to feel connected to my younger self, the girl I'd been, and even the adult I was meant to be. I started to imagine maybe I could be that woman.

Maybe it wasn't too late. ◦

# CHAPTER 36
## Cindy

I'VE ALWAYS CONSIDERED MY SISTER, Cindy, a war buddy. Twenty months apart, we were two vulnerable little girls attached to each other for love and support. We experienced the chaos, abuse, and neglect together. We both turned to drugs at a young age to help us cope, and we both became addicted. We smoked our first joint together. We used alcohol and other drugs together many times in our youth. And I put the first needle in Cindy's arm.

Heroin became her drug of choice for much of her adult life, although she varied her primary chemical dependence through the years as she was less committed to her favorite than I was to meth. She worked intermittently and mostly had lived in dives, often with abusive boyfriends, or spent months homeless.

A year into my recovery, I felt a powerful urge to try to save Cindy. I understood her suffering from the abuse and addiction and felt guilty that I'd survived the war when she still might not. I envisioned her dying from an overdose or living her current miserable existence for decades more. I wanted my sister back, her true self, and hoped to shine a light on the path to happiness.

When I visited the family for Christmas, I invited Cindy to break-fast. To pick her up, I pulled off the expressway onto a dirt road. The complex, if you could call it that, was eight small duplexes, four on each side of a narrow, rutted driveway. The muddy brown paint matched the color of the soil, visible between the buildings and under-neath the broken-down cars and abandoned furniture. I honked, as instructed. I guessed because Cindy was too embarrassed to let me inside the apartment and wanted to avoid a confrontation with her asshole boyfriend.

She'd gussied up for our date, her hair smoothed behind her ears, and she had put on a bit of makeup. Although her clothes were faded, they were clean. The leather jacket she'd bragged about had discolored patches as if it had been in the rain a few too many times. She tossed her purse to the floor and slammed the door shut. A quick peck and a "let's get going," and we headed out.

"Where are we eating, Mary Beth?"

"Crackers. Mom said they make excellent French toast."

"Oh, wow. That's expensive. I figured McDonald's."

"I think it's just regular breakfast prices."

We chatted about how much she enjoyed Arizona, where Mom and her latest boyfriend had moved the year before—with Cindy's kids as the court had awarded Mom custody due to Cindy's substance use disorder. That is why Cindy also lived in Arizona, so she could keep her visitation rights.

At the restaurant, after we updated each other on how mutual friends were doing, I talked up Chrysalis, telling her how it wasn't perfect but still offered a solid recovery foundation for a reasonable price. I described how Doc and I were getting along, and I was paying off debt now that I could hold a job. And how surprised I was that I could, in fact, stay clean. I reached over to hold her hand and grab her full attention.

"Any interest in rehab?"

"Aw, Mary Beth. Yeah, sure, it would be great to change my life. But I can't afford that."

"What if I paid for Chrysalis?"

"Really? I don't know. Steve would try to stop me."

"Ninety days. You could clean up. That would help your relationship. You could work again. Wouldn't that make him happy?"

"Maybe. Let me think about it."

The following week, in tears from a Steve blowup, she called me collect and agreed to treatment. I convinced Chrysalis to push her up the list and admit her two weeks later. I paid for her ticket and picked her up at the airport.

"I don't know if I can do this. Chrysalis said I couldn't even talk to Steve for a month. A month! He might figure I'm never coming back and get a new girlfriend."

"Look, Cindy, I went through my own fears around Doc, because we were in a bad place at the time. Try to focus on where you could be in a month. Sober. Healthier. Calmer. Ready to start a better life."

"All right, all right. I'll go."

And she did. And three days later Chrysalis called and said Cindy insisted on leaving. So I drove to Oakland and did my best to convince her to stay—to no avail. I was so upset from fear and so angry that she was letting herself down like this that I sent her home on a Greyhound bus.

Afterward, through the years, now and again, I'd share some thoughts about recovery. But mostly I let her see the value of sobriety by my example. And I kept a lifeline open between us. I tried not to be judgmental about the consequences to her kids from living with our mother, who wasn't a good parent. I did struggle with trepidation that I'd lose her, and soon, especially when she disappeared for months. But I didn't harangue her about it when she showed up again.

I understood Cindy's inability to drag herself out of the hell of addiction. Damage from a horrendous childhood and from early drug use becomes deeply embedded in the brain. A tremendous effort is required, over a long period of time, to recover from trauma and addiction. I knew I had some advantages over Cindy, such as a better partner and living environment. And I considered that perhaps addiction and trauma had altered Cindy's brain differently than mine, in a way that made it more difficult for her to find recovery because, even today, the science cannot explain why some addicts succeed in their initial efforts whereas others require multiple attempts to stabilize.

Fast forward a few years, to when I traveled to Arizona for work and arranged to meet Cindy at a lovely café. As I entered, I saw her hunched over a table in the back. I realized I probably should've selected a McDonald's as she wore her typical attire of worn T-shirt and faded jeans. She hadn't dyed her hair in a while, so the red stopped midway. Today she perhaps could pretend she paid a lot of money for the ombre look, but at the time this just announced a lack of self-care. As Cindy appeared somewhat emaciated but had gained weight since our last encounter, I presumed she was using drugs less frequently. Still, any stranger who guessed her age would overshoot by ten years.

As I approached, Cindy attempted a weak grin. She hated to smile broadly because two teeth had been knocked out by a boyfriend and several others had half rotted. "Thanks for taking the time to see me. You look great. Love the suit." We both laughed.

For the next thirty minutes, I listened to her litany of difficulties. Her live-in boyfriend couldn't find a job, purportedly despite best efforts. The landlord would evict them shortly if they didn't catch up on their rent. She just had been laid off because her boss was a bitch and didn't like her. Could I please, please, please help?

I told her I was frustrated that she continued to live with the abusive dick. I reminded her that I'd paid their rent just three months prior. She'd promised to repay me but never mentioned the debt again. Not that I'd expected to recoup, but she'd made such a big deal out of giving her word. Cindy shrugged. And I wrote a check, to the landlord. And I paid many times after that over the years, which I resented sometimes—not because of the money, but because I was aggravated that she continued to live in the chaos created by drugs and abusive partners who refused to work.

I am happy to report, though, that Cindy eventually attended community college and earned an associate degree. While her boyfriend choices remain problematic, she has worked steadily for several years and is in much better health. And our war buddy bond continues as strong as ever. •

# CHAPTER 37
# Recovery Year Two

IN 1995, YEAR TWO, I continued to tackle my sobriety but also targeted what I called Big R Recovery. That requires me to reconnect to my authentic self and develop my healthy and competent parts, to minimize the residual effects of the abuse and neglect, and to blossom into the best Mary Beth that I can be.

I focused on the WFS and SOS tenets of self-empowerment and being responsible for my own recovery. Witnessing others succeed without God lifted a great weight from my shoulders. I tried to release my resentment toward those who put my recovery at risk with the falsehood that there was only one path. Still, I believed it important, in my early recovery, to pause before I rejected suggestions. So I persisted in my search for ideas, 12-step meetings included.

I agreed with Rational Recovery that substance use disorder recovery shouldn't require constant and eternal focus. I wanted to reach the point where my urge to use speed, or any mood-altering substance, faded into the background. Considering the depths and length of my addiction, I wasn't concerned I'd forget the horrors. Yet, as 12-steps and SOS disagreed with this premise, I reinforced my

decision not to play around the edges. So, for example, I now refor-
mulated Step 1's powerlessness into the precept "I lack the power to
use in moderation" and avoided addictive medication and even des-
serts made with alcohol.

As another technique, I reviewed my core strengths. In childhood, before the worst abuse and addiction, I'd been smart, verbal,
and precocious. In high school, even as my substance use disorder
escalated, I'd excelled. In college, when I'd had partial control over my
drug dependence, I'd achieved impressive grades and worked part-
time and dealt with trauma and Martin's abuse. I'd been accepted to a
prestigious law school. I'd managed my money, contrary to the spend-
thrift modeling of my mother. I'd learned to cook, not well but well
enough, built friendships, negotiated with roommates, and satisfied
my shared-housing responsibilities. These memories were excruciating because I had lost so much, yet they were also encouraging.

For the next ten years, in the midst of my post-college addiction, I'd developed computer and organizational skills. My declining
income and periods of unemployment, rather than excessive spending, caused my financial problems. I'd partnered with Doc, so I had a
stable living environment. I had some friends, several of whom didn't
abuse drugs. Lucky in my health, I'd dodged the intravenous drug use
diseases such as HIV and hepatitis. As a middle-class white woman,
I didn't have an extensive criminal record, notwithstanding that I'd
carried drugs every day and had interacted with the police multiple
times due to traffic violations.

Also, in meetings, I realized I didn't have unique pain. Many
people had been abused or raped or both, yet now thrived. Others
had navigated losses, family challenges, or mental health issues. Even
friends without addiction histories could lose their bearings, but then

climb out of the abyss. This knowledge convinced me that the promised land existed if I worked hard to reach it. As long as I kept the chemicals out, my brain could guide me forward, and I could evolve into a capable woman.

Considering all this, I decided to expand my recovery to include the trauma as a prerequisite to living my ideal life. If I didn't better manage my anguish, I risked turning to speed to ease my pain or, to state it in positive SOS terms, dealing with emotions will desensitize you to the drug's pull. Without meth, I felt more deeply. My knee-jerk reaction was to box up my feelings and shove them down, which cut me off from myself and prevented further growth. Plus, terror often washed over me, sometimes for days, when I thought of facing my abuse wounds. I needed to overcome this despondency, which threatened to drag me down into sober misery.

So I located a therapist with abuse and addiction expertise. During this work, I grieved my short-changed childhood and related adult destruction. I even considered how much easier it would be if I turned the wheel of the car and drove off a cliff. Yet, as promised by my counselors, feelings and memories became prominent in pieces, not all at once. I started to learn how to allow my emotions to bubble up so I could examine them and discover what they were telling me, whether about the past, the present, or my fears for the future.

All my recovery work taught me a fundamental concept. Trauma and neglect probably were the primary drivers of my substance use disorder. But the parents and abusers who broke me were not going to fix me. I had to repair myself. As WFS teaches, I would no longer be victimized by my past. This didn't mean I had to travel this path alone, though. Self-empowerment also means seeking out the assistance you need: professional help, support groups, recovery buddies, or family. If one avenue fails to yield the desired result, reevaluate and give it another shot.

For an effective recovery plan, I needed to counterbalance the negative parts of being meth free. I missed the rush and the high, so I would glamorize the experience. Plus, my life could seem mundane as I slowed down the pace and no longer raced from crisis to crisis. I'd relive the joy as I anticipated the first shot and the power of the meth. Then I'd force these images from my mind and remind myself that if I picked up crank, I'd be lost again. When I reminisced about intense telephone discussions, I reality checked myself. On most drug days I couldn't concentrate long enough to chat or was so manic I dominated the conversation. To talk myself out of labeling my new lifestyle boring, I reviewed the parties I'd skipped because I was in the tweaky phase of a drug run. Now, I visited with friends, remembered birthdays, and attended recovery events. I didn't create chaos and new problems but instead set goals and moved forward. On occasion, I could believe that from this base I could handle unexpected challenges, if something went amiss, instead of sinking into a pit of despair.

In this second recovery year I reduced down to three recovery meetings per week to pursue other activities. I'd gained seventy pounds, I think due to an imbalanced metabolism from the crank, so I joined Weight Watchers to educate myself on weight loss and food management. I quit smoking, which I'd started so young, puffing on a Salem as I played jacks behind the bowling alley with Cindy and Sharon. Doc and I attended various speaker events and joined a film club. I was appointed to the board of the local chapter of the National Organization for Women and later accepted a role at the state level. I volunteered for my political party during elections. These steps enhanced my confidence, provided intellectual stimulation, and allowed me to develop new relationships. As Women for Sobriety says, I was a competent woman who had much to give life.

I slipped up along the way. I overreacted to slights or any hint of criticism when I felt weak or vulnerable. Foreboding could consume me as I imagined my achievements yanked away due to a mistake. I judged myself weak for my failure to shake off these thoughts. At times I ate to excess and smoked like a chimney to regulate my mood, or I'd resort to tweaky behaviors like playing solitaire or solving crosswords for hours. And I'd be aggressive with Doc, such as when I realized he'd never investigated how to help me, even though each year I further deteriorated before his eyes. In response, he'd express anger and pain about things I did in my addiction, which enraged me because I didn't want to accept responsibility for my behavior during a meth haze.

As a result, for much of my early recovery, neither of us knew whether we would stay together, and we struggled to steady our relationship. I found it difficult to see Doc's heartache or address it when I did and, instead, overwhelmed him with logical arguments to prove him wrong. I failed to appreciate the generally calm Doc and worried he didn't love me when he didn't explode every time I pushed him.

Yet, as I recovered and settled down, Doc's natural good nature began to reemerge. He supported my positive steps and encouraged me to continue to stretch myself, always confident I could succeed. We grew more skilled at responding with kindness to the other's thoughts and feelings, which built trust and bonded us. I now could relax and savor the peaceful joy of being together and appreciate how Doc nurtured me. I believed this partnership would sustain me in recovery and in life. At the end of year two, we booked a wedding venue. ●

# CHAPTER 38
## Mom

MY DIFFICULT RELATIONSHIP WITH MY MOTHER continued in recovery. Before getting sober, I'd not admitted my addiction to her. After I'd left home for college, she'd never mentioned my drug use. I almost wrote "she must have known," but perhaps not as I didn't see her often and she paid little attention to my life or my behavior. Six months after I graduated from Chrysalis, I came out to her during a phone call.

"So, I went to drug rehab and I'm clean and sober now."

"I know. I read the letters you wrote Cindy from that place since you sent them to my house. Don't worry. I won't tell anyone. Would just embarrass us both. You girls and your drugs. I thought you'd outgrown all that."

"Jesus, Mom, those letters were private."

I later pondered this conversation. My mother had volunteered she'd violated a basic rule of life—don't read other people's mail—with no indication that she considered this problematic. She suspected her daughters kept secrets from her, secrets she had a right to know, so the letters were fair game. Plus, I was reminded again that Mom accepted no responsibility for two of her children developing drug addictions. Yet she rejected any suggestion that our upbringing was a root cause. From my mother's point of view, I believe, our substance use disorders arose out of thin air.

But, on the positive side, although Cindy regarded Mom in the same vein as I did, Albert loved her. He even moved in with her to help them both financially, which benefited my relationship with him because he wasn't much of a phone talker. And I could spend time with him when Doc and I went to Arizona every Christmas.

On one hand, Mom did accept custody of Cindy's kids, which probably was better than foster care. Her mothering skills had improved somewhat, too. She was more affectionate, and her over-reactions to mistakes or irritants, and the hitting, seemed to be at a lower level than with my generation. But, Mom also left them alone to pursue her gambling addiction. When the oldest was seven, she woke up in the middle of the night to find my mother gone. To try to alleviate some of Mom's stress, we took the kids for a week or two every year so she could visit her sister in New Jersey. I even tried to talk Doc into taking custody, but three children were too much for him.

Since she was raising our beloved nieces and nephew, the kids, as Doc and I call them, I felt obliged when Mom demanded financial help. The difficulty was that, in addition to her general spend-thrift habits, she had a gambling addiction to the point where she'd declared bankruptcy. I believed she often turned to me to offset her losses although she would cite house maintenance or car repair bills to justify these requests. I tried to find balance, to give appropriate help but not waste my hard-earned money. Rather than hand over cash, I would wire funds to the mortgage company and paid vendors directly.

I once refused to send five hundred dollars a few days after she'd returned from Las Vegas. In hysterics, she tried a new tack. "Well, you clearly don't care about me. I might as well kill myself." I didn't believe she would carry out the threat but called the local sheriff's office and asked them to check. An officer phoned an hour later to report they'd found her washing dishes.

A brief respite occurred when Mom received an inheritance from Grandmom O'Connor. However, instead of paying off her home, within two years she'd gambled away the money and confronted foreclosure. She insisted I purchase her house. Instead, I researched her local real estate market and encouraged her to downsize. I located a realtor, explained my mother's requirements and budget, and discussed options. I flew to Arizona to spend a weekend house hunting with her.

As she dressed, I noticed an unopened envelope on the kitchen table.

"Mom, you didn't review the packet the realtor sent?"

"Why bother? I'm only doing this because you're making me."

"If you don't want to move, that's your choice. What alternative plan do you have? Other than me borrowing against my house to buy you out? Which isn't going to happen."

"Why? I can pay you instead of the bank."

"But you don't pay the bank."

She glided out of her room, full makeup and hair well-coiffed yet slightly too blond. Her white slacks and satin blouse suggested upscale Scottsdale rather than the remote edge of Phoenix. In this costume, I thought, she intended to charm the realtor's attention away from her financial straits.

I grabbed my purse and headed to the rental car. Once inside, I closed my eyes and took a few deep breaths to calm my "I've got to deal with my mother all day" anxiety. Then I found myself jolted back into the world when Mom slammed the passenger door. I swiveled toward her with a sideways grin.

"Really? How about you don't break the car?"

As I drove, I mentioned a few of the listings. "The larger one in Apache Junction has a good floor plan and a deep lot."

"Apache Junction. You want me to live in the ghetto."

"It's a working-class town. And it's not far from the rest of the family."

"You are so selfish. Fill out a couple of papers and they'll hand you the one hundred twenty thousand dollars. I'd be happy to sign a contract. You could kick me out if I don't pay. I wouldn't even argue. You reject this simple solution. You refuse to help your own mother."

My mind considered various rational responses. However, my reserves already had been depleted.

"I've paid your bills in the past, and it doesn't solve the problem. Plus, it's not my fault you gambled away your inheritance."

I glanced over. My mother's eyes widened, then hardened into a harsh squint. Her mouth opened and closed as she sputtered incoherent sounds.

"You—fucking—bitch."

I activated the turn signal and peered into the left mirror, then I moved us into the middle lane of the expressway.

A punch landed near my right ear. I closed my eyes as my head bounced forward from the blow. She pounded my skull with both fists twice more. Then twice more. My heart wailed and my mind shrieked. *Jesus Christ. Not again.*

I slammed on the brakes and lifted my arm to protect my face. The car behind us screeched to a halt. The horn blared. She grabbed a clump of my curls and pulled hard. My neck jerked toward her. Searing pain. Extracted hair floated in the air and glistened in the sunlight.

"Mom! Mom. Knock it off."

I seized her arm. We were rolling forward. I released her and threw the car into park. Awash in fear and frustration, I wanted to pummel her. But she was my mother. I pivoted toward her with both hands upturned in a defensive posture.

A driver, forced to go around, screamed at us. "Get outta the road, you crazy idiots. You'll get someone killed."

Mom pounded the dashboard. "Who the fuck do you think you are?"

My every muscle contracted. My chest heaved. Her fists loosened to open palms. She indiscriminately slapped me several times, then lowered her arms. She whispered, "I'm the mother. I'm the mother."

I scowled at her and shook my head. I put the car in gear and maneuvered us into the right lane. I pulled into a parking lot and exited the car. I paced back and forth. My shoulders rose and fell as I struggled to control my rage.

My mother jumped out. She raced around the rear of the vehicle and toward me. I turned to face her. I straightened my spine and stood tall. I held my hands by my side. I clenched and unclenched my fists. She stopped three feet from me.

I stared at her. She had attacked me when I was driving fifty miles per hour on a busy thoroughfare. Her rage had overcome even her basic survival instincts. And her furor could be triggered so easily. I could not trust this woman, ever, on any level.

"Do that again, and I will have you thrown in jail."

She glared at me as she walked back to the car. Neither of us spoke as we continued the drive to the realtor.

In the following weeks, I recognized that my comment had spurred the assault. I often could not predict when she would fly off the handle. This time, though, I knew I'd upset her if I criticized her over the lost inheritance. When I returned fire, I satisfied the angry little girl inside me but then suffered the consequences. Moreover, although I spoke the truth, no positive outcome would result from such a discussion. She would deny gambling or money management problems. So I'd put myself in danger for no good purpose.

I reflected on all her abuse, which took so many forms: physical, emotional, verbal. But I also evaluated my own worrisome reactions. I did not want to behave this way. I almost cut her out of my life. But really couldn't because we wanted access to the kids to maintain our close bond with them. Still, at thirty-five years old, taking a beating from my mother eliminated any remaining hope we could formulate a deeper relationship. I needed to accept that she would never transform.

I decided to disengage from her emotionally since I could not change her, only myself. In the long run, I hoped this would be enough to find a new equilibrium. I would control my words and my actions. I would approach her with civility yet establish and maintain strong boundaries. I would not retaliate when verbally barraged. I would have her arrested if she struck me again. I realized it would help if I could stop feeling the hurt and anger induced by our interactions. So I began to view her as a damaged person who did not tell the truth and who did not love me, at least not in a meaningful way. I also better understood that she had nothing positive to offer.

Although it took years to perfect, I learned to ignore her, laugh off her comments, hang up the phone, or leave the room. I helped her financially, when necessary, and refused to engage in debate when I said no to a request. I sometimes helped resolve her chaos but did not allow the insanity wave to overcome me. And I used Doc as a reality check. Was I being unreasonable, seeing things right, responding correctly?

As I distanced myself, my mother stepped up her attempts to force me to react. She created emergencies and made urgent demands. One day, years into my recovery, frustrated with another failed effort, she called me a junkie whore. This, I noticed, slid off my back. I no longer cared what she thought of me or what she said about me. To me, this was success. My mother had earned the relationship she had with me. I didn't owe her an emotional connection. My self-protection wasn't linked just to the way she'd treated me in childhood. It was that her same poor behavior continued.

The total lack of trust doomed our relationship more than anything else. Even on her deathbed, twenty years into my recovery, I could not bring myself to say a loving word to her, though I did my daughterly duty. The last few months I visited her regularly and spent the last week by her side. I spoke with her doctors and worked with the hospice so she received proper care. I brought her treats and spent time with her to make sure she was comfortable and had everything she needed. Neither of us attempted to have a final conversation. I saw a lot of risk and little potential benefit and did not feel it appropriate to say anything that might trouble her. I think she felt the same.

I did reassure Mom that we would watch out for Cindy's kids and do our best to guide them forward, and stay connected to Albert.

I believed she knew this but, to be certain, wanted to alleviate her primary concerns. As much as she did not parent me and for all her mistakes, she deserved respect because she took the kids in and raised them and because, while the benefit was mutual, she did help Albert by letting him move in.

Many people said I would be more unsettled by her death than I anticipated, but I wasn't. I was a bit sad. And I felt sorry for her that she died at a relatively young age. But I did not grieve the loss. To me, this evidenced the depth of separation that already had occurred. ❧

# CHAPTER 39
## Recovery Year Three

DURING MY THIRD RECOVERY YEAR, I attended one or two meetings per week, mostly to share what I'd learned. I then stopped because I had confidence in my recovery foundation as to my substance use disorder. I had prevailed in my battle over the obsession to shoot crank or imbibe other drugs. My brain had been rewired, and not using was my new normal. I believed the addict pathways remained but had receded. The healthier patterns now dominated. I thought little about my meth-obsessed life, and even drug dreams were rare. Maintaining sobriety was easier on every level. The struggle was over.

I experienced my addiction as a brain disorder. I know it sounds simplistic, but the ultimate basis for recovery is to stay sober long enough for your brain to heal. Some improvement happens when you no longer pour chemicals into your body. But the process also can be proactive. When I made positive choices and these unfamiliar behaviors morphed into habits, I helped my brain rebuild and augmented my recovery. Every decision that supported sobriety was part of that evolution. Each step forward reinforced my progress. Success breeds success.

Still, I struggled to integrate the Mary Beth I had been for twenty years with the clean and sober version. I'd analyzed my pre-drug strengths, which had increased my fortitude and guided me. But for these initial recovery years, I'd focused on forward momentum rather than resolving the damage from my past. As a result, I now worried I'd put on a different mask since I felt disconnected from both my selves, as if I'd stepped out of one role and into another. And sometimes the addict identity seemed more solid than this new variant, as if that crank-shooting, out-of-control teen was closer to my true self. I empathized with her because I understood that her pain drove her toward self-destruction. And I'd moved past any shame about my substance use disorder. I began to wonder if this was sufficient synthesis. I realized that to push to the next level, to reach Big R Recovery, I had to work harder in therapy to address the abuse and neglect.

Overcoming the trauma proved to be an uphill battle that took many years longer than conquering my addiction. I continued individual counseling and joined a therapy group for women with abuse histories. At an early session, our therapist asked what we needed from our partners and family, which confused me. Needed? I barely wanted things from my family, except Doc's love. It never had occurred to me that actual emotional needs existed. Even considering the idea terrified me. If you need something, what happens when you inevitably don't get it? And yet, the women in the group had answers to that question. My astonishment at my comrades' ability to express their feelings underlined how cut off from my core self I remained.

Also, the variety and depth of the abuse consequences in these women's lives allowed me to better understand the ripples in my own. I began to appreciate the strain of living in high-risk situations and how this had affected me. My childhood, and the adult traumas, had crushed my spirit and forced my true self underground. Because the people who should have protected me instead harmed me, I'd turned off most feelings and developed detrimental methods of dealing with my anger and fear, like dissociation and my addiction.

And this had a name: post-traumatic stress disorder. I'd thought only war vets experienced PTSD, so this diagnosis surprised me but then made sense as I learned more. With trauma, the body/mind connection can shut down, which carries an enormous price as the same parts of the brain that convey distress also transmit joy. Trauma also can cause unconscious acting out, for example having accidents or exposing yourself to danger, and can trigger freezing into helpless immobility when trapped. Plus, trauma can stun the psyche such that you don't adjust to updated information unless you make focused efforts to heal.

All this resonated. I thought about when, as a teenager, I'd flipped from rage to avoidance, part of my fight-or-flight impulse. This reminded me of the molestation as well, when I just lay there and waited for Allan's assault to be over. From this and so many other episodes, I'd been taught I had no control, not even as to my own body or safety. I'd turned to drugs to avoid this truth and ease the agony. In light of this, and from my recent knowledge about PTSD, I reevaluated my penchant for self-harm, such as when I wandered dangerous Hollywood streets, stuck with abusive Martin, and cut myself. At the time, I viewed these actions as signs that I was "crazy" and doomed to live in chaos my entire, probably short, life. I now also recalled when I initiated counseling at Berkeley and phoned the rape hotline during a particularly bloody wrist-slashing episode. Overwhelmed with anguish and sorrow and rage, with no idea how to process these feelings, I'd thrashed through life but also had searched for methods to help me survive one more day.

For me, the most prominent of PTSD evidence was my ongoing anxiety. I'd been called high-strung since early childhood. During this recovery work, I flashed back to the noise-reduction rituals for opening the Bordentown house door and how I put away one dish at a time. I'd learned so young that the world is dangerous, I was alone, and I shouldered responsibility for my siblings' safety. To me, life's core tenet was "no room for error" since any mistake likely would result in life-threatening or life-altering repercussions. Similar to many abuse survivors, my enhanced ability to identify peril could turn background risks into uncontrollable stress. This skill explains why, in my first two years of addiction recovery, I'd assumed all my worries were irrefutable since I could provide multiple reasons why the worst-case scenario was about to happen or at least might well happen. My therapist pointed out that, while I was smart enough to create seemingly valid explanations, the depth of my despair was disproportionate to the actual threat. Plus, these emotions wouldn't change the outcome regardless.

Yet I had trouble identifying anxiety as a fundamental problem. When my therapist prodded me about specific experiences, such as Allan beating me, or even current concerns, I would scrounge through my brain as I tried to remember what I'd felt during or after or right now. She had to give me a laminated list of emotions to help me name them. I suffered from other PTSD symptoms, too. I jumped at loud noises, stood in the back of elevators so I could keep tabs on everyone, and continued to have nightmares. In public, I always held my purse tight, walked at a fast pace, and surveyed my environment constantly. I once pushed a woman hard when she'd grabbed my shoulder from behind. I did not trust men, in particular, which rolled onto Doc. With over a decade together, part of me expected that, one day, he would turn around and punch me. When we took the kids on vacation, I considered whether Doc could be trusted with two young girls, despite having no reason to think otherwise.

As I mulled over the input from my counselor and the women in group therapy, I started to agree that my natural state was clenched tight as I waited for everything good to explode into chaos and horror. To illustrate, if I arrived home when Doc should be elsewhere but his car was in the driveway, my heart dropped and tears spurted. In my mind, the only possible explanation was he lay dead in our bed. Even when I recognized the flimsy underpinning for this emotional certainty, I couldn't shake off the trepidation. I would tiptoe through the house and hope for signs of life, like an open back door or keyboard clacks. At my jobs, I dreaded making a calamitous mistake or being judged unfairly, to the point that I left myself up to a dozen voicemails most nights, in which I justified my performance that day because my ruminations had convinced me I faced immediate termination.

As I became more aware of these ingrained patterns and my negative thinking, I could begin the repairs. When triggered, I'd try to talk myself off the ledge or share my distorted thoughts with Doc, who would hug me and reassure me I was safe. He showed me a comic in which a woman just won the lottery and saved the world yet asked, "But what about tomorrow?," a succinct commentary on my never-ending foreboding. After Doc's friend spent the night, as I readied for work, I told him all the bad events I expected that day. He responded, "It's good to have a goal." This captured my attention and reinforced the self-perpetuating prophecy side of expecting misery.

With all this, by the end of this year I almost trusted that mistakes or setbacks wouldn't annihilate me or my accomplishments. When I took new risks and experienced success, I built a sense of mastery that offset the impetus to sink into the mire of my anxiety. While still overly aware that life can change in an instant, I began to believe I would survive and perhaps flourish. Plus, it was counterproductive to diminish my emotional reserves by living with constant trepidation. My hyperintense misgivings arose less often and resolved in hours to days.

For me, childhood abuse led to childhood addiction. Both had long-term multifaceted consequences. So it is not a surprise that I still struggled after I eliminated the chemicals. At first, I felt deep anxiety although I took appropriate steps forward despite my dread. But difficult emotions made for an unpleasant existence. My achievements, though, created confidence in my competence and assisted me when I faced the next challenge. With hard work, bucked up by professional expertise, by the end of my third year of sobriety I was on track to conquer the unjustified and disproportionate fear. And getting closer to Big R Recovery. ❧

# CHAPTER 40
## Professional Success

AFTER I LEFT CHRYSALIS, I reentered the workforce. Not ready for a full-time career position, I accepted a part-time temporary job as a low-level administrative assistant. I answered phones, opened mail, typed correspondence, and boxed samples. When I interviewed, I felt self-conscious as I had to explain away my employment history, but they didn't scrutinize my resume due to the limited commitment. While I appreciated the opportunity to transition back into the work-force, I had twinges of embarrassment that this was the best I could do despite my age and education.

Nonetheless, I showered, blew out my hair, showed up on schedule, only called in sick if seriously ill, and strove to impress with quality output. Work changed from a mandatory activity that I couldn't pull off to an avenue to enhance my finances and confidence. This half-time job also enabled me to focus significant energy on my recovery. They retained me for nine months, and, for the first time since college, I left with a good reference.

At this point, I could handle forty hours per week and more responsibility. I landed a mid-level administrative position at a small software company. The not stellar salary was similar to my pre-Chrysalis compensation. I promised myself I would never earn less. As a reward for my excellent performance, my boss promoted me to office manager within the year. I continued to absorb new duties, like the accounting. Adding in my second raise, my income had increased by one-third. I applauded my success at climbing these rungs up the corporate ladder.

And yet I struggled with starting from ground zero and fell into the comparison trap. I obsessed over the lost years and the squandered opportunities. I could crumble, awash in anguish, when I interacted with people who enjoyed the achievements or material trappings I'd let slip through my fingers. I tried to counter the feelings logically, remembering I had a good life and had made huge strides. With time, I could recoup some losses and buy pretty things. But I already had enough. I recited a phrase I'd heard at WFS: "Never compare your insides to someone else's outsides." Maybe that person wasn't happier, even with the nicer car or bigger house. Plus, regardless, I only could move forward from where I was, a thirty-two-year-old newly sober woman.

Sometimes I convinced myself. Still, in particular, I agonized over law school. I'd had a stimulating and lucrative career within my grasp, but my substance use disorder had forced me to abandon this opportunity. Reminders caused deep twinges of pain, such as when law school friends complained about complicated research or difficult judges, which to me sounded like heaven. I smiled and nodded when they mentioned favorite professors although I drew a blank because I'd been so drugged and missed so many classes. I considered a return to law school, but Berkeley had warned that my credits would expire and I couldn't imagine they'd readmit me. If I applied to other law schools, I'd have to justify the multiple withdrawals and mediocre grades, the thought of which nauseated me.

I revisited the beneficial aspects of my tarnished work history. While I couldn't control my erratic behavior, this had resulted from my addiction rather than inherent limitations. With each position, I'd grasped the tasks quickly and had offered ideas for efficiency or better results. True, these jobs had been below my inherent abilities, but, regardless, I had demonstrated I could absorb new tasks and adapt to new environments. And I'd continued to perform well intermittently despite my excessive absenteeism. When counseled on my deficiencies, I hadn't been defensive. "You're right, of course. I understand, I'll straighten up." I'd known I couldn't do better, but all this bought time and goodwill. I'd always been laid off, never fired. This could've been due to legal concerns or, more likely, they'd thought I had mental health issues rather than I wasn't capable.

Near my three-year recovery anniversary, I secured a job as an administrative supervisor at a much larger company, which presented fresh challenges. One of the women I oversaw said I was aggressive and harsh—familiar words, yet disturbing since I'd improved from my meth-fueled attack mode. I once walked into a common area to find a temporary employee, whom I'd hired, loudly complaining that I made her feel she couldn't do anything right. Because I felt betrayed, I ordered her to pack up and leave. Apprehensive about another professional catastrophe, I wanted to improve but wasn't sure I could. Even when I acknowledged my rough edges, I believed some intensity was a positive attribute, so I rejected some of the criticism. Still, I tried to observe how people reacted in discussions and to modulate my approach. With time and attention, I augmented my interpersonal skills although perfection eludes me even now. Then, with the company downsizing on the horizon, I realized my position, not so much me, might be at risk, so I looked around for another spot. As Doc will tell you in one of his "she's amazing" examples, I maneuvered a promotion during these layoffs, which reassured me as to my overall work reputation.

At five years sober, because this job didn't stimulate me intellectually, I reconsidered law school. To repair this loss would be wonderful. But I'd be devastated if I was rejected or failed again since I hadn't studied or taken an exam in fifteen years. I almost persuaded myself to let it go and not dream the impossible. That Christmas, my mother laid out her plan to spend her impending, in her mind, huge lottery win. Then she asked what I would do with a million dollars. "I'd go to law school." I paused, then looked at Doc. "You know, I don't need a million dollars to do that." He smiled and squeezed my hand.

We discussed this over several months and, with Doc's encouragement, I wrestled my fears into submission and decided to take the risk. If Berkeley wouldn't take me back, I might be accepted elsewhere. To prepare, I reduced my spending, cashed out my stock options, and built my savings. I enrolled in a class to prepare for the standardized admissions test, then scored in the top 1 percent. Even with this, I doubted Berkeley would accept me but hoped nearby Hastings might. When I had to address my law school withdrawals, in the applications, I didn't trust the process enough to admit to my addiction. Instead, I referenced the related, but more vague, personal and financial problems.

Berkeley did reject me. But as I watched television one day, Doc walked into the room, gave me an "I told you so" look, and tossed the fat envelope from Hastings. As I walked up the steps for orientation,

I felt invigorated and terrified. I was six years sober but still struggled with anxiety, so the gamble loomed large. Although I enjoyed my courses, stress overwhelmed me during finals and while I waited for grades, even though I'd attended every class, read every case, and prepared for every test. After one exam, I suffered for weeks when I realized that, though I ultimately provided the correct answer, I'd flubbed a tangential point. As the "stupid, stupid" tape replayed in my brain, I rehashed every exam because, if I had made this mistake, there must have been others. I damned myself for fantasizing that I could succeed. When grades came out, I'd earned an A. The professor said I received full credit for my excellent analysis but had lost a point for this minor blunder.

Despite getting in my own way, my grades put me in the top of my class, so Berkeley accepted me back as a transfer student. I was beyond thrilled. Doc and I reviewed all my recovery accomplishments, which reinforced my pride in my evolution. My return to Berkeley's law school was exceedingly delicious icing on that lovely cake. ◦

# CHAPTER 41
## Gina

WHEN I ENTERED LAW SCHOOL, I intended to fight for my people, the working-class, by studying labor law or personal injury. But my grades qualified me for a big firm, big business, big money job. I debated these alternatives for months.

"Gina, I can't decide. These Silicon Valley firms litigate important cases. And their clients make cool tech products. Plus, I could earn beaucoup bucks and get rid of my debt. Maybe buy a fancy house. Still, the workload is insane."

She grabbed my arms and peered into my eyes. "Don't sell yourself short. If you don't like it, after two weeks' notice, you're outta there—with a bright and shiny resume."

I accepted an offer from Cooley, where I specialized in securities and complex business litigation. The lawyers were smart and talented. The atmosphere was collegial. Cooley assigned me interesting cases about off-label marketing and the variants of business fraud. I excelled my first year, so advanced fast. I argued motions in court and oversaw other attorneys. I paid off my loans in fifteen months. Doc and I moved into a stunning home in a better neighborhood.

Yet I'd sold all my time to Cooley. I lived up to that bargain and prioritized my job over my life, almost living at the firm—ten to twelve hours weekdays, most weekends, and even one Thanksgiving. I checked my Blackberry as soon as I woke, right before bed, and hourly whenever not in the office. I answered calls at the beach and during family gatherings. My colleagues and I compared hours, more bragging than complaining. And I made sure my performance exceeded expectations so I received outstanding reviews and large bonuses.

Three years in, Doc and I went to see *The Lion King* in San Francisco. This was one of the few instances when I actually used my theater ticket rather than sending a friend in my place because I had to work. Gina lived in the city, so I asked her to lunch with us, before the show. I thought about how she and I had struggled to manage our pain and build a happy life. Despite our "let's have fun" attitude at Berkeley, underneath neither of us had believed we could find joy or even stability. I was wrong, but at least up to this point Gina was correct. By the late '80s, she'd succumbed to a heroin addiction. When I was still using crank, we'd talk on the phone and meet up when we both could manage it, which wasn't often. Then, even though our paths diverged as I recovered and she did not, our deep love and appreciation for each other remained, and we kept in touch. I'd tried to get her into recovery, off and on, but she would shake me off. As I waited outside the theater, I wondered if I had put in enough effort, even though I knew I couldn't control her decision.

When Doc pointed to indicate Gina on the approach, I focused on her as she sashayed down Market Street, dressed in a hippy dippy loose skirt with multiple layers of nuanced shades of black, an intricate lace top, and long necklaces of skulls and Grateful Dead logos. Lovely as ever, her fair skin glowed. I never understood how a heroin addict could retain such beauty. She hugged me tight and then Doc, her obvious adoration for him warming my heart.

We hoofed it to a nearby Thai restaurant, caught up on recent events, and reminisced. I only remember snippets of the conversation. Our move to the new house excited Gina because she could see us more often since we lived closer to San Francisco. She did her best to present a positive life, that she was in a good place, that she was not using that much. I didn't pursue this topic further because I didn't want to ruin our visit with a difficult discussion that would fail to accomplish any positive change. I chose to stay quiet and sink into our loving bond.

A few weeks later at Cooley, I plopped into my chair, slid my potato chip dinner onto the desk, and glanced at the Westlaw logo that flickered on the computer screen. I squeezed my eyelids open and shut, to clear the fuzz, then examined the legal research list. As I reached for my Diet Pepsi, I noticed the red message light blinking on my flip phone.

*Area Code 702. Vegas? Hmm. The only people I know there are Gina's parents.*

I gulped and pressed *86.

"Oh! Mary Beth, Mary Beth. Call me. Call me right away."

These words and Mrs. Barranti's anguished sputter informed me that my Gina was dead.

Dizzy, I shoved my head between my legs. I rested there for a minute. A half smile formed as I recalled meeting Gina at the Bear's Lair. In my mind, dazzling light surrounded her as her luminous gaze locked on me. A searing heat flowed from my heart to my fingertips. I looked down at my silk blouse and linen pants. *Jesus. That was twenty-two years ago.*

I raised my head from my lap, leaned forward, and stared out the window at the parking lot. I realized I still held my cell. My hand shook as I punched the buttons. Mrs. Barranti's phone rang and rang. I decided she must be on the other line and ignoring call waiting.

"She's notifying the family," I whispered to myself.

I lurched to the doorway and scanned my office neighborhood but found myself alone. My footsteps echoed as I paced the halls. I wriggled my shoulders, hopped in place, and repeated reassuring thoughts. *It could be just an accident. Or her parents need me to go to the hospital.* But I'd expected this call for years. I knew Gina probably had overdosed or died in a drug-related accident.

At my desk again, I hit redial. No answer.

I spun around in my chair, which slammed my knee into the credenza and sent several manila folders sliding to the floor. I thought of Gina's piercing blue eyes, soft laugh, and gentle spirit. I envisioned myself sitting with her as we ate bad pizza and watched our favorite soap opera. I shook my head to pull myself into the present. Mrs. Barranti answered on my third try.

"She's gone, Mary Beth."

Tears streamed down my cheeks as I gathered the details. Found near her apartment door. Maybe crawling for help. Drug paraphernalia nearby. Autopsy next week.

I rubbed my belly and repressed the bile rising up my throat. My temperature increased five degrees and I felt disoriented. My jaw ached, and I realized I'd been clenching it since I'd listened to the voicemail.

I compelled myself to stop crying. What should I do about work?

Simon, the partner leading the case, expected the legal brief I was writing by Monday because we had a court deadline. It was impossible to get an extension. Since it was already Friday night, I elected to go home and finish it over the weekend.

Unable to sleep, I arrived at the office at the crack of dawn Saturday and pounded my computer behind closed doors for a couple hours. On my fourth coffee run, a colleague approached me. He scanned my pale face.

"Are you all right?"

I buckled over as the sobs exploded from my chest. "My Gina, my dearest friend, died. She died yesterday. I don't know what I'm supposed to do."

He strode toward me and then retreated. I straightened up, swallowed my tears, apologized, and returned to my office.

When I turned in the completed document, I informed Simon about Gina's sudden demise. "I won't be able to work Saturday. That's the service."

He leaned over and patted me on the back. "Whatever you need."

I knew he didn't mean this. That one day off exhausted the available accommodations. Simon never offered to extend a deadline or transfer an assignment. I could have insisted although doing so would have breached my bargain with the firm. After all, Gina was not a parent or a sibling. Those deaths would have bought me a few days leave. A spouse might have justified two weeks. But not even a weekend off for the loss of a friend, no matter how heartbreaking.

I wept every day on the drive to my office, then freshened my makeup before I headed upstairs. I felt stunned and distressed, but the pace of the job allowed no time to grieve. I began to reconsider my career path. I asked myself if I wanted the big firm life, with the mandatory sacrifices. Even the partners worked at this pace. I'd once lamented to Gina, "There's no light at the end of this tunnel."

As I evaluated my options, I recognized that guilt was intermixed with the pain over losing my beloved. Had I tried hard enough to help her? Had I abandoned her for law school and a prestigious job? So busy I'd averted my eyes from the impending disaster? I tried to console myself with the knowledge that no one could have forced me into recovery until I was ready, but this only partially assuaged my remorse. Even if my dereliction had not caused her death, did I want to continue to be absent from the lives of those I loved?

One night, when I arrived home at 9:00 p.m., I rushed into Doc's arms. He held me tight and I held him tighter. "Maybe I should resign. I just don't know if I can do it any longer. Or if I ought to."

"I'm surprised you stuck it out this long." Doc tilted my chin up and kissed my forehead. "Of course you're tired of the ridiculous demands."

"My family won't understand if I choose to walk away from so much money. For God's sake, my bonus is more than my mother's annual salary. Plus, will I regret it? Because there's no turning back."

I carved out time to consider the impact of the job on my personal life. I contemplated the long-delayed trip to China, the missed birthday parties, the books unread. I reminded myself that I had not signed a lifelong contract. I'd climbed to the top of the mountain, but what did I want my mountaintop to look like? Perhaps making partner at Cooley wasn't the right goal. I could select a different path and find a better balance. True, I thrived on challenges and wanted financial security. Yet I also needed to engage with family and friends. I craved a life in which Doc and I could buy season tickets to the theater, take long vacations, and enjoy spontaneous weekend get-aways without work interruptions.

Six months after addiction stole my Gina, as I stepped into my black pumps, I paused and summoned her memory. I could feel her hug and her love pulsed through me. I imagined Gina nudging me forward, down a steep cliff, and into a meadow filled with fragrant flowers. I drew in a deep breath, stood tall, and smiled. I wiggled my hips and shimmied my shoulders. I laughed and sang out, "They can't make me. They can't make me do it."

I seized the calendar from the wall and flipped to the one-year anniversary of Gina's death. With a red Sharpie, I inscribed RESIG-NATION DATE. I slid into my jacket and ambled down the stairs. ●

# CHAPTER 42
## *Conclusion*

IN 2008, I SECURED A JOB with the Social Security Administration, which I chose for the fair salary and reasonable hours, along with varied and engaging work. I soon oversaw much of the California litigation and led high-profile class actions. I regularly interacted with agency executives, guided and directed numerous attorneys, resolved problems, and made important decisions. I juggled overlapping deadlines and managed to keep each case on track. Doc called me ambitious, but I didn't agree. My superiors asked me to take on these roles, I was willing to do so, and did my best. But, by this time, I no longer needed to prove myself.

In 2013, I applied to become a federal administrative law judge. Thousands of people competed, but most failed to survive all the tests and interviews. I was in the first group hired, despite having been grievously ill during much of the process. I said to Doc, "I can't fathom how I did so well when I was so sick." Doc responded, "You're the only one who doesn't understand."

With this achievement, I revisited the arc of my life. From childhood abuse to adult traumas. From sipping Boone's Farm Strawberry Hill wine to slamming meth. From law school dropout to federal judge. From deeply pained to horrendously anxious to Big R Recovery. The abuse and trauma had beaten down my true self. Then addiction had become my prison cell. Conquering the substances had released my potential, but I'd had to figure out how best to utilize this newfound freedom.

If I had accredited the premise that I could not recover without a higher power, I would have given up. Luckily, instead, being forced to find my own path transformed me. As I clawed my way out of crank hell, I began to believe I wasn't just the lunatic I had become in active addiction. Although I sometimes felt defeated and overwhelmed by the losses, my trajectory encouraged me to remain on the recovery path. I proved my meth-free brain could make rational decisions and gained confidence in my ability to guide myself forward. I applied my intelligence and analytical skills, made mostly good choices, set goals, persisted, learned patience with incremental progress, grew honest about my mistakes, and cared about others.

I achieved ambitions beyond the wildest imagination of my druggie self. I am happily married and a reliable aunt and sister and friend. I went to law school, became an attorney, and then a judge. I also contribute to my community. I am a board member of LifeRing Secular Recovery and She Recovers Foundation, an essayist, and recovery speaker. This book is part of that work too. My hope is to put another face to long-term recovery from addiction and childhood trauma. To reassure those suffering, their families, and their friends that they can lead productive and fulfilling lives. To show what recovery can look like, including for atheists or agnostics or those who prefer approaches other than the 12-steps.

All this—and the gift of enjoying the journey—is a result of working hard for the infrastructure that so far has provided 29 years of sobriety.

And it is all because I did it my way.

# Recovery Guidelines

WHEN I DECIDED to take a hybrid approach to my recovery by incorporating ideas from multiple sources, I did not have access to success stories of others who took this tack. But you, my reader, have my example, which I hope reassures those inclined toward this method. Moreover, several peer-to-peer recovery organizations explicitly promote this idea. This includes LifeRing Secular Recovery's personal recovery program philosophy, She Recovers Foundation's acceptance of individual pathways and patchworks, and Women for Sobriety's emphasis on empowering its members to make their own decisions.

While I do not believe any one strategy is right for everyone, I offer the following guidance, intended to help you create the best plan for you.

First, consider whether you would benefit from inpatient treatment, intensive outpatient treatment, a therapist with addiction expertise, and/or a recovery coach.

Second, familiarize yourself with a variety of support programs. I would suggest this include She Recovers Foundation, LifeRing Secular Recovery, Women for Sobriety, SMART Recovery, and Alcoholics/Narcotics Anonymous. You can locate more options with an internet search. Peruse the websites, read the written materials, and attend meetings. Many individuals also utilize ideas available through recovery books and podcasts.

Third, review what you've learned. Decide whether your sobriety would advance most from participating in one program or from a hybrid approach. Regardless, filter all ideas for those you find valuable and modify suggestions as needed, so the concepts assist you.

Fourth, develop a specific plan for your recovery at this point in time. What are your priorities? What are the top three to five areas you want to work on *now*? Recovery examples can include the number of meetings to attend per week, analyzing which relationships are supportive and which are problematic, and deciding which activities you can participate in without risk. Non-recovery goals might include improving your work performance or becoming a better parent. Write a specific plan for each priority, including steps to take and obstacles to overcome. Distinguish what you can accomplish in the next few months from what has a longer time horizon.

Fifth, study your core strengths. Which characteristics will aid you in recovery? What's your optimum problem-solving style? Evaluate your success thus far, focusing on how you achieved these goals.

Sixth, update your plan every month or two. Which objectives did you accomplish? Do any plans need to be amended, such as when you didn't fully succeed? Do you now have the bandwidth to target a new area in your life?

Seventh, never forget the misery of your addiction. For me, this is knowledge to which I still feel connected. For others, ongoing support meetings are useful.

In addition to laying out these seven guideposts, I want to summarize some core doctrines that assisted me in the hope that you might find value as well.

Taking charge of my own recovery strengthened me. Rather than follow orders to submit to the program being offered, I viewed all ideas presented to me as suggestions. I did my best to keep an open mind, even to those teachings I wanted to knee-jerk toss out the window. I analyzed each concept against this standard: "Will this help me build a strong recovery foundation?" I then accepted, rejected, or modified the recommendations. This process invigorated dormant decision-making skills and improved my ability to make solid judgments. I learned to guide myself forward. And I gained expertise that I continued to apply to my recovery and to use when making decisions in any arena.

The key to my recovery was my motivation and my efforts. In my family, only a weak connection existed between my actions and what happened to me. No matter what I did, I could not avoid the abuse. Building a hybrid recovery program taught me that my labor had a significant impact on the likelihood I'd triumph. I couldn't control everything, but by making good choices, I came to trust my ability to guide myself to a drug-free, and happier, future. This confidence smoothed the path to improving in all areas.

Try to find hope. I entered rehab hopeless about attaining sobriety. My goal was to learn to use less because that was the extent of my imagination. Meeting sober people, listening to their stories, and witnessing their progression allowed me to believe that perhaps I could follow that path, too. So, I went from hopeless to somewhat hopeful to cautiously optimistic, which empowered me and justified the exertion required to attain long-term recovery.

Recovery results from incremental improvement. Most addicts I know, me included, expected to repair all aspects of their lives in a couple of months or maybe a year. This is unlikely, particularly for my peers with extensive drug histories. I noticed that those who tried to race through the process often failed, whereas those satisfied with putting one foot in front of the other, again and again, succeeded. I took this approach, such as when it took me six years to work my way from a temporary, part-time job to law school. What helped me was to regularly look behind and congratulate myself on my progress. That is, to notice and value each step forward.

It's drugs *or* happiness. I know this sounds simplistic, particularly to those who have suffered from a substance use disorder, but it took me a year to understand and accept this. I realized that I could use drugs *or* be happy and productive. I had to make a choice because for me it is one or the other. As my life improved, the losses I would suffer, if I were to return to active addiction, increased. I'm not willing to pay that penalty.

Recovery is hard for a while, but active substance use disorder is hard forever. Recovery takes focused practice, but that's often for just the first few years or intermittently thereafter. Addiction is hard every day because the beautiful highs of the beginning are long gone and the destruction is ever increasing. In addition, whatever challenges the world throws your way would be worse if you are in active addiction. Choose the easier way. Choose recovery. ☉

# Recovery Checklist

## TREATMENT

❑ Do you need professionally supervised detox?

❑ Would inpatient treatment be beneficial because your substance use disorder (SUD) is exceptionally severe or because you would be better able to focus if removed from your home environment and daily activities?

❑ Would an intensive outpatient program (IOP) be a good option, either because this provides sufficient treatment or since you are unable to leave your life for inpatient treatment?

❑ Are there any mental health issues that need be addressed, too, such that a dual diagnosis program would be valuable?

❑ Will a faith-based program be a good fit or do you need to verify that the treatment facility offers options other than 12-step programs?

❑ Even if you believe in a higher power, do you view yourself as powerless over your addiction, or do you believe that your motivation and efforts will be the foundation for your recovery? If the latter, verify that the facility offers options other than 12-step programs.

❑ Even if the 12-step approach might be a viable option, do you want to verify that you also will be exposed to other approaches?

❑ Does the facility offer evidence-based treatment?

❑ Would you be more comfortable in a female-or male-only environment, or is an integrated program acceptable?

❑ Is the length of the program a good fit when considering factors such as insurance coverage, cost, work flexibility, family demands, and personal preferences?

❑ Is there an aftercare program for when you return home?

## PEER-TO-PEER SUPPORT

❑ Will you, like many of those in early SUD recovery, benefit from peer-to-peer support groups?

❑ Review the online materials for LifeRing Secular Recovery, She Recovers Foundation, Women for Sobriety, SMART Recovery, and 12-step programs (AA/NA).

❑ Consider searching for other options, of which there are many.

❑ Consider attending multiple programs and combining ideas from different programs.

❑ Give yourself permission to reject or modify ideas to develop a program that works for you.

❑ Even within one program, meetings have different personalities, so consider trying new meetings for fresh approaches and ideas.

# PROFESSIONAL HELP FOR SUD

❑ Would individual therapy with an addiction specialist be of value?

❑ Would your relationship with your life partner benefit from couple's counseling?

❑ Would a recovery coach assist you in staying on track or by offering guidance?

❑ Would medication for your SUD help you maintain sobriety?

# OTHER PROFESSIONAL HELP

❑ Mental health conditions can make it more difficult to maintain sobriety. If this is true for you, consider adding appropriate professional help.

❑ Should you find a therapist with relevant expertise in trauma or your specific mental health diagnoses?

❑ Would group therapy provide additional insights and support?

❑ Would mental health medication improve your symptoms and your life?

# OTHER SUPPORTS

❑ Do you benefit from reading substantive recovery materials?

❑ Would understanding the science of SUD be useful?

❑ Do you benefit from reading memoirs or inspirational recovery stories?

❑ Do you benefit from listening to podcasts about recovery?

❑ Do you benefit from journaling?

❑ Do you benefit from mindfulness, meditation, or yoga?

## HOME ENVIRONMENT

❑ Has your home been cleared of alcohol and mood-altering drugs (other than those medically indicated and taken as prescribed)?

❑ If you cannot clear your home of alcohol or drugs, such as when a partner or roommate continues to imbibe, can you establish any limits such as keeping the drugs and alcohol out of sight or locked up?

## ACTIVITIES

❑ Are you comfortable with exposure to alcohol and other drugs in social situations?

❑ Do you need to limit your activities to situations without alcohol or other drugs?

❑ Do you need a plan or specific supports when exposed to alcohol or other drugs during social gatherings or other activities?

❑ Are you comfortable in all size groups, or do you need to limit the number of people you interact with at any one time?

❑ Are you comfortable engaging in activities with anyone or only with people supportive of your recovery efforts?

❑ Which activities would you like to add into your life to replace the hours spent consuming alcohol and/or other drugs?

❑ What positive habits can you develop that will increase your odds of success, such as attending a support meeting after work rather than heading to the bar, making a date with a friend at the time of day you typically smoke a joint, or starting each day by reflecting on your recent success?

## RELATIONSHIPS

❑ Partner: Supportive? Sufficient SUD understanding? Able to work productively to address lingering feelings from active addiction period or other issues? Willing to engage in counseling if needed? SUD of his/her own? Good partner overall, or should you terminate the relationship?

❑ Family: Same questions as partner, but also considerations as to when to reveal SUD/sobriety, with the caveat that you are not obligated to share with everyone at the same time or at all.

❑ Friends: Same factors as family, but also are any relationships based on using alcohol or other substances such that the friend pressures you to do so? Or is there no true bond without shared substance use, so the relationship should be terminated?

❑ Children: Much depends on the age of the child, such as how much to explain about your SUD and recovery, whether you have custody or want to regain custody, the child's feelings around your behavior while under the influence, and alienation from the child. Consider these factors and develop an appropriate plan.

❑ Sobriety support network: Have you built the network you need? Do you utilize this network when facing challenges? Does your team support your recovery plan, or do some pressure you to do it their way? Is anyone stepping outside their role of sobriety support and inappropriately inserting themselves into other areas of your life?

# WORK

☐ Evaluate your current ability to work, such as how many hours a week and what levels of complexity and stress you can manage.

☐ If unemployed and looking for work, consider this analysis before applying for a job.

☐ If you have a job, is your position consistent with your current abilities?

☐ If your job exceeds your current abilities, can you ask to modify the job temporarily or get additional help or support so you can succeed?

☐ Is your sobriety at risk in your job, such as sales meetings involving alcohol? If so, can you modify your duties, or do you need to develop a plan for these situations?

☐ Due to your SUD, did you have performance problems that you need to address?

# PRIORITIES

☐ List the top three to five areas in your life on which you most need to focus.

☐ What are the primary obstacles to improvement?

☐ What specific aspects in this arena do you need to improve?

☐ Write up related goals.

☐ Write up the first three to five steps needed to move toward these goals.

☐ What are you able to implement now?

# RELAPSE PREVENTION

❑ Plan how you will handle cravings. Attend a support meeting? Call some-one in your recovery support network? Make a list of all your reasons for choosing sobriety? Distract yourself with activities? Meditate?

❑ Talk to others about how they handle relapse impulses to gather ideas that might help you.

❑ Look for patterns that lead to cravings or relapse, then develop a plan to disrupt these cycles.

❑ Even if you relapse, remind yourself of your overall improvement, such as longer periods of sobriety, shorter relapses, or your refusal to give up on achieving your sobriety goals.

# PERIODIC REVIEW OF PLAN

❑ Review and congratulate yourself on your accomplishments.

❑ Review the new positive aspects of your life in recovery.

❑ Review your successful plan periodically to ensure it's still the optimal approach.

❑ Review your plan if it isn't working, including analyzing relapse patterns.

❑ Evaluate if you now want to explore other peer-to-peer support options.

❑ Have you met some of your goals so you now have the bandwidth to tackle new challenges?

❑ Did any of your plans fail because you hadn't considered all the factors, so you should revisit these approaches?

❑ Did you simply fail to carry out part of your plan and need to do an honest assessment as to why you allowed this to occur?

# Acknowledgments

I AM SO GRATEFUL for the encouragement and dedicated guidance provided by my agents, Anne Marie O'Farrell and Caroline Fanelli, of Marcil-O'Farrell Literary, LLC.

I also thank my team at HCI Books, including Darcie Abbene, Allison Janse, and Lindsey Mach, for bringing this book into being with so much enthusiasm and support.

For the past several years, I've received valuable input from the members of my critique groups, for which I am indebted.

And to my husband Doc, words cannot express the depth of my gratitude for your incredible support during my recovery and while writing this book. Your confidence in my ultimate success helped immeasurably during the long slog of crafting my story into a form that I hope will be useful to others. ●

# About the Author

A RECOVERY ADVOCATE, Mary Beth O'Connor has been sober since 1994. She also is in recovery from abuse, trauma, and anxiety. Mary Beth is a board member, secretary, and founding investor for the She Recovers Foundation. She also is a director for LifeRing Secular Recovery. She regularly speaks on behalf of these organizations and about multiple paths to recovery. This includes conferences, podcasts, radio, and recovery houses. She also develops relationships with other organizations, such as Women for Sobriety.

Mary Beth's opinion pieces have appeared in the *Wall Street Journal* and the *Philadelphia Inquirer*. Her memoir writings have been published in *Memoir Magazine, Awakenings, The Noyo River Review, The Fault Zone, Carry the Light,* and *Ravens Perch.*

Professionally, six years into recovery, Mary Beth attended Berkeley Law. She worked at a large firm in Silicon Valley, then litigated class actions for the federal government. In 2014, Mary Beth was appointed a federal administrative law judge, a position from which she retired in 2020. ●

For more information, visit https://junkietojudge.com/about